Folklore in Motion: Texas Travel Lore

Folklore in Motion: Texas Travel Lore

edited by Kenneth L. Untiedt

Publications of the Texas Folklore Society LXIV

University of North Texas Press

Denton, Texas

Permissions:
University of North Texas Press
P.O. Box 311336
Denton, TX 76203-1336

The paper used in this book meets the minimum requirements of the
American National Standard for Permanence of Paper for Printed Library
Materials, z39.48.1984. Binding materials have been chosen for durability.

Library of Congress Cataloging-in-Publication Data

Folklore in motion : Texas travel lore / edited by Kenneth L. Untiedt.
     p. cm.—(Publications of the Texas Folklore Society ; v. 64)
     Includes bibliographical references and index.
     ISBN-13: 978-1-57441-238-3 (cloth : alk. paper)
     1. Texas—Description and travel—Anecdotes. 2. Texas—Social life and customs—
Anecdotes. 3. Texas—Folklore. 4. Travel—Folklore. 5. Travelers' writings, American—
Texas. 6. Folklore—Texas. I. Untiedt, Kenneth L., 1966–
     F386.6.F65 2007
     917.64'0463—dc22

                                                                            2007028412

Folklore in Motion: Texas Travel Lore is Number LXIV in the Publications of the
Texas Folklore Society

CONTENTS

III. *The Modern Era: Tales of Rails and Highways*

IV. *Still Movin' On, Any Way They Can*

PREFACE

We're all travelers of some kind. Many of us have traveled great distances, roaming all across this nation or even to foreign countries to explore cultures that vary widely from our own. Some of us have come from faraway places to get to where we are. Americans in particular are travelers—this country was founded by people from other places. The history of our state was written by adventurers who came from many different places: Thomas J. Rusk, Stephen F. Austin, Davy Crockett, Sam Houston. The same is true for many key individuals in the Texas Folklore Society—half of our secretary-editors were born in other states, and none of the men responsible for establishing the organization were native Texans. As a group, the members of the Society value the experiences of our travels, and the travels of our ancestors, because those experiences are what make us who we are. Many of the stories in *The Family Saga,* one of our most popular publications, are about how we (collectively) got here.

Travel affects—and is affected by—many things: economics, social customs and interactions, superstitions, and personal beliefs. Folklore itself travels, and changes as it does. As we move from one place to another we take our customs and beliefs with us, and we share them with others. However, sometimes they are what compel us to embark on journeys in the first place. Travel—and the many various means of transportation—is a big part of the traditional knowledge of any culture. The adventurous spirit of Texans has led to much travel lore, from stories of how ancestors first came to the state to reflections of how technology has affected the customs, language, and stories of life "on the go." As travelers, we are all involved in crossing barriers, invading territory, and continuously effecting change everywhere we go.

During the Folklore session at the 2005 meeting of the Texas State Historical Association, Joyce Gibson Roach shared a traveling anecdote that got me thinking about how folklore moves about. A traveling anecdote is not necessarily about travel; it is a story that moves around from place to place, and it can be serious, didactic, or humorous. However, some traveling anecdotes are actually about travel. I remember fondly an account Paul Patterson shared during a hootenanny once, of one of his boyhood moves (an excerpt from his *Crazy Women in the Rafters*), when he so eloquently stated that he was "small for his age and dumb for his size." That was a hook; I've been a fan of Paul's wit ever since. From days of traveling by covered wagon to the twenty-first century, stories of the road are equally compelling. In "The Traveling Anecdote" (*Folk Travelers: Ballads, Tales, and Talk*, PTFS XXV, 1953), J. Frank Dobie relates many traveling anecdotes, and he explains that they will always exist, no matter how advanced we or our forms of travel become.

Traveling has changed significantly for the average American, just in terms of advances in automotive technology. One could view these changes as positive or negative. I remember family vacations with nine of us in a car during the sweltering heat of summer, cramped and unseatbelted, entertained only by songs we taught each other or made up as we went along. We covered hundreds of miles, played games without the aid of electronic devices, told stories and, probably, wore our parents' nerves pretty thin. Do I now appreciate our minivan and our children's personal CD players or Gameboys? Yes, I do. Still, traveling was once much easier and, therefore, probably more enjoyable. Before Homeland Security placed restrictions on where and how we get from one place to another, limiting what we can take on airplanes or who can fly them, people viewed trips as adventures, not just tremendous inconveniences. But neither technology nor government regulations will really affect our desire to travel or the lore that surrounds it.

The preface for *From Hell to Breakfast* (PTFS IXX, 1944) reads, "How Far is it From Hell to Breakfast? Out in the cow country a man upon returning from a trip might say that he had traveled from hell to breakfast. Nobody could tell you in miles just how far he had been, but everybody would know that he had traveled a far piece and covered a lot of territory."—Mody Boatright and Donald Day. Texas is a vast territory, and the folklore of East Texas is different from that of West Texas. The roads within this state cover not just land, but also the cultures of each area they cross. This Publication of the Texas Folklore Society features articles that examine all kinds of lore about travel. These articles examine people and the places they go, and the methods of travel used in getting to those places, as well as the vehicles (including wagons, trains, cars, and boats), the traditions, the food, the songs and games, and the stories along the way. The first chapter examines how folklore is related to travel, specifically in Texas (or for Texans). The title of the second chapter—Back in the Day—is a new folk expression that stands for something from days bygone, and it features articles that relate how some authors' ancestors came to the state—traditional "Gone to Texas" accounts. Also included are articles about methods of travel that are no longer prevalent, although their influence lingers on.

Another chapter is dedicated to trains and cars, two machines that changed the face of our entire nation. This year's throwback article, Newton Gaines' "The Ford Epigram," tells about creative signage painted on car fenders. The art of customizing vehicles is probably more popular today than ever, as can be evidenced by looking at a car frequently parked several blocks from my home; it is emblazoned with large metallic letters across the rear quarter panels identifying its owner as "Cut Dawg" in stylized script. (The ridiculously large tires are another folk way of modifying, and thereby personalizing, the appearance.) The last chapter includes articles that examine the lore associated with different types of modern transportation, including two-wheeled machines, machines that fly, and machines that scream across the land at dangerous speeds. It concludes with articles that consider how we fuel our machines and ourselves, and the rituals in which we engage when we're on our way from here to there.

Readers interested in Gretchen Lutz's article on drag racing may want to revisit Hermes Nye's article on drag strip speech in

Tire Shrinker to Dragster (PTFS XXXIV, 1968), as well as the other article that gives that volume its title, E. J. Rissmann's "The Tire Shrinker." Those two articles, as Wilson Hudson notes in the preface of the book, show just how far we've come in a short time. Everyone has a horror story or two about the old days of traveling, and those days are not far gone. Although my school wasn't several miles away from my home (or uphill, whether going to or coming from), I can honestly share with my children the story of how I walked to school one bitterly cold morning when the temperature was seventy degrees below zero—with the wind chill, of course. We would never subject our children to such dangers today.

Jim Harris's "Texans on the Road: The Folklore of Travel" was not the original inspiration for this publication, but it does fit well with the topic and is, therefore, the kick-off article. It is an overview of all that follows: unique places around the state, family vacations, folk expressions about life on the road, modes of transportation, and the very motivation people have for deciding to hit the road at all. In the article, Jim suggests many ideas for further study, which I also encourage readers to consider. Hopefully, all of our books provide impetus for or generate further interest in continued research on a particular topic. Remember, these publications are not the final word on the research of the various topics, but rather just the beginnings.

I give thanks to several people, including all of the contributors, my colleagues and administrators at Stephen F. Austin State University, Karen DeVinney and the staff at the UNT Press, and especially to Janet Simonds, who continues to provide innovative ideas that breathe new life into this organization and its publications. We used a slightly different process for collecting submissions for this book: email. It was extremely effective, and we will continue to solicit contributions this way in the future. Everyone who reads a Publication of the Texas Folklore Society should know that anyone can contribute to the publications, and all are encouraged to do so. These books are created by the Society's members, and the more that contribute the better. Not only does it make my job easier by giving me more selections from which to choose, but it makes the publications better because they are more diverse and personal.

This publication is dedicated to all the members of the Texas Folklore Society who travel across this great state each year to attend our annual meetings. Gathering in a different city—big or small—each year is an added bonus to membership in this organization. We get to see interesting exhibits, visit historical sites, and experience distinctive local culture in a different location each year. In addition, we get to experience all the sights and sounds and foods and culture of all parts of the state along the way. I know that for many who attend, the trip is a much anticipated event, perhaps the most enjoyable one all year. As always, I look forward to seeing you all again next Easter.

Kenneth L. Untiedt
Stephen F. Austin State University
Nacogdoches, Texas
June 8, 2007

FOLK TRAVEL

IN TEXAS

Jim Harris, Road Scholar

TEXANS ON THE ROAD: THE FOLKLORE OF TRAVEL

by Jim Harris

If the interior world of our minds reflects the exterior world in which we live, the American mind must look like a road map. Or better yet, if we could peer into the national mind, it would look like a road. It would be Interstate Highway 95 from Maine to Florida along the East Coast. Or it would be Highway 101 from Oregon to California along the West Coast. Or still better, it would be Route 66, the mother of all American roads—in the twentieth century anyway.

In 2001, Route 66 was seventy-five years old, although as everyone knows, the fabled artery has been plowed up, paved over, and renamed in recent decades. That didn't stop people from remembering Route 66 in 2003, when the Smithsonian National Museum of American History in Washington D.C. celebrated a transportation exhibit. At that celebration, a concrete portion, saved from a part of the route in Oklahoma, was put on exhibition.

Route 66 is the road John Steinbeck wrote about in the 1930s in *The Grapes of Wrath*. It is the road jazz singers celebrated in the 1940s. "Get your kicks on Route 66." It is the road television producers featured in the 1950s with a popular television show: two guys in a Corvette traveling from adventure to adventure along its twists and turns.

It is our hallowed highway, but it is not just Route 66 that we have loved. Americans have always been lovers of the open road. It is a national tradition and an historical fact. Frederick Jackson Turner saw all of American history as a road trip west. Walt Whitman, our great Democratic poet, wrote a 14-section, 224-line poem he called "Song of the Open Road." The poem begins:

> Afoot and light-hearted I take to the open road
> Healthy, free, the world before me,
> The long brown path before me leading wherever I choose.

Our roads are no longer "long brown" paths, but we still see the road as a symbol of the kind of freedom we have here.

Some folks think America's greatest novel is Mark Twain's *Huckleberry Finn,* the story of a young man taking a trip down the country's super highway of the nineteenth century, the Mississippi River. On the surface, Huck floats down the Big Muddy, but he is really traveling down a mythical American road.

Texans have always had a special place in their hearts for the road. We had only a little part of Route 66 up in the Panhandle, but the open road has always been a romantic place for us. "Just can't wait to get on the road again," Willie sings. It's his signature song, and as far as I am concerned it could be the state's signature song. Let's sing it at our TFS meetings instead of "The Eyes of Texas" or "Beautiful, Beautiful Texas."

For how many of you is our annual Easter gathering an opportunity to get on the road again? For how many of you is the yearly TFS meeting a pilgrimage that has its comings and goings on the road that are also an important part of our Easter experience? Up in northern New Mexico this time of year hundreds of my fellow New Mexicans make a pilgrimage to some holy ground at El Sanctuario de Chimayo. Easter weekend with the TFS has become my family's equivalent of that pilgrimage. We haven't missed Easter weekend with the TFS since 1975.

At our annual meeting in Nacogdoches, I told John Lightfoot that I wanted to do this paper on the folklore of travel in Texas. In 2000, the state's most famous fiction writer came out with a book about his travels on American interstate highways: Larry McMurtry published *Roads: Driving America's Great Highways.* It is a book in which he acknowledges his addiction to being on the road. In his introduction, McMurtry writes, "From earliest boyhood, the American road has been a part of my life—central to it I would even say."[1]

Now, McMurtry's *Roads* is no literary masterpiece. It is no "Song of the Open Road" or *Huckleberry Finn*. However, it does say a few things about my topic. For instance, he writes, "I had no river to float on, to wonder about. Highway 281 was my river, its hidden reaches a mystery and an enticement."[2] And still later in his introduction, he says, "Three passions have dominated my more than sixty years of mostly happy life: books, women, and the road."[3] That's pretty good company, being third only to books and women.

McMurtry is a collector of books and claims that he has read and thought about over 3,000 travel books. He says, "I have also read a fair amount about the great roads or routes of old, the famous caravan routes, particularly the Silk Road out of Asia and the spice and salt routes in Africa, mainly out of an interest in nomadism itself and in the desire humans seem to have to migrate, even though the routes of migration are hard. Trade has usually been the motive for travel on the routes, but the need to be on the move may be an impulse deeper than trade."[4]

Perhaps that should be my title for this paper—an impulse deeper than trade. It is certainly a deep impulse for me. My childhood of the 1940s and 1950s is filled with many fine memories. Despite the fact that those years were on the heels of the Great Depression and sandwiched between two wars—World War II and the Korean War—I had a childhood oblivious to all but the world of my family and friends.

In those two decades, we lived on the edges of a mushrooming urban Goliath—in a part of West Dallas called Cockrell Hill, and then in far south Oak Cliff. We were lower middle class, my parents having been brought up on farms east of Big D and struggling for the necessities and luxuries afforded the pastor of several small Missionary Baptist Churches. Most of our neighbors talked and acted like they were just a few steps from the plowed fields of Texas farm life.

The memories of those times are overwhelmingly good: going to the Cockrell Hill indoor theater or the Chalk Hill drive-in theater; visiting my grandparents, Momma and Poppa Ausbrooks, on their farm outside of Garland, where they lived in the house where I was born, a house in the middle of a cotton field; staying a couple of weeks each summer on a farm with my country cousins; and taking annual vacations with my parents, my brother, and my sister.

In fact, most of the truly great memories I have of my youth involved some sort of travel. These are the things that have stuck with me. For instance, we made more than one vacation out of trips to Carlsbad Caverns. In 1952, when I was nine years old, we drove a gray 1950 Plymouth four-door on one of the grand adventures of the Harris family. My parents still recall it fifty years later. We went west along Highway 180 through Fort Worth, Snyder, Lamesa, and Seminole before jumping off into exotic New Mexico. We went through Hobbs, New Mexico, to Carlsbad, and then south out of the town to the caverns and into country that seemed like the edge of the earth. Sometimes I think it odd that Mary and I have lived only a few miles from those caverns for the past twenty-six years.

On another one of our annual vacation trips, my family drove up Pikes Peak. That trip was made in the same 1950 Plymouth, and when we reached the top of the mountain I thought we had ascended Everest. The road had been important in the families of both my father and my mother. My grandfather's great-great-great-great-grandfather on my father's side came from Wales. My grandfather Harris came to Texas from Arkansas in 1914. On my mother's side the Ausbrooks family came from England in the early 1700s, settling first in Virginia. My grandfather Ausbrooks came from Tennessee to Texas around 1904. He took the family to Hall County, west of Childress, where a storm blew away his house while he and his family huddled in a storm cellar. A blacksmith and a farmer, grandfather Ausbrooks put the family in a wagon and drove to Dallas County, country not so wild as the Panhandle. They settled northeast of Dallas near Garland.

Many of my memories of the 1940s and 1950s involve some sort of travel, and getting on the road was as much of a tradition in my family as was Wednesday night prayer service. Well, perhaps that is a bit of an exaggeration. The trips, though, were customs in the Harris house that had a tremendous impact on me. I think I would go so far as to say that there were no other experiences more important in impacting the way I have lived and the way my own immediate family has lived. Being on the road has been at the center of my life and of the lives of my wife Mary and my son Hawk. Life has been a highway for us. We have carried on the vacation tradition and developed it. And I think that has been the case for many Texans and, indeed, for many Americans.

Here are some of our proverbial expressions about the road that are part of American speech:

> A man never got lost on a straight road. Don't cross the road till you come to it. Every road has a turning. Follow the straight road. It is a long road that does not end. It is a long road that goes nowhere. Keep in the middle of the road. No road is long with company. The middle of the road is safer. The road of life is lined with many milestones. The road to hell is paved with good intentions. There is no royal road to learning.

The folklore of travel is an enormous subject, and I would like to suggest in the remainder of this presentation some of the possibilities for detailed study of Texans on the road. First, a definition. I have used the expression "on the road" several times already. What I mean is just movement that involves some time and distance. It might be temporary movement, such as a vacation, or it might mean permanent movement, such as in pulling up stakes and finding a new home. It might mean movement for business, as a modern truck driver might experience, or it might mean movement for pleasure, such as a trip to South Padre Island. Being on the road might be movement that is voluntary or movement that is forced.

Here is my list of the top ten approaches to the study of travel lore:

1. Modes of transportation, such as by car, truck, train, motor home, plane, bicycle, or foot.
2. Destinations—where the traveler goes, such as traditional locales like Galveston or Big Bend.
3. Stopping places along the way, such as motels, camp sites, roadside parks, and rest stops.
4. Reasons for traveling, such as business, recreation, and health.
5. Psychological impulses and ramifications, such as a need for mobility or a need to escape the routine of ordinary life.
6. Who it is that travels, such as individuals alone, people in tour groups, families, or different economic groups. Recently, I learned that private pilots have clubs for owners of particular types of planes, and that they rendezvous in different locations for annual celebrations.
7. When we travel, such as during summer vacations, on religious days, or on designated national holidays.
8. Traditions within certain businesses that depend on travel to make a profit, such as UPS, the postal service, airlines, and outfitters who take hunters into the outback of the Valley.
9. Differences between true folkways of travel and travel created by advertising, popular culture, or mass media.
10. Differences between different kinds of travel traditions, such as stories a family might tell about a particular vacation trip, games they might play traveling down the highway, or the foods they consume along a traditional route.

To illustrate just how enormous is this subject, the folklore of travel, I will mention just one topic that I think has potential for study. Mary has wondered for several years how I was going to work into a TFS presentation something that has become a hobby for me and for hundreds of other folks in the Southwest and in America. The subject is running. Distance running. Road racing. I think my love of the sport and hobby has come partly from my love of travel.

For more than two decades, I have been a jogger interested in keeping off a few pounds. For the last five years, I have been a racer, running in competition against individuals who are roughly my own age. I have run road races in several states, including Texas, New Mexico, Arizona, and Nevada. I belong to several clubs; the Hobbs group is called The Road Warriors. I also belong to the Arizona Road Racers, the Roswell Running Club, and the Midland Running Club. The West Texas Running Club, headquartered in Lubbock, is the one I am closest to; I run thirteen club races each year with them, and then several other races in town that the club helps organize. Last year I ran twenty-five races, the shortest a two-mile sprint, but most of them three, four, or five miles, and the longest a 10k, or 6.2 miles. I run about thirty miles a week in training.

This year in Austin, on April 1, I ran in the 24th Annual Capitol 10,000, in which over 15,000 runners participated. My son Hawk is the real runner in our family, having run cross country races since he was in junior high school. He is the one who inspired me to start running competitively when I was 53 years old. Hawk finished 25th out of those 15,000 runners in Austin. The *Austin American-Statesman* carried the story of Austinite Sid Smith, who is 90 years old and has run each of the races since 1983. The Saturday headline read, "Still in the running. At age 72, Sid Smith raced his first Cap 10k. At age 90, he sees no reason to quit."

Hawk started me racing, and going to the races has become a custom that has kept our immediate family close. On February 10, 2001, we traveled to Las Vegas, Nevada, where Hawk ran a half-marathon and Mary and I ran a 5k race in the streets of the glittering gambling capitol. I think of our road races as an extension of our love of the road. Running six miles around Buffalo Springs Lake outside of Lubbock is just a long road trip in miniature.

I think the numbers of individuals doing it, and the length of time that it has been popular, make road racing more than just a fad. It is true that its popularity has something to do with the love of professional and amateur sports that has consumed the nation. It is also true that the popularity of running has something to do with our consciousness of the importance of staying fit, of the baby boomers and the rest of our aging population wanting to stay healthy, and of all of the medical data that reminds us of how important it is to be active.

But in October of 2001, I will run in the 20th annual Red Raider Road Race, which is run on homecoming weekend at Texas Tech University. It is sponsored by the WTRC, and it will be the sixth year that I have participated. I would love to spend some time talking to you about the traditions, customs, and practices of road racers, the marathoners and those who run the shorter races. Their rituals and customs are just as elaborate and complex as any other group formed by common interests. For instance, if you are a runner, you don't want to mention certain four-letter words, such as "rain" or "wind" in the days before a race. Some runners wear a particular article of clothing for good luck. For some, a particular meal the night before a race will result in a good finish. Runners have their own vocabulary. The term "hit the wall," for instance, means to arrive at a point in a race when it feels like all the body's fuel has been used.

Runners are different. They think differently, they act differently, and they are a unique group of men and women who have their own heroes and legends, who have their own superstitions, who have their own practices that some would think as fanatical. For the last ten years, I have spent a week the first part of June on a lake in the bush of northern Saskatchewan with some Canadian friends. When I run in the mornings on the northern Cree Indian Reserve, I wear a bell to make sure I do not startle a bear and get a leg bitten off, which would probably slow me down a bit.

Have you heard that joke? The park ranger is guiding hikers through the woods and telling them to be very careful because they are in bear country. The ranger says, "Always wear some bells so you won't surprise them, and be careful when you come across bear scat on the trail. And be especially careful if you come upon some grizzly bear scat." One of the hikers asks the ranger how you tell grizzly scat from black bear scat. The ranger says, "The grizzly scat is the one that has the little bells in it."

There's a road joke for you. But back to the running. When I travel today, wherever I travel these days, I spend some time exercising on the roads of that place. I have run on farm roads in Ireland, on the city streets of Papeete, Tahiti, in the deserts of southern Arizona, on the beaches of the island of Kauai, in the mountains of New Mexico's Sacramento Range, along the Kenai River in Alaska, along the harbor in St. Thomas, and many more places. It is a different way of seeing and knowing a place.

Road racing is not just a fad. It is here to stay. The Boston Marathon and the thousands of small club races held around the country will continue, partly because they are for amateurs as well as the professionals. This is not going away. I have a feeling that at a TFS meeting 100 years from now some man or woman may be giving a presentation on the beginning of the road racing clubs back in the 1960s.

Road racers make up just one small part of the thousands of individuals crowding the American road. Do they represent a folk group? Not as we have defined folk groups in the last century-and-a-half. But as everyone is aware, as we move into the twenty-first century, as we move along the information super highway, we are going to be rethinking our ideas about who constitutes a group.

Geography, language, and ethnicity do not divide us as much as they once did in America, and I think one of the many ways that we might help decide who we are is to study our traditional lives along the roads that connect us. Perhaps one of these days we should designate one of our annual publications to the subject of Texans on the Road—this impulse deeper than trade.

ENDNOTES

1. Larry McMurtry. *Roads: Driving America's Great Highways.* New York: Simon & Schuster, 2000. 11.
2. Ibid., 11.
3. Ibid., 11.
4. Ibid., 14.

Archie McDonald

TRAVELING TEXAN

by Archie P. McDonald

People just can't stay put. As much as we love hometowns, or Texas, or America, curiosity and horizons summon us to adventures beyond the seas. Texans, no less than Connecticut Yankees, wander the world with itchy feet and wide eyes at the wonder of it all.

I joined the caravan late. Apart from occasional excursions across the Rio Grande, I was dangerously close to the epitaph I read in an old novel a half century ago: "Here is my butt, the very watermark of all my sails." Title and author escape me now, so this is as much attribution as I can muster for a line I wish I had written.

Then, in 1986, Ab and Hazel Abernethy tolerated my tagging along with them to Australia for three weeks on a folklore exchange. Ask Ab about our assignment to entertain the inebriated crew of the USS *Joseph Kennedy,* in port at American River on Kangaroo Island, South Australia, or the controversies that come with comparison of Queensland versus South Australia beer.

The passport acquired for visiting Australia got another stamp in 1990, when the fellow slated to escort fifteen high schoolers on a three-week summer trip to Germany had to withdraw. "Have passport and will travel," says I, when the chairman of the exchange committee asked me to take over. The deal involved round-trip airfare and home stay with Rotarians in three cities. How could a schoolteacher turn down such an invitation?

We gathered in Houston for the Lufthansa flight, and the Rotarian in charge of all this sternly, but I feared futilely, attempted last-minute lessons in etiquette and deportment; I told them we were going to have fun. When we arrived in Frankfurt for the transfer to Bremen, I asked my high schoolers to stick close until we found the gate for our next flight. I needn't have bothered. When they saw security guards patrolling with automatic weapons, my charges went to big-eyed but becalmed anxiety.

In Bremen, the kids scattered to homes in various cities and I was taken to the home of Dr. and Mrs. Viehoffs in a small town. We all gathered on a farm near Bremerhaven a week later, which enabled me to confirm that there had been no hasty marriages, broken bones, or international incidents; we scattered again—my next billet was in Mella—rendezvoused for a three-day tour of the German Democratic Republic and Berlin, scattered once more with me visiting with the Rochmanns in Achen, and finally reunited at the Bremen airport to return to Houston. Here are some memories:

- all my hosts had been prisoners-of-war after WWII, with all but one grateful to have been in the custody of American or British forces instead of Russians;
- in those days, a West German could say "GDR" and make it sound like profanity;
- German beer really isn't better than American, French, or Italian beer, but it is more pervasive;
- in East Berlin, still communist then, I attempted to switch a purchase in mid process to a more expensive item, which irritated the clerk—my host explained that the amount of my purchase was irrelevant to the clerk, whose pay was decreed by the government;
- most Germans speak English—I mean BBC English—which leads me to the following tale.

Before departure, my wife suggested that I get out the German books that helped me pass that language test I needed to receive a Ph.D. at LSU in 1963. I declined, fearing I would give offence. I couldn't wait to tell her of my visit to a plastics factory conducted by proprietor Claus Spies. His explanations were all in German, then translated for me. Finally, he conducted us to his office for coffee, where he spoke the only English of the visit. Gesturing politely to a chair, and with a smile, Claus invited me to "Sit on your arse." A perfect description of the anatomical action involved.

The author on the street in Beaune, Germany

In March 1991, my colleague at SFA, Jere Jackson, led about forty of us on a fiftieth anniversary, World War II tour of London, a channel crossing to Normandy, and on to Paris. I fell in love with Paris. The saying is "See Rome and die," but I believe everyone should see Paris—as often as possible—and live! The "us" cited above included my wife, Judy, who served as a city commissioner and then mayor of Nacogdoches for nine two-year terms, so until 1996 we traveled with Jere only in non-election years, always over Spring Break—though we left early and stayed late to enjoy twelve days in, by now, every country in western Europe and one memorable trip to Egypt. Judy's mayoring also enabled four trips to Japan as part of a sister city/sister university exchange with Naze City, Amami Island, and the Nissho Gakuen Educational Corporation, headquartered in Miyazaki. Along the way, granddaughter

Kelly accompanied us on trips to London, France, and Ireland. (I have now every grandparent's dream: an excuse to tell you about my perfect granddaughter. Some may call this "bragging" but grandparents will recognize it as just good reporting.) Here are some memories, and lessons learned, from a Texan perspective, about these marvelous adventures.

For most of the year Kelly then lived in North Texas with her parents. She spent some of the summer in Nacogdoches with Papa and MiniMac, the moniker our mischievous son taught her to call her five-foot grandmother. MiniMac determined one or two weeks insufficient, so she contrived an extension—after Kelly's visit in Nacogdoches, they'd have another week's vacation for the whole family. At age four, this meant that MiniMac took *my* granddaughter and her parents, *my van,* and *my credit card* to Colorado after I had started fall classes. They got away with this just one year. For ages five and six, I accompanied them; age seven, we took the Inland Passage cruise to Alaska; age eight, we visited London—the real London, where Big Ben lives. We had read about him in numerous books, and on our first day there we experienced his solemn tolling of the time.

We visited the War Cabinet Rooms, petted the horses at the Horse Guard station, marched with the band to change the guard at Buckingham Palace, toured the Tower of London, attended Evensong services at St Paul's, viewed the tables and tombs honoring monarchs and poets in Westminster, and bounced in the red double-decker busses above and swayed in the Underground below to various destinations in the city. And on the flight home, Papa got to visit the flight deck of the British Airways *777* just because a flight attendant thought an eight-year-old girl ought to have the experience—and let an old man tag along. What is not "perfect" about that? How can you build a better memory? Maybe in Paris.

I already had promised Kelly that Judy and I would show her Paris when she became twelve years old. Never make promises to little girls unless you intend to keep them. She never forgot; even in London, when Judy had asked her something about that trip, she replied, "Yes, and when I'm twelve I get to go to Paris." She made it at eleven years, nine months because I couldn't let the chance to show my best girls the City of Lights escape me.

We departed the day after Christmas and spent the next six of them in the most beautiful city in the world. We included museums on our itinerary because one simply cannot travel to Paris without visits to Musee D'Orsay or the Louvre. Impressionism *is* French art to most Americans, and one *must* view the *Venus de Milo, Winged Victory,* and the *Mona Lisa* without the filter of photography, if such is ever possible. DaVinci's most famous work disappoints most tourists because it is small and displayed so darkly, and because so many others want to see her that guards literally exhort viewers to remain in motion as they pass by. I expect we spent about as much time in museum shops and restaurants as we did with the art, but hey, it's Paris—it's *all* art.

A tour by bus of historic Paris and another to Versailles helped fill some days, as did frequent visits to Galleries Lafayette, Paris' most famous and interesting department store. Metro rides to explore Montmartre, La Chapelle, a special Sunday visit to St. Sulpice for the organ concert, the *Arc de Triumph* and *Tour Eiffel* (as the French call Mr. Eiffel's tower), filled our days, as did lingering dinners at various street cafés evenings.

A special New Year's Eve dinner aboard a *Bateau Mouche,* followed by watching midnight fireworks in the *Place de Concorde* while standing in the middle of what seemed like a million people on the *Champs Elysees,* topped the trip. On the way home, Judy asked Kelly for her best memory of Paris. "All of it," she replied.

While Judy served as mayor of our town, she helped develop a sister-city relationship between Nacogdoches and Naze City, Japan. The moving force from the Far East was Daiji Goto, chairman of the Nissho Gakuen Educational Corporation. Goto is a man of means who uses some of his wealth to promote world understanding. This relationship resulted in several trips to Japan to visit Goto's schools. I was permitted to tag along, and soon learned that my name in Japan is "husband." It is almost a promotion when sounded in that patriarchal society. Our trips involved more than schools, for the Japanese are marvelous hosts. They wanted us to understand as much as possible about their geography, culture, and cuisine. About the latter, I really think they just wanted a good laugh while we confronted unaccustomed creatures from the sea with chopsticks.

On one visit, they took us to Nagasaki. The historian in me was eager to examine the site of our second nuclear bomb, delivered on August 9, 1945, as the *coup de grace* to end World War II without an invasion of Japan. The American in me was a little anxious about the visit. We sat for photos at Ground Zero, which is marked by enlarging circles in a now tranquil park. We visited the memorial museum, which includes no politics in its exhibits—only consequences. I'll never forget the display of mangled, gold eyeglass frames.

A day later, Goto asked our reaction. We pussyfooted a bit until he seized our attention with the admission that the bad bomb had produced a better Japan. Goto explained: a boy of seven in 1945, he was trained to defend Nippon with only sharpened bamboo. His father, a soldier survivor, came home and founded schools, because, he said, education was the only route to peace. His best pupil was his son. Goto did not *like* that bomb, but he accepted it as necessary shock treatment to stop the war. The co-pilot who dropped the first atomic bomb recorded only "My God . . ." when he looked back into the mushrooming cloud in his wake. I don't know his inflection then, but after our visit to Nagasaki and Ground Zero, that sounds like a prayer.

Our visits to Japan made us prime targets to host Japanese guests when the John Manjiro Whitfield Foundation chose Texas for its twelfth Japan-America Grassroots Summit with Nacogdoches as one of the host cities for forty Japanese for a weekend emersion in American culture. For forty-eight hours—noon Friday to noon Sunday—they were dealt out for homestay. Since Judy was in charge of the dealing, we got two guys—Fukuda Asushi and Matsuo Hitoshi. This was an act of faith—we can say good morning in Japanese—"*ohayo gozaimasu*"—and a few more pleasantries; their command of English exceeded ours of Japanese, but not by much. Nonetheless, it is amazing how much communication can be achieved with pointing and facial expressions—especially a smile—and good will.

"Good will" is the whole point of the Summit and of the sister city relationship between Nacogdoches and Naze. We are peoples of polar opposites. Their society is remarkably homogenous—imagine a street, a school, an auditorium, filled with folk of black hair and dark eyes and copper skin, and mostly dressed in dark, formal clothing. Similar settings in America offer shades and hues of all these aspects, and casualness of dress.

Japanese are compulsive about the exchange of "business cards," which tells as much about what they are as who they are. There is a protocol to the presentation, acceptance, and fate of the card that Occidentals simply have to be taught—it would never occur to them that the card must never be stored in a pants pocket.

Here is a moment of the visit others might like, at my expense. One of our city's guests, Yoshie Nakayama, a bright and attractive lady of fifty-two who was billeted with a friend, seemed always around me when we gathered for dinner or a ranch party. On the final day of the visit, she told me why: "You remind me my father." She spoke *that* English plainly enough for everyone to hear and to the amusement of all but one.

On our Spring Break trips to Europe, Judy and I join a group of old friends. We have numbered as few as twenty-five and as many as fifty on these trips, always led by my History Department colleague Jere Jackson. Jere does this better than anyone I know, and most of us, who are decision-makers in our real lives, luxuriate in not having to decide much for a fortnight—Jere plans everything and we are just proud to show up at appointed places and times. A 4:00 A.M. departure from Rome strained us a bit, but not so much that any wanted to be left behind the next year.

We are sufficiently experienced to wear comfortable shoes, carry travel-sized umbrellas, and know when it is safe to drink the water, though some of our friends will appreciate me not mentioning names of those who prefer to sample local wines as much as possible. I have learned that it is always best to travel with good

friends, especially if they are doctors. Our little band had two medical crises one spring and it pleases me to report that when needed,
both of our traveling medicos responded promptly, competently,
and without apparent concern for malpractice suit.

First, one of our friends fell in the street of a small town in
France. The blow opened the skin on a good portion of his fore-
head and his glasses plowed a deep furrow across the bridge of his
nose. Hand surgeon Dr. Dennis Stripling responded immediately.
Dennis cleaned the wounds, produced bandages from a store in his
luggage, and gave our friend a non-narcotic pain medication. For a
while he kept an ice pack supplied from a nearby *brassier* on his
wounds. Though he had bled like a stuck pig, as we say in East
Texas, he healed nicely and only those of us who know can even
detect a scar.

Two nights later, another of our number stoppered her
esophagas with a hunk of lamb. Our other doctor, Hamp Miller, a
gynecologist/obstetrician who treated my sinuses in Vienna one
year, responded immediately. Relieved that the obstruction
involved the esophagus rather than the trachea, which meant there
was no danger of suffocation, Hamp nonetheless tried the Heim-
lich Maneuver, to no avail. Then, abandoning dinner, they spent
much of the night in an emergency room in Nice, getting the lamb
to lie down. It is a great comfort to us to know that we have com-
petent, caring, and willing medical providers to minister to us in a
time of need, in a foreign place, when we know not where else help
is available.

On one of our spring trips, we visited the Burgundy area of
France and Jere arranged for us to examine the vineyards operated
by the Duchess of Magenta, and to lunch with her at Chateau de
Sully. We arrived at the vineyards late of a cold but bright, sunny
morning, and there awaited the Duchess. I don't know what the
others expected, but I had envisioned a dowager making a living by
capitalizing on her title. Only part of that was true.

A tall, dark-haired woman, perhaps forty-five years of age, met
our bus at the edge of the vineyard. She did so quite democratically
for a duchess, shaking hands all around and greeting us with a

decidedly English—turned out she was a Scot—not French, accent. The Duchess set to her work, which was more tell than show because, in March, vines have been pruned to a single runner not far up a gnarled old stump, and await only warmth to spring into annual renewal. Afterwards, the bus followed her auto to Chateau de Sully. Upon arrival I received a warm greeting from the friendliest golden Labrador retriever I ever met, and we had lunch and samples of the yield of grapes of previous years.

The Duchess visited each table-of-eight during the meal and the sampling, never volunteering personal information but also never declining to answer a question. In doing so she revealed much about herself and her culture. She, a daughter of Scotland, had met the Duke of Magenta, her senior by about twenty-five years, at a wedding of mutual friends. Their eyes met, said she, "across a crowded room," and it was love at first sight. The Duke's reputation as a man of many lady friends did not discourage her, for indeed, both had found the love of their lives. So they married, had a boy and a girl, and . . . lived "happily ever after" if "after" describes their fifteen or so years before his fatal illness. Anticipating that this might happen, perhaps because of their ages, the Duke insisted that the Duchess learn the process of wine making from the ground up—literally. Now she was preserving the chateau, winery, and their way of life for their son, the next Duke of Magenta, still a schoolboy.

At this point all the ladies, whether or not they had ever read a romance novel with Fabio on the cover, had melted. What got the guys came later, when we departed, and that tall, brave, and determined lady—the Lab looking up at her—kept her eyes on our bus traveling all the way down the lane through the grapevine stumps back to the road and lives beyond the sea. Then she turned and walked, alone, slowly, back into her future. Where in the world is Fabio when you need him to make a story have a happier ending?

The group that Judy and I accompany on our Spring Break trips to the Old World makes every attempt to understand foreign cultures. Here is part of what we have learned—every quality European bathroom has a particular plumbing device called a bidet. I asked all our Texas travelers plus a few others attending a late afternoon gathering in one of our rooms, how one used a bidet. None would admit to possessing this knowledge. One did say that his Daddy had encountered a bidet back in the 1950s, and that it had spit right in his eye when he inspected it. Our tour director, an experienced European traveler of several decades, said that he had washed his feet in many a bidet back in the days when the actual bathing and toilet facilities were always "down the hall" with only this curious commode of a creature available in sleeping quarters.

The item in question looks a lot like the johnny one might find in any American home, except the manufacturer did not supply it with a seat, so imagine a toilet or commode without a wooden or plastic seat. Also, without a water tank. But there is a faucet controlled by valves marked "hot" and "cold." Officially this appliance is, "a fixture . . . for bathing the lower parts of the body." I'm not sure that means Jere's feet, but it may. Anyway, a pair of roommates found a use for the bidet at their party for the group. They filled it with wine bottles and everyone had their photo taken with it, even the Baptists.

We have, at last, moved to the bottom of the list of things Texans learn by traveling. The Department of State can advise you on the relative safety of other nation destinations, and your travel agent gives counsel on prices. But who will teach you how to flush a foreign toilet? You may think this a simple function, what with the nearly standardized American practice of slapping a lever beside a standup urinal or toilet, or depressing a handle on the front of a tank. This is not necessarily so in places outside our great state—or nation. In Asia and the Near East, one is likely to discover no toilet at all in the water closet. Instead, there is an opening in the floor, and places to locate one's feet. In Japan, a cup-shaped riser to the front provides directional orientation. Most westerners will shun these devices until pain levels approach Mach 4 or 5.

Most of what follows grew from a fact-finding expedition to France. The subject came up when one of us returned to our restaurant table and apologized for being unable to resolve the riddle of eliminating elimination. Each of us made the attempt; none found a solution. Turns out there was a lever beneath what appeared to be a small oxygen tank above the facility that had to be twisted with considerable torque. After considering the likelihood of obtaining a National Humanities Endowment grant to investigate this important cultural diversity, we judged this report sufficient. So, when "over there," here is what you may find:

- some ancient equipment with a chain—pull hard;
- some tanks will have a button in the middle and, depending on no circumstance I can decipher, you push it or pull it, and sometimes you twist it;
- some will have a plate in the wall above the tank, which has a butterfly function—you press at the bottom and sometimes must press again at the top to stifle the flow;
- one had the outline of a human hand on the top of the tank and when a real hand covers it, *voila!*
- And in downtown Paris, there are vending machine pay toilets on some street corners.

I didn't go for the NEH grant, but I wonder if this publication makes the trip deductible from my income tax. After all, I returned absolutely flushed with information about foreign cultures.

[Some portions of these reports on Texans abroad were drawn from Archie P. McDonald's weekly commentaries on Red River Radio, a National Public Radio affiliate network serving portions of Louisiana, Texas, Oklahoma, and Arkansas. McDonald's commentaries may be heard each Friday morning at 7:35 A.M. at 88.9 FM, or accessed via http://www.redriverradio.org.]

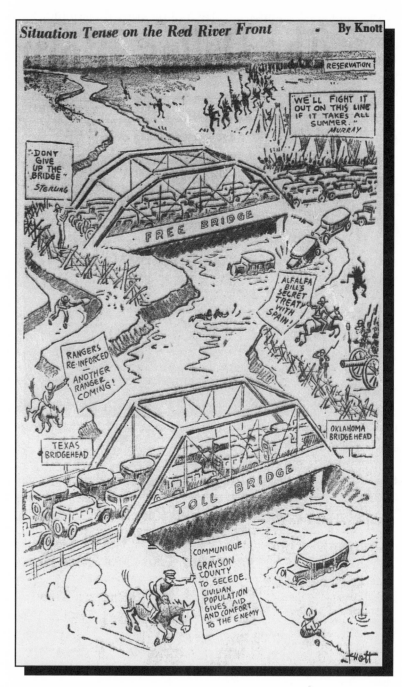

John Knott's July 23, 1931, editorial cartoon in the *Dallas Morning News*

RED RIVER BRIDGE WAR

by Jerry B. Lincecum

On Thursday, December 6, 1995, the old three-truss bridge spanning the Red River north of Denison was destroyed with 750 pounds of dynamite strategically placed by the Texas Department of Transportation. The blasting of this structure, which in 1931 became the most famous public free bridge across Red River between Texas and Oklahoma, marked the end of an era. However, few people know about the heated controversy it provoked six decades earlier.

This bridge was involved in a war—the Red River Bridge War of 1931. The magnificent new bridge was completed in April of 1931, through the joint efforts of Texas and Oklahoma, after their offer to purchase the Colbert Toll Bridge and two others was rejected by the toll bridge company. But its use was blocked by an injunction obtained by the Red River Bridge Company in Federal Court in Houston. Soon the controversy led to a confrontation involving the governors of both states.

First some background history. Colbert's Crossing had its beginnings at least as early as 1853, when B. F. Colbert obtained from the Chickasaw Indian Tribe a charter for a ferry across Red River. With language typical of Indian treaties, the charter was to last "as long as grass grows and water flows." The toll was $1.00 for a two-horse wagon, $1.25 for a four-horse wagon, $1.50 for a six-horse wagon, 25 cents for a man and horse, and 10 cents a head for loose cattle or horses. Immigration was heavy through 1871 and 1872, and the number of wagons crossing each day varied from twenty-five to two hundred. The boat ran on a cable across the river and could make a round-trip in twenty-five to forty minutes.

In 1872, the first Missouri-Kansas-Texas (Katy) train crossed the new railroad bridge across the Red River into Texas, and on September 23 of that year the city of Denison was established. Colbert soon built a wooden bridge across the river, but it was washed away in 1876. Then the Red River Bridge Company was established, with most of the stockholders being Denison residents. They claimed that in 1875 a franchise had been given to Colbert by the Chickasaw and Choctaw Nations for perpetual use to operate a ferry, and that they had purchased this franchise, which extended two-and-one-half miles on either side of the bridge they constructed. Their bridge served until the historic flood of 1908, which also destroyed the MKT railroad bridge located farther west. The replacement bridge built by the Bridge Company became highly profitable as auto traffic increased in the 1920s and '30s. The toll had risen to 75 cents for one-way or $1.00 for a round-trip.

As auto traffic increased, highway commissions of both Texas and Oklahoma decided it was time to free their citizens from the burden of paying tolls by buying up all the toll bridges between the two states. However, stockholders of three of the bridge companies refused to sell. The two highway commissions then agreed to build free bridges at the location of these toll bridges and thus force them out of business. In 1927, Senator Jake J. Loy of Grayson County shepherded through the Texas legislature a "free bridge" bill that empowered the State Highway Department to make some settlement with the bridge owners. This bill passed in the record time of twelve minutes, and it greatly advanced the career of Loy, who went on to serve several terms as Grayson County Judge.

Bowing to the inevitable, the toll bridge company finally agreed to sell for payments totaling more than $200,000. There was to be an initial payment of $60,000 and fourteen monthly payments of $10,000 each. The new bridge was authorized under a contract for just under $240,000, and construction began May 14, 1930. This triple span was to become the crowning feature of Grayson County's first new concrete highway, voted in as part of a bond issue in 1929, before the Great Depression hit. However, as the new free bridge was nearing completion in April of 1931, the owners of the toll bridge company had not been paid as promised. On July 10, 1931, before the new bridge opened, their lawyer obtained a temporary injunction in the U.S. District Court in

Houston, prohibiting use of the bridge on the grounds that the Texas Highway Department had not fulfilled the settlement agreement. In obedience to the injunction, Texas Governor Ross Sterling ordered barricades erected at the Texas end of the bridge. Signs at both ends of the bridge warned that the bridge was closed by court order.

Then entered Oklahoma Governor William H. Murray, known as "Alfalfa Bill." Born in Grayson County, Texas, in a small community named "Toadsuck" on the outskirts of present-day Collinsville, Murray had run away from home at age twelve. He did farm labor, chopped wood, punched cattle, sold books, taught school, and practiced law. Having settled in the Indian Territory, he got into politics, helped write the Oklahoma Constitution, became Speaker of the Oklahoma House of Representatives, served a term in the U.S. Congress, and served as governor of Oklahoma from 1931–35. To say he was colorful would be an understatement. He smoked long cigars and loved a good fight. He escalated this little dispute into a war.

On July 16, 1931, Governor Murray ordered an Oklahoma Highway Department crew to plow up the approaches to the Colbert Toll Bridge on the Oklahoma side of Red River, making it impassable, and then had the crew remove the barricades from both ends of the new bridge. Alfalfa Bill opened the free bridge by executive order, asserting that Oklahoma's half of the bridge ran lengthwise, north and south across the river; moreover, he claimed that the state of Oklahoma owned both banks of the Red River under the Louisiana Purchase Treaty of 1803, and contended that since the injunction issued by the U.S. District Court in Texas failed to name Oklahoma, he wasn't bound by its terms. He then invited the public to cross the bridge, and the response was enthusiastic to say the least. *Denison Herald* reporters counted 493 vehicles crossing in a forty-five-minute period, and estimates were that during a twelve-hour period, more than 3,000 vehicles crossed and recrossed the bridge. The exhilaration at finally being able to cross the Big Red without paying a toll bordered on hysteria.

Former Grayson County Judge Jim Dickson, who was county auditor in 1931, recalled that he was in a lodge meeting in Sherman when someone came in and excitedly broke the news that "The Bridge" had been opened for traffic. Judge Dickson said he and the others were caught up in the excitement. They quickly adjourned the meeting, put on their hats, jumped into cars and drove rapidly up to Red River, where they were among the very first to cross the free span. He emphasized the charge of excitement they experienced as a result of the opening of the bridge. But the celebration was premature.

Texas Governor Sterling, viewing "Alfalfa Bill" Murray's actions as defiance of the federal court order and an insult to Texas, immediately sent a detachment of Texas Rangers to re-erect barricades at the bridge and keep it closed until further ordered. In charge was Ranger Captain Tom Hickman, whose many publicized encounters with bank robbers gave him an international reputation. Meanwhile, the bridge company lawyers went to a federal district court in Muskogee, Oklahoma, and on July 24 a federal judge enjoined Governor Murray from blocking the northern approaches to the toll bridge. However, Governor Murray was not to be outdone. Acting a few hours before the injunction was issued, he declared martial law in a narrow strip of territory along the northern approaches to the toll and free bridges. He argued that this action placed him, as commander of the Oklahoma National Guard, above the federal court's jurisdiction. He ordered five companies of Oklahoma National Guardsmen to the north end of the bridge, stating that the bridges were to be defended "against all authority except the President of the United States." He dared the courts to take any action against his blockade of the highway leading to the toll bridge. The Oklahoma Guardsmen included a machine gun platoon and brought along a howitzer. They pitched camp on the north ends of both the free bridge and the Colbert Toll Bridge, with the howitzer and machine guns strategically placed. By now the *Dallas Morning News* coverage of these events included daily front-page stories and pictures.

In response, the Texas Rangers were reinforced by two additional Rangers and four Grayson County Sheriff's deputies. The Rangers' only armaments consisted of their .45 Colt revolvers. The *Dallas News* reported that some Texans, in an excessive display of state pride (or perhaps levity), claimed the odds favored the Texas Rangers. Armed with an antique revolver, Governor (or "General") Murray visited the "battlefield" and set up a tent on the banks of the Big Red, from which he inspected the troops and continued to govern the State of Oklahoma. Now each side was dug in, ready for battle. The situation was tense. A miscue could lead to a violent confrontation.

Having the toll bridge shut down as well as the free bridge was a major inconvenience, and local residents found a detour. Soon informants advised Murray that traffic was being routed across a toll bridge owned by the Kansas Oklahoma & Gulf Railroad, five or six miles downstream, at a location called Carpenter's Bluff, east of Denison. Determined to keep the pressure on and force a settlement, Murray ordered his troops to plow up the approaches of that bridge also.

In summary, the objective of the Rangers was to keep traffic on U.S. 75 from crossing the new bridge. Their Oklahoma counterparts kept traffic from entering the Sooner State on a toll bridge owned by a Texas company. The net result was that on the heavily traveled highway that ran from Galveston in the south all the way to Winnipeg, Canada, in the north, traffic ground to a halt.

Local citizens in particular were upset. The closure of the bridges, the shutdown of traffic, and the potential danger galvanized people in the affected area. Public meetings were held in Sherman and Denison on July 20 and 21. Resolutions demanding the opening of the free bridge were passed and sent to state officials. On July 23, 1931, an editorial cartoon drawn by the well known artist John Knott appeared in the *Dallas Morning News* with the headline, "Situation Tense on the Red River Front." At this point the *News* reported that "Alfalfa Bill" suggested a novel solution. He said the women of Texas and Oklahoma could solve the impasse and get the bridge open if they would meet there for some quilting and gossip. Undoubtedly, this was intended to send a message that he was open to a peaceful solution. However, Texas Governor Sterling was not receptive, calling the proposal "tomfoolery."

At this time the Adjutant General of Texas was William W. Sterling (no relation to Governor Ross Sterling). He accompanied the Texas Rangers to the south end of the free bridge and oversaw the erection of a stronger barricade than the one which had been destroyed by Governor Murray's men. Displaying a sense of humor as well as downplaying the seriousness of the "bridge war," Adjutant General Sterling sent a message to Murray, which can be paraphrased as follows: "If you are sending a brigade of Oklahoma National Guardsmen to the free bridge, I will have the four Texas Rangers remain on duty there; if you send only a regiment, I will allow two of the Rangers to return to Austin." He then returned to Austin and directed operations from there.

The Texas Rangers arrive

The only shooting that occurred resulted from the Texas Rangers amusing themselves with target practice. They used their Colt .45s to split playing cards and strike matches at twenty paces. The only casualty of the war came when an Oklahoma guardsman fell and ran his bayonet through his leg. This led to a short truce, as Rangers helped carry him over the bridge to the Texas side and then rushed him four miles to the nearest hospital in Denison.

On July 23, 1931, the Texas legislature, meeting in a special session, passed a bill which granted the Red River Bridge Company the right to sue the state in order to recover the sum claimed in the injunction. Governor Sterling immediately signed the bill into law. The bridge company then joined the state in asking the court to dissolve the injunction. Finally on July 25, Judge Kennery made an armistice possible. He dissolved the injunction and permitted Texas to remove the barricades. One of the first cars across the free bridge this time was the black limousine carrying the triumphant governor of Oklahoma.

With the barricades down, the Texas Rangers went home. However, on July 27, Governor Murray announced that he had learned of a plot to close the free bridge permanently, and he extended the martial law zone to the Oklahoma boundary marker on the south bank or Texas side of the Red River. Oklahoma Guardsmen were stationed at both ends of the free bridge, and Texas newspapers spoke of an invasion. The Oklahoma Guard refused to leave because Judge Kennery had not decided whether to make the dissolution of the injunction permanent. On August 6, he did make it permanent, and the guardsmen returned home. The war was over, and the Red River Bridge was assumed to be forever free of tolls. That is, unless the legislature sees fit to extend the current pattern of rapidly expanding toll roads to include another bridge over the Big Red.

The delayed opening celebration for the free bridge took place on Labor Day, September 7, 1931, but there was little enthusiasm. Local newspapers described it as a day of "good fellowship and feeling." Miss Jeanne Murray, daughter of the governor, broke a bottle of Red River water on the bridge, saying "I dedicate this bridge in the name of the governor of Oklahoma." But the governor of Oklahoma was not there; neither was the governor of Texas, nor even Senator Jake Loy, who started it all with his Free Bridge Bill back in 1927.

The legal war dragged on in the courts, as the toll bridge owners sought payment for their losses. Eventually they negotiated a new contract with Texas for $165,000, but that one was later repudiated. They also won a judgment against the state of Oklahoma in the amount of $168,000, but that was reversed by a federal appeals court. Finally, in 1938, peace was assured when Texas handed over $50,000 for full title to the toll bridge. Oklahoma also agreed to a settlement but never paid off.

The "bridge war" was brought back into public attention in the late 1930s when *Life* magazine reported (Nov. 21, 1938, page 11) that Hitler was using the incident for propaganda purposes. Photos of the armed Texas Rangers at the barricades were published in German newspapers with commentary suggesting that there was "continuous civil war" in the U.S.A. Nazi propagandists presented the bridge controversy as a dispute between the governors of Texas and Oklahoma, as evidence that the U.S. was not a nation but "a chaos of little states with different laws." Actually, as this paper shows, the dispute was between the owners of the toll bridge and just about everybody else.

In the mid-1950s, a new bridge was built near the 1930s span. U.S. 75 traffic was divided, with northbound using the new bridge and southbound on the old one. In 1960 the old toll bridge was closed to traffic because of its poor condition. Later the bridge burned when a natural gas line underneath it caught fire. The north truss of this bridge fell into the river during the fire. By the time the old three-truss bridge that sparked the controversy was destroyed in 1995, hardly anyone in Grayson County remembered the "Red River Bridge War" of 1931.

Sources Consulted

Dallas Morning News. July 17–25, 1931.

Handbook of Texas Online, s.v. "Red River Bridge Controversy," *http://www .tsha.utexas.edu/handbook/online/articles/RR/mgr2.html (accessed June 20, 2006).*

Life. Nov. 21, 1938, p. 11.

R. C. Vaughan. "Red River Bridge War." *The Life and Times of Grayson County, Texas.* Sherman, TX: Big Barn Press, 2006.

Wagon Train on break, but ready to go

WAGON TRAIN EXPERIENCE

by Carol Hanson

⌒

Nineteen-eighty-six was the Sesquicentennial of Texas—a mouthful to be sure—but a year in which our State attempted in a variety of ways to celebrate, memorialize, discuss, and make all sorts of tributes to all our Texas ancestors and the history of all that's "Texan." One of the more unique events of the year was the Sesquicentennial Wagon Train that began on January 2 in Sulphur Springs and wandered around the entire state for six months until it pulled into the Fort Worth Stockyards on July 3 to celebrate the Fourth of July there. It was my privilege to have the experience of riding a few days on the Wagon Train in May of that year, along with two of my brothers—who thoroughly enjoyed it as well. This is my account of our short journey.

I had contacted the Wagon Train Association in mid-March of 1986 to inquire as to the possibility of our traveling with the train. Since we had no wagon, horses or other appropriate animals, we were at the mercy of whatever arrangements were available to the general public. But the Association wanted to involve as many citizens of Texas who wanted to be there, so they had a wagon set aside specifically for folks like ourselves who just wanted a chance to experience the ride for a short time. Our confirmation, postmarked "No Trees, Texas," came about ten days later, saying that we could meet them in Tahoka.

Upon arriving, we quickly found there were basic rules for all participants, including taking care of the campsites, and having no firearms or alcoholic beverages. And those who had responsibilities for animals or wagons (which were a majority) also had to know this: "Be sure your teams can keep up. The Wagon Train will NOT be delayed by slow vehicles. . . . All teams must be shod and remain shod. . . . Wagons must carry water and provisions for their own team, teamsters, and occupants for the day. . . . Have your equipment in shape . . . will not be delayed for breakdowns and equipment failure."

The Wagon Train traveled at four miles per hour. No stallions were permitted. If a horse or mule kicked, its owners or caretakers were to put a red ribbon on its tail, to alert others in the animal's vicinity. "Wagons Ho!" was called around 7 A.M. There were water breaks about every two hours, but they were really for the animals, not the humans involved; it was well recognized that the journey's progress, in every way, depended on the animals and their health. More than one person told me that participants really had to love and understand animals, and most of those involved had nearly constant contact with the animals. After any animal was either unhitched or unsaddled, they still had be watered, fed, cleaned, given first aid, and often shod—as well as making certain they did not get loose during the night!

The wagon in which we were to ride was called "Big Pop's Wagon" and was designed for passengers, with bench-box style seats along each long side of the wagon. Above the seats were open windows with plastic window-covers which could be snapped in place, if needed. The wagon was painted a pale blue, with a loading door on the right side and three ladder-type steps and one wooden step to get inside. There was a storage area partitioned off at the back with a wooden wall; there were provisions there that the teamsters may need, but passengers could store whatever they needed for the day there as well. Across the top was a white canvas top in a slightly curved fashion, reminiscent of the old Conestoga wagons but not as tall.

Big Pop's was normally driven by a young man named Apache Barrett (isn't that a great name?), who was short with a wiry build, dark hair, and tanned skin. He rather looked like he could actually be of American Indian descent; that is, until you noted the beard, which no Indian that I have ever seen had, either on television or in old photographs. He was married to Vicky, who on occasion would drive the wagon to relieve her husband. We eventually learned that they had met on the U.S. Bicentennial Wagon Train in

Big Pop's view from behind the Georgia wagon, when Train is on the move

1976 (which I had never heard of), and both are native Texans from Sulphur Springs. They married a year later, and rode in a Conestoga wagon from the wedding to the reception! They had three children with them on the Texas Wagon Train—two daughters under the age of four, plus a son, James, who was older and attended the Wagon Train School.

The number of wagons varied during the six months of the Wagon Train's journey, but during the four days we rode that May, there were usually thirty-six. Two wagons did join while we were participating; one was a stagecoach that only stayed about three days. There were wagons from many other states beyond Texas' borders, which sort of surprised me. Big Pop's place in line was between the Georgia wagon and the two green wagons from the South Dakota Boy's Ranch. The Georgia wagon was probably the prettiest wagon, because it was more "artsey" looking than any others that I saw.

The "artsey" wagon from Georgia

We met several folks from other wagons during our time with the train. One was the wagon from Arkansas driven by Mr. & Mrs. Williams, whom we talked with our first night in camp. They had really sacrificed a lot to be on this journey. They had lived on a small farm and had sold almost everything they had to be there, including their tractor. Then there was Albert and Alice Nicely from Goshen, Virginia. They shared one of their riding horses with us one day on the trip. The horse's name was "W.T." (for Wagon Train), and he was probably the largest horse on the train. Most everyone had to mount W.T. from something—he was that big. The Nicelys decided to sell their wagon at the end of the trail in Fort Worth on July 4. They had hoped to get several thousand dollars off that sale, because the wagon had also been on the Bicentennial Wagon Train, but it only brought them $1900.

The oldest wagon was the Maryland wagon, which also had a sign attached which read, "Maryland: More than you can Imagine!" I was never sure whether that was an old Maryland travel slogan, or if it referred to their trip and experiences getting to Texas for the Wagon Train. The two Boys' Ranch wagons from South Dakota were both pulled by four large Belgian horses. The horses were rotated each day, so they actually had more than eight horses to care for, and the caretakers of those horses were the boys, who at each water break had to get buckets of water to take to their horses. Some of the other teamsters got rather peeved at how pushy the boys would be at the water tank, but when one of the boys told me that each horse required from four to six buckets of water at each break (and the breaks were no more than thirty minutes), I decided that it wasn't really too surprising that they might be a little pushy!

Depending on what the schedule dictated, each day's ride varied from ten to thirty-five miles per day. The schedule had been made earlier, taking into account the terrain of the area and, to some extent, the climate and expected crowds. The long days lasted from 7 A.M. till between 4:30 and 5:30 P.M.; short days might end around 2:00 or 3:00. Big Pop's Wagon used mules for pulling, and Apache explained rather early his primary directions for them: "Step up mules!" means "Let's go!" "Gee, mules" is "Go to the right," and "Haw, mules" is "Go to the left."

The Wagon Master was Gary France, a key factor to the functioning of the Wagon Train's routine. He was very experienced with animals and recognized as an excellent leader. My impression was that he carried the responsibility very well, helping where needed, but most importantly keeping the Wagon Train on schedule. It took me a while to understand the out-rider system, but each wagon had to have at least one out-rider. If the wagon was using a "four-up" team (four animals pulling) on the wagon, then there were two out-riders. They were to help the teamster with the animals in any way necessary during the day, and let the teamster know if there were any problems that he couldn't see with the wagon as it was moving. Also, they were the primary communication system between the Wagon Master or his deputies, or another teamster. Plus, there were additional out-riders designated by the deputies to assist the train as necessary and occasionally relieving some of the teamsters. During the final week of the journey, it was expected for the train to have 150 wagons and 300 teamsters!

Lunches were relatively short—no more than forty-five min-utes, if possible. Because every minute was valuable, there was a chuck wagon, but not the old-fashioned type you've seen on the old westerns. This was a modern one, motorized with a genera-tor, and not even resembling a typical wagon. It was really more like a small snack bar that you might see at a sporting or concert event. It wasn't any larger than one of the big wagons, however. Its services were available to anyone who was hungry or thirsty, whether a participant or spectator. We usually tried to have our own lunches, but we took full advantage of the chuck wagon for breakfast and drinks! Its normal eating fare at lunch was sand-wiches, burgers, hot dogs and the like, as well as lots of non-alcoholic beverages.

It didn't take long for us to realize that this was just one very long continuous parade. People came from *everywhere,* bringing their kids and grand-kids, just to watch and wave and take pictures. Of course, some of us (like my brother Phil and I) were taking pic-tures too, of the spectators! Some tried to ride along with us in their own vehicles. Others brought banners, saying: "Welcome Wagon Train!" or "Cooper/Levelland [town name] Welcomes the Wagon Train"—"Cooper/Big Spring Welcomes Y'all Folks!" The three of us enjoyed the heck out of it, and fairly soon became experts at waving and getting some of the children to wave back! My brother Phil is a bit of a ham, so he really loved that experi-ence, but my brother David commented early that first day, "I've never waved so much in my life!"

Our second day's ride was probably the most exciting. For some reason, Apache had to use a pair of mules which belonged to the Wagon Master, but they had never worked together. Apache had only used one of the mules before. Also, one of the mules had only pulled the lead wagon, and so was not accustomed to being behind any other wagon. Plus, the train had a couple of false starts that morning. The first "Step up Mules!" called went fine, but the second time, one mule balked a little at starting. Then, when we stopped a few minutes later, we were on a hill, so when we started forward, that mule's hooves slipped a little (the pavement was probably wet with dew) and apparently that frightened him, because he bucked a couple of times and then both animals took off at a run! The Wagon Master yelled for Apache to go off the roadway onto the grass, so they could get their footing, which they did. Apache told us, "Hang ON!" because we would be going over a curb and it would be rather bumpy! And it was pretty rough for a bit. I was a little worried the mules would just get worse and perhaps upset the children on board, but I was really glad to be wrong when Apache got them under control after a short distance. After going just over the crest of the hill, we re-crossed the curb and returned to our place in line.

During this entire episode, my brother Phil was at the front by the driver's seat, near the brake lever. Because Apache had his hands full with the reins and the whip, he asked Phil to help with the brake. Phil was happy to oblige by pushing the brake on and then off; that really made him feel a part of the wagon driving experience!

After lunch, Apache told us the troublesome mule's name was Frank, which Apache decided fit his outlaw ways, and that his full name must be Frank James. When the train started again, Frank was lying back and not pulling, making the other mule, named Lady Bird, pull extra hard. During the afternoon break, Apache asked Willie (his out-rider) and another rider to bring one of his mules to exchange for Frank. Unfortunately, they had to make the

Apache Barrett, the driver of Big Pop's wagon, with Mr. Truelock, one of our fellow passengers

change just after the break ended, and we had to pull over and watch the train pull off, leaving us behind for a bit. But it didn't take them long to make the change, and sure enough, Elvira (Apache's little red mule) pitched right in and gave Lady Bird a break. Lady Bird lay back for a while, but soon picked back up. The trade-out of mules put Big Pop's at the very end of the train, in the middle of the out-riders, and that made the rest of the day rather interesting and fun!

Every day was a little different. Our third day provided a rotating group of fellow passengers aboard Big Pop's, because the town of Levelland, which we were leaving from that day, had held a drawing for tickets to ride Big Pop's for a day. Since it had been decided to stretch the experience to several people, between two to three new people would get aboard at the end of each break.

Willie Hazelwood, outrider for Big Pop's wagon

We met Mr. Truelock, who was eighty-four years old; he had been raised west of Springlake, but had lived in Levelland for a long time. His son had won the ride, but wanted his father to ride instead. He told us he'd driven teams with both horses and mules; Apache asked which he preferred driving and Mr. Truelock responded, "That depends on what I'm doin'." Apache seemed to really appreciate that answer, and they both agreed that mules can usually last longer in a wagon's traces. Later, a young mother and her two children, Bonnie and Nick, rode with us. Poor Nick had a bit of an identity crisis, however. When he was asked his name at first, it didn't come out very clear, and Apache claimed he said "Heck" instead of "Nick," so for the remainder of his ride, Apache called him "ol' Heck." Nick would just sit there with a little grin and turn red every time Apache used the new nickname.

Bonnie was older and we enjoyed a good conversation. There was also something different about the wagon's team on the third day—Big Pop's was using a "four-up" team which, of course, helped distribute the wagon's weight better. The two animals nearest the wagon were the larger pair—Lady Bird (from the second day) and Belle Starr received most of the wagon's weight, while the front two (which included Apache's Elvira), were smaller and helped to keep up the pace for the ride. Apparently, it made things work better, because Apache did not have to use the whip at all that day.

I should tell a little about Willie, Apache's out-rider. Everyone liked him—he was a wonderful character. Apache enjoyed teasing Willie about riding at the end of the train, visiting the female out-riders. One evening, I ate with Willie and asked him about his old job in the oil-drilling business. He told me the places he had gone, including California, New Mexico, and several northern states. I

The Texas Wagon Train School, Gainesville, Texas

asked him if he'd ever gone to Alaska, and he said he'd had several opportunities to go, but had always turned them down—"Just didn't care to be that cold!" he said. He'd worked in the Dakotas . . . and that was as far north as he'd care to go. My brother Phil kept in touch with him for a few years after the train ride.

Apache was a very cheerful sort who enjoyed telling stories at any opportunity, which he had plenty of while he was driving passengers who had only time to listen. He was not one to withhold criticism, when he believed it was deserved, though he was equally generous with praise for those who'd earned his respect. Apache never seemed to mind explaining the details of the Wagon Train's routines or other information, although I'm sure our questions were probably ones he had answered dozens, if not hundreds of times in the previous four months before we rode. He obviously

The author, during a water break, beside the Big Pop wagon

The author's brother, Phil Stanglin, checks out the blacksmith's wagon

enjoyed his work, and he did what he could to make the ride pleasant for the passengers.

Although the Wagon Train's spectators, or short-term participants like us, didn't realize or appreciate this, the Wagon Train Association's participants considered the Wagon Train School an essential element. That was because of the need and desire to involve as diverse a group of people as possible. Without the school, the train would have only consisted of older folk, or those without children. Certainly they were welcome as well, but it was felt to be very important for such an historical event that people of all ages should be included. And since it would last six months, to include families with school-age children was an absolute necessity. Unfortunately, I didn't have the opportunity to meet the teacher or go inside the school wagon, but I was told they had computers aboard, as well as old-fashioned McGuffey Readers to work with. What a contrast!

Altogether, our journey was a rather surreal experience, albeit a rather peaceful one. Since we were primarily traveling in the north-west portion of Texas, there were times as we rode across the terrain that, except for the occasional fence-line or telephone pole, you could look out on the land and imagine how it might have appeared to those real pioneers of a hundred-plus years ago. We saw flat prairie as far as the eye could see, and since we were riding at the approximate pace of those distant ancestors, it provided the unique perspective of the land appearing to stretch on forever. Of course, we were riding on modern built road-ways, and even high-ways, and probably made much better time than they could. They would have probably been lucky to travel thirty to thirty-five miles in one day.

My brothers and I had a great time being involved in a never-to-be-forgotten experience that we will always treasure. What really impressed me about the entire experience were the people who were a real part of the train. Among those we visited, there was a definite attitude of neighborliness and team-work to accomplish whatever was needed that day. Whether it was loaning someone else a mule, offering a ride to the nearest store, or helping to repair someone's wagon or other equipment, they were all (as far as I could tell) ready and willing to do those things and more, if needed. And I believe that camaraderie alone was an appropriate memorial to the spirit of those original pioneers of our great state, and indeed, of our country. Besides that quintessential attitude, most of the "core group" of the Wagon Train folk were truly *committed* to making this idea work—for the train to function smoothly and for it to truly reflect, as much as possible, the spirit of those hardy ancestors who traveled west to Texas, through Texas, and for some, who traveled beyond Texas, to find and make a home for themselves.

Certainly, there were some modern conveniences permitted in this contemporary version of a wagon train. But surely our ancestors would have taken advantage of anything they could have used, depending on what they could afford, to make life easier on the trail, had it been possible. The trip was hard on both the original pioneers and those of the modern Texas Wagon Train's participants: sacrifices were made by both groups to be involved in the journey. Of course, loss of life or that looming possibility were not such a threat to this modern-day version of the wagon train, thankfully. But many folks put their routine life on hold for the entire six-month period; others could only make a part of the trip. And there were those who began a new life as a result of the modern Wagon Train: there were three marriages during the last month on the trail. In addition, in the animal world, there were two colts born near the end of the journey.

Everyone on the Wagon Train was there because they *wanted* to be, and would do it again, as several did, in smaller versions. Special friendships were formed while sharing the same feelings and similar activities as our state's ancestors. Some of those feelings included:

- RESPECT for the land traveled over (even if this trail was a paved one).
- EXCITEMENT of being on this unique journey, and the eventual BOREDOM of the routine drudgery and exhaustion after each long, rough day.
- FRUSTRATIONS caused by uncooperative animals and/or people and the RELIEF at the end of the long, rough days in bad weather, whether it was cold, hot, windy or wet.
- A TEAM SPIRIT, previously mentioned, to help each other make it to the end of the trail.
- A need for ADVICE/WARNINGS from someone who knew what was ahead or was needed, such as the Wagon Master or his Deputies. (In the old days, of course, that may have included Indian scouts and the like.)

The *modus operandi* was this: *"If the wagons are scheduled to move, they will—no matter what. If you can't come with us now, join us later when you can!"* There were many who rolled along on all 3,000+ miles of the journey: from Sulphur Springs south to the King Ranch, west to El Paso, north to Lubbock/Amarillo, and back east to Fort Worth, which *of course* is WHERE THE WEST BEGINS!

The author doing field research

FARM AND RANCH ENTRANCES IN WEST TEXAS

by Mary Harris

In Elmer Kelton's novel *The Man Who Rode Midnight*, the grandson of the old-time rancher and protagonist Wes Hendrix thinks about city folks moving to the country and pretending that they are ranchers. Kelton writes:

> Along the road, especially near to town, Jim Ed saw perhaps twenty fancy gateways of stone and steel and brick, bearing names like Angora Acres and Rancho Restful and The Poor Farm. He looked twice at a sign that declared Heavenly Days Ranch. These were the harbingers of an urban invasion, ten- and twenty- and fifty-acre ranchettes, homesites for city folk who wanted to play at the rustic life without suffering its discomforts.[1]

The novelist's references to "fancy gateways," and what he later refers to as an "entrance gate" or a "decorative arch," are called in this paper "decorative entrances." These decorative entrances are those highway and county road structures that announce to the passer that here is access to a Charolais ranch or a cotton farm, or as Kelton writes, smaller places where the people want "to play at the rustic life."[2]

These structures, that are *not* just gates, and may or may not have cattle guards, appear across Texas and the Southwest, but for this paper the study is limited to parts of West Texas along the Pecos River and east, with a few examples from the southern part of the state. In West Texas the entrances appear infrequently north of the area around Seminole and Lamesa. In the Panhandle, rarely do you find them along the major interstates and highways. South of the Seminole-Lamesa area, though, they appear regularly and seem to dominate some stretches of highway. In Elmer Kelton country, along Highway 87 between Big Spring and San Angelo, for example, it is rare that a rancher or farmer does not have some decoration at the entrance to his or her property. It appears that when one person erects an entry, others spring up like Johnson grass. Everyone wants to keep up with the Joneses, some would say.

Of course, some of these entrances are strictly functional, permitting or discouraging entry by particular groups. This study is limited to the decorative entries, or at least to those parts of the entrances that are non-functional, the intent being to see them as an aesthetic expression of the folk, a way of demonstrating originality by the rancher or farmer, while serving to mark his or her territory.

I might add as a footnote, that my husband, our son, and I traveled to the East Coast, then New England and eastern Canada one summer. And another summer, we traveled the entire West Coast and some of western Canada looking for entryways as we went. We saw very few in our informal survey.

Functional *and* personal

These structures may be thought of as a part of folk architecture, which includes, of course, fences, gates, and other structures outside the family dwelling. Warren Roberts in his essay "Folk Architecture," states, "In folk architecture . . . traditional plans are followed in that the owner or builder . . . follows a design or plan with which he is familiar, either in that it is the prevailing pattern in the area in which he lives or it is one employed by his forebears, while the materials, tools, and building techniques are traditional."[3] Based on Roberts' definition, the West Texas entries considered in this paper are definitely an expression of folk architecture. Rather than seeing them as attempts to keep up with the Joneses, builders of these seem to be following "prevailing patterns" and using materials native to the region.

In fact, using native materials is one of several important characteristics of the entrances. Where there is abundant rock, the rock entries dominate. Types of wood used in building them depend on the region. When wood or rock (other than caliche) are not available, brick or stucco entries are plentiful; or, when there is an

Incorporating native materials to supplement design

abundance of iron piping (as in the oilfields), the rancher becomes a welder and creates his own works of metal art. Sometimes the folk will use old telephone poles to decorate the entrances, or the driver across Texas can even see corrugated metal used.

Beyond the use of existing materials, some other characteristics include the following:

1. Often the entry is an extension of a fence; but when it is decorative, it will appear apart from it. The fence stops and the decoration begins.
2. The entry usually makes a portal, with a horizontal cross piece either curving from or at right angles to the vertical pieces.
3. Often the decoration will be in harmony with the house— the same type of brick, for instance, may be used on the house and on the entry.
4. Many times the decoration is added next to an existing gate, emphasizing again the non-functional nature of these structures.
5. Most of the entrances demonstrate the builder's need to express symmetry. Often the two sides are mirror copies, and only when an additional gate or cattle guard is added is balance violated.
6. Sometimes, as with an expression of folk art or architecture, the builder or craftsman will lean to extravagance of expression. Just across the West Texas line in Tatum, New Mexico, two welders decorate gates and entrances for many area ranchers and farmers. This father and son team, O. J. and Tex Welch, has been so successful that they have made the street signs for their town, and they do many advertisements for businesses in eastern New Mexico and West Texas.
7. Other characteristics of the entrances include the ranch or family name displayed, trees and shrubbery as a part of the decoration, hobbies of the owners announced and, finally, they may serve a commercial function.

Several times I have mentioned that these are ranch and farm entrances. Mostly they appear at the roads to ranches.[4] In fact, very few farmers build them. When the farmers do put them up, they usually build very small ones or tend to be very reserved in their expressions. There may be several reasons for this, other than the belief some people might have that the rancher is just showier than the farmer. For one, farmers usually drive wide farm machinery, such as cotton pickers, and cannot maneuver them through narrow entrances. It may also be the case that the farmer values every foot of the land for planting and feels it would be wasteful to use even a small space just for decoration. However, farmers also use "live fences" or entryways, which can be used as windbreaks or "as a method of demarcating their farms."[5]

As to why they appear at all, several reasons come to mind:

1. Psychologically, they may be ways to satisfy territorial instincts, or they may be just a way to say "I am."
2. Socially, the entries are a way of being a part of a larger community, identifying with neighbors, or they may become customized, economic status symbols.[6]
3. Artistically, the entrances may be an expression of folk art, the highway equivalent of the yard art and kin to mailbox art, documented by other Texas folklorists and various folk art organizations in other states.[7]
4. Practically, the entrances serve several functions, including welcoming visitors, rejecting unwanted guests, identifying a family in wide-open spaces, and notifying the traveler that out of the many gates and roads on a multi-sectional ranch, the decorated entrance is the one road to the house.

As to why these entrances came into existence in the first place, research is sparse. However, it may be these originated in wealthier parts of cities and towns where commercial architects have the opportunity to make the estate stand out with a fence and decoration.[8] Perhaps they were then picked up by rural folks. Second, if they originated in the country, they may be just an extension of the fence. Third, the entrances can be an elaboration of the gate, which often is the place where the structural integrity of the fence is reinforced with a crosspiece as a fence anchor.

According to Steen in his Texas history, in the 1870s when ranchers in West Texas put up thousands of miles of barbed wire, they were required to have gates at three-mile intervals, and they needed some way to designate the one entrance to the ranch house.[9] These entryways could have come into existence as spontaneous creations of the rural folks of the region, a product of the environment or necessities of West Texas or ranch country. Other folks might think of these entrances as originating far back in history, as elaborations of decorated heavenly gates.

In the Texas Folklore Society publication *Built in Texas*, C.W. Wimberly writes of elaborate gates built by individuals who wanted not only to mark boundary lines, but also to suit taste; they were "something to see."[10] Wimberly believes that the first cattle guards were built in the late 1890s, and it is a possibility that decorative entrances appeared after that time—that the entrances were extensions of the work that went into putting in a cattle guard. Regardless of the intent of the builders, the entryway is, in this part of the country, an often regular, familiar, and interesting structure to watch for while traveling. It is hard to explain why I became interested in the entryways. But somewhere along the road during our family trips, I got used to watching for them—these architectural expressions of the folk. These entrances may be functional or decorative, plain or fancy, homemade or professionally built. They are constructed of a wide variety of materials and probably for a variety of reasons. And whether or not research will ever show when or why these entryways came into existence, they will continue to be an enjoyable visual statement of folk architecture.

This paper began with a quote from an Elmer Kelton novel. I'll end it with a recommendation for the reader of his novel to find and enjoy some of Kelton's early artwork that shows that he too is interested in all kinds of entryways. And the next time you're on the road, be on the look out for farm or ranch entryways.

ENDNOTES

1. Elmer Kelton. *The Man Who Rode Midnight.* New York: Doubleday and Company, 1987. 20.
2. Ibid. 20.
3. Warren Roberts. "Folk Architecture." *Folklore and Folklife: An Introduction.* Richard M. Dorson, Ed. Chicago: The University of Chicago Press, 1972. 282.
4. Wildhorse Ranch [Culberson County, TX]. Retrieved January 8, 2007, from *http://www.reatarealty.com.*
5. S.D. Cherry and E.C.M. Fernandes. "The Overstory #38: Live Fences." *The Overstory: agroforestry ejournal.* Retrieved January 8, 2007, from *http://www.agroforestry.net/overstory/overstory38.html.* par.8.
6. Farm and Ranch Construction. Retrieved January 8, 2007, from *http://www.farmandranchconstruction.com/index.html.*
7. Wyoming Arts Council. Retrieved January 8, 2007, from *http://wyoarts.state.wy.us/.*
8. Amazing Gates. Retrieved January 8, 2007, from *http://www.amazinggates.com/.*
9. R.W. Steen and F. Donecker. *Texas Our Heritage.* Austin: Steck-Vaughn, 1962. 267
10. C.W. Wimberly. "Gates." *Built in Texas.* Francis Edward Abernethy, Ed. Waco, Texas: E-Heart Press. 1979. 192.

BACK IN

THE DAY

American settlers move into East Texas in this painting (detail) by Nola Montgomery. *Courtesy of the Interpretation and Exhibits Branch, Texas Parks and Wildlife*

LEGENDS OF THE TRAIL

by Francis E. Abernethy

~~

[A legend is a traditional prose narrative that has a historical setting and real people as characters. It deals with extraordinary happenings, even supernatural events, in a realistic way. Legends are folk history which document heroic or dramatic events of a culture's life.—*Abernethy*]

The following happened in August of 1886 on the Camino Real de los Tejas, where the Trail crosses Onion Creek southwest of Austin.

1886 was the drouthiest year in over a generation, and the wells had dried up, and the black land on Tobe Pickett's farm had cracks in it wide enough to swallow a jackrabbit. María, who with her husband Pablo were Tobe's hired help, walked alongside a great wide crack on her way to cut prickly pear for the hogs. As she looked into the depths of the crack, thinking to see a trapped jackrabbit, her eyes caught the gleam of old metal. A closer look revealed a crack's-width view of a large chest with an iron chain around it.

María had found the chest of gold the Spaniards had buried on the Camino Real when they were attacked by bandits a hundred years earlier—before Spaniards became Mexicans. María marked the spot and told her husband, and they waited and planned how they would get the chest out when nobody could see them.

They waited three days for Tobe to go into Austin and give them some privacy—and the night before the day that Tobe was supposed to go to town, leaving them time and space to dig up the chest and become richer than the governor of Texas—they heard a rumble of thunder in the northwest. It began to rain. It rained for a day and a night. And the creeks flooded and the wells filled and the black land became a gumbo that could bog a burro. And everybody rejoiced. Everybody, that is, except Pablo and María, who searched for days for evidence of their crack and the hidden treasure the Spaniards had buried along the Camino Real de los Tejas. But the land had swelled with the moisture and the crack had closed.

Finally they searched no more. "Sea por Dios," said Pablo, in resignation. "The gold is not meant for us."

"You are right," said María. "We will live the lives we have."

And that great chest of gold with a chain wrapped around it is still buried alongside the Camino Real de los Tejas. We have had a drouth this year; perhaps the earth is cracked once more down to the old Spanish treasure chest. Es la voluntad de Dios that some traveler—some day—on the King's Highway will find it. Let it be one of us.[1]

Now, I do not absolutely vouch for the veracity of that tale. I tell it as it was told to me. I can also tell you about several pack loads of Spanish church crosses and chalices and plates of gold and silver that to prevent their theft were dumped into the Attoyac River at the Camino Real crossing in San Augustine County.[2] And there are six jack loads of unimaginable wealth secreted at the bottom of a pond that lies close by the Camino el Caballo, the Smuggler's Road that left the Camino Real and looped around Spanish customs in Nacogdoches.[3]

The Camino Real is a corridor of myths and legends as ancient as the tracks of the first people that walked it. The Caddo Indians, who traveled the Trail and lived alongside it over a thousand years ago, have a tale which says that they came to East Texas out of a land of darkness. They brought corn with them and seeds for squash and pumpkins, and they journeyed from their dark, unknown past in the east to a new world of light on the Angelina and the Neches where the Trail crosses those rivers. And they met travelers with their greeting of "*Tejas*"—meaning "friend"—and gave Texas its name.[4]

The first Europeans to travel the Camino Real came as the result of the tales of great wealth hoarded among the Indians of the Southeast. Hernando de Soto and seven hundred men set out from St. Petersburg, Florida, in 1539 to find this wealth. Three years later the De Soto remnants were down to three hundred men and *up* to seven hundred hogs, but no treasure. Now under the command of Luis de Moscoso, they reached East Texas, tattered and torn and much poorer than the Caddo Indians they found at Guasco. These Caddos lived near the Old Spanish Trail where it crosses the Neches River in Cherokee County. Desperately searching for a route back to Mexico, Moscoso sent ten mounted scouts down an Indian trail that would become El Camino Real. They reached the Guadalupe River near present-day New Braunfels, but finding the natives to be as destitute as they were, they turned back up the Trail to Guasco. Moscoso and his men did get back to Mexico, but by boat, unfortunately not by the Camino Real.[5]

In 1690, 150 years later, when the Spanish came again to the Camino Real—this time to the land of the Hasinai Caddo, whom they called the Tejas—they followed the legend of The Lady in Blue. The Spanish began, however, in 1685 following *not* the legend but the reports of the landing of the Frenchman LaSalle on Spanish soil near Matagorda Bay. The Spanish were on him like a hound on a rabbit the moment he landed, and in 1689 Alonso de Leon found his pitiful French remnants at Fort St. Louis.

Franciscan Father Damian Massanet accompanied Alonso de Leon on the 1689 search for LaSalle. Father Damian came to New Spain following the legends of the miracles of Mother María de Jesús of Agreda, Spain. She was The Lady in Blue, who—according to stories she had told sixty years earlier in 1631—had by the miracle of bilocation (an enviable miracle of being in two places at one time) visited the land of the Tejas without leaving her convent in Spain. She said that while she was in the New World she had instructed the Tejas in the mysteries of Catholicism and had saved many souls for Christ. Father Damian encountered a group of these Tejas Indians in the vicinity of La Salle's Fort St. Louis.

The wily Tejas, as eager after gifts as my six-year-old grandson, with utmost sincerity told Father Massanet that they were familiar with the stories of God, his Son, and the Holy Mother—

La V: M: Maria de Jesus de Agreda. Predicando á los Chichimecos del Nuebo-mexico. Ant͛ d. Ca͂o͛ f:

The Lady in Blue preaching to the Indians of New Spain

and of course, The Lady in Blue. They begged that Father Damian send missionaries among them to teach them Christianity—and don't forget the presents!—even as a Lady in Blue had taught them years before when she had come down from the East Texas hills to their villages. Father Damian, ecstatic and convinced that this was the miracle of the Mother María, promised that he would return with Catholicism—and gifts—the following year when the corn was ripe.

In the spring of 1690, an entrada under Alonso de Leon and Father Damian Massanet came to "Cenis," a large Hasinai Caddo settlement near the Neches River (in the same general area as the village of Guasco that Moscoso had visited), and established a Franciscan mission. The Spanish dedicated Mission San Francisco de los Tejas on June 1, 1690. This tribute to The Lady was the first permanent European establishment in Texas on the Camino Real.[6]

Now that the Spanish had this Imaginary Kingdom at the far end of what was to be the Camino Real they decided to equip it with a governor. Consequently, in 1691 the viceroy appointed Don Domingo Terán de los Rios as the first governor of this newly created province among the Tejas. Terán planted the royal standard at every campsite on his gubernatorial entrada, claiming the land for Spain. His standard was *not* the flag of Spain, however, but was a banner that had the Crucified Christ on one side and the Virgin of Guadalupe on the other. Then he gave the land of the Tejas the unhappy title, "Nueva Reyna de Montaña de Santander y Santillana." Imagine, if you will, singing "The Eyes of Nueva Reyna de Montaña de Santander y Santillana are upon you"!

Governor Terán's bitterly cold tenure in Texas was not a happy one. His explorations in the winter of 1691 were expeditions out of hell, if there is an icy hell, and he reported to the viceroy that "the difficulty was so great that I [can] not find words to describe it." Our first Governor of Texas concluded his report with words to the effect that if he owned hell and Texas, he'd rent out Texas and live in hell. This catchy insult was later copied by other intruders into the Lone Star State.[7]

According to popular legend, Louis Juchereau de St. Denis is the trailblazer of the Camino Real. He was not, of course. The many trails from East Texas to the southwest had been traveled for centuries, but St. Denis, with his Frenchman's élan and panache, became the most famous. In 1714, St. Denis and a small band of Frenchmen and Caddo Indians rode the Camino Real corridors

In this sketch by Charles Shaw, St. Denis arrives at San Juan Bautista on the Rio Grande after traveling the Camino Real through Nacogdoches from his Red River trading post at Natchitoches, Louisiana

from Natchitoches through the camps of the Nacogdoches, then through the southern route to Paso de Francia and Mission San Juan Bautista on the Rio Grande.

The St. Denis story is hard to believe, even now. Can you imagine Diego Ramon's surprise when this *Frenchman* showed up on his doorstep at San Juan Bautista? Now look who's coming to dinner! And then St. Denis spent two years successfully playing bureaucratic politics with the Spanish, marrying Diego Ramon's granddaughter, and finally being hired (Can you believe it?) in 1716 to guide the Domingo Ramon expedition up the Camino Real, this time all the way to the founding of six missions and a frontier outpost at Los Adaes, the end of the Trail for the Spanish. I think St. Denis fully qualifies as a semi-legendary figure on the Camino Real.[8]

I would like to cite the St. Denis-Domingo Ramon entrada of 1716, as the coolest, most casual and laid-back expedition that ever went up the Camino Real. It has to be legendary in some sense. The troops were supposed to march twelve to fifteen miles per day, but they were continually stopping to chase deserters or find lost horses, or children. They spent all day March 17 fishing, and the churchmen claim that they caught 300 fish. Several other days were spent hunting and fishing—or when somebody got sick. March 26–29: "These four days," Ramon says, "I remained in this place because a soldier's wife gave birth to a child." Ramon camped on the Conchas River five days "so that all of the people would have plenty of time to confess their sins and pass Holy Week." They also went wild horse hunting on this stop. May 5 was a wedding day: "a soldier was to be married to Anna Guerra, an occasion that was celebrated with a feast prepared by his companions." June 2: "This day I remained here, because it was such a fine day." Eight days later: "This day I remained here, because it was a good camping place and because we wished to celebrate the Feast of Corpus Christi." Captain Ramon almost did not finish his diary because on the fourth of May he ran a horse race with a Frenchman that included snatching his hat from the ground while riding at full speed, and Ramon fell off his mount.[9]

The Domingo Ramon travelers were welcomed to East Texas—when they finally got there—by an Indian woman speaking Spanish. This was Angelina, an enduring legend of the Camino Real. Friar Isidro Espinosa tells in his trip's diary about "a learned Indian woman of this tribe (Hainai Caddo), reared in Coahuila," who met the Domingo Ramon entrada and thereafter acted as an aide and interpreter between the Spanish and the Indians.[10]

Artist Ancel Nunn's painting of Angelina, who helped shape the Spanish frontier in East Texas. *Commissioned by Claude Smithhart of Lufkin Printing Company for Bicentennial Project*

Angelina assisted the Spanish and the French during the period of exploration and settlement between 1712 and 1721 and was described by contemporaries as being "learned," "sagacious," and "famous." She was obviously greatly valued by the Spanish who named the Angelina River after her, and she would have shaken her head in wonderment had she known that she achieved such legendary stature that a county, a college, a river, and whole page in a Lufkin telephone book would carry her name—and that

In this etching by James Snyder, Father Margil is joined by the Indians and the Spanish to drink from the holy springs

nationally famous artist Ancel Nunn would draw a picture of her that made her look like a movie star. I think I see Linda Darnell in that role.[11]

If the Camino Real ever decides it needs its own saint or the blessing of one who definitely has the ear of God, it should appoint Father Antonio Margil de Jesus as its guardian angel. Father Margil walked the length of the Texas Trail twice—barefooted! sixty years old! and with a double hernia!—and this was after he had walked all the way from Costa Rica, with side trips through the Yucatan. Father Margil carried no food, only a staff, a cross, and a breviary. He ate one meal a day consisting of a broth of herbs and greens. He slept only three hours a night, the remaining time being spent on his knees in prayer with arms outstretched in remembrance of Christ's suffering on the Cross. Father Margil's religious zeal was already legendary before he traveled the Camino Real to East Texas, and stories about his walking on water and turning water to wine had sprung up wherever he had preached.

Margil's Nacogdoches legend grew out of the terrible drouth of 1717–18, when the Indians' crops failed and La Nana and

Banita creeks dried up and the Spanish were surviving on crow meat. According to legend, Father Margil spent a night in prayerful supplication and received a vision. On the next morning he proceeded to a high bank of La Nana Creek, about a hundred yards upstream from the Camino Real crossing. Here he struck his staff against the rock bank and two springs began to flow. The people were saved, and the springs were known thereafter as Los Ojos de Padre Margil, the Springs (or Eyes) of Father Margil. The City of Nacogdoches has purchased the traditional site of the Holy Springs, and it has now been cleaned and protected. The holy waters still flow (or trickle or seep), and I regularly bottle some for my friends who need its curative and procreational powers.

Another legend of Father Margil of the Camino Real was the tale of his encounter with the panther. The padre was traveling the Trail from Nacogdoches to Bexar when during the night a panther (sic "tiger") killed his baggage mule. When Father Margil awoke to the deed the next morning, he indignantly summoned the panther in from the woods, ordered him to kneel, and then loaded him with the dead mule's baggage. That panther had to carry the gear all the way to San Antone, where he was finally unloaded, pardoned, and allowed to return to his hunting ground. He was also sternly lectured about molesting mules that belonged to Roman Catholics.[12]

Legends on the Camino Real stuck to Father Margil like ticks on a bird dog. He is credited with starting the flow of the San Antonio River[13] and with conferring the name on the Brazos River.[14] I would strongly recommend that the name of Father Antonio Margil de Jesus be invoked at all deliberations involving El Camino Real.

And in the dramatic history of the Old Spanish Trail, who can forget that bloody conflict, The Chicken War. Two mighty nations,

Spain and France, faced each other in an uneasy truce across a gulley called the Arroyo Hondo, the eastern boundary of the Province of Texas. In Europe, this fragile truce broke into warfare, and the French in Natchitoches happily heard about it before the Spanish got their news. Thus, on the morning of June 19, 1719, French Lieutenant Philippe Blondel mounted a sneak attack on the mission at Los Adaes on the Spanish frontier. His army of seven soldiers surrounded the mission and captured all the occupants, which consisted of a lay brother and a soldier. The battle fought and won, the dastardly Frenchmen raided the mission's henhouse and captured all of the chickens. Unfortunately, when the lieutenant tied his squawking brace of hens across his saddle, they made such a racket that it spooked his horse, which plunged bucking through the pines and dashed the Frenchman to the ground. In the confusion that followed, the lay brother escaped and spread the word through San Augustine, Nacogdoches, and finally to Domingo Ramon's fort on the Angelina. Panic ensued and the Spanish fled down the Camino Real to Bexar. East Texas was once more devoid of Spaniards, which vacuum gave the bellicose French second thoughts: they had *won* the war but they had *lost* their best and only market.[15]

Antonio Gil Y'Barbo was the founder of Nacogdoches, a mercantile village begun in 1779 at the crossroads of the Camino Real and Trammel's Trace. The enduring and much circulating legend of the Y'Barbos—and all of the old Spanish families of East Texas—was that they were pure Andalusian Spanish, who had come straight to East Texas from Seville, through French New Orleans, if you can imagine! This put them a cut above the more recent Mexican imports.

Antonio Gil Y'Barbo, founder of modern Nacogdoches, as drawn by Charles Shaw

As it turned out, the Aguayo entrada of 1721, which was the time of the arrival of the First Families, brought a very mixed package of beggars, debtors, and jailbirds—much like colonials elsewhere. Of the 110 men recruited, 107 were taken from the jail at Celaya and one was sent by his father. As to the legend of ethnic purity: forty-four of the settlers were indeed classified as Spanish. The rest were classified as such ethnic mixtures as *mestizos, coyotes, mulattoes, lobos,* one free Negro, and one Indian from Sapotlan. These settlers reproduced and married among the French in Natchitoches and the Indians all around them. They soon created a Spanish-Creole colonial culture that grew along the Camino Real from Los Adaes back toward the missions around Nacogdoches.[16]

In East Texas, "A True-Born Spaniard is a Contradiction."

These "Spanish" settlers were brought up the Camino Real by the legendary Marques de San Miguel de Aguayo, who (as one story goes) excused himself from a card game in Mazapil, rode fifty miles back to his hacienda near Saltillo on the Camino Real, slew his wife and her lover, rode back to Mazapil and finished the card game. He rode ten horses to death and silenced five mozos in the process, and his card playing friends never knew he had left the building.[17]

All the tales of the Camino Real have not been told. Spanish treasures still lie hidden along the Trail—and The Lady still walks. The Lady in Blue appeared at Sabine Town, at the Camino Real

Uncle Matt Pantalion. *Photo by the author*

crossing of the Sabine River, two hundred years after she had first appeared to the Caddos of East Texas. She came this time in 1844 to nurse and care for the victims of the black-tongue plague. And when the sickness was over, she disappeared again.[18]

Seventy years later, in 1916, Uncle Matt Pantalion of Nacogdoches saw The Lady on the Camino del Caballo on the dusk of Christmas day. She was dressed in a flowing white and blue robe, and she was standing by a large white-oak tree on the side of the road. She looked at young Matt, sighed sad and lonely, and then ghostily faded away into the darkness of the forest background. You very well might question some of the tales I have told, but I *know* that this legend of the Camino Real is true because I took a picture of Uncle Matt standing by that very white-oak tree.

ENDNOTES

1. J. Frank Dobie. "In a Drouth Crack." *I'll Tell You a Tale.* Boston: Little, Brown and Company, 1931. 282–290.
2. J. E. Mayfield in Blake Papers, Vol. 45, p. 287, Special Collections, Steen Library, SFASU.
3. Uncle Matt Pantalion. Letter to author, in March 1972.
4. F. Todd Smith. *The Caddo Indians: Tribes at the Convergence of Empires, 1542–1854.* College Station: Texas A&M Press, 1995.
5. James E. Bruseth and Nancy A. Kenmotsu. "Soldiers of Misfortune: The de Soto Expedition Through Texas." *Heritage* (Vol. 9, No.4, Fall 1991): 12–17.
6. William C. Foster. *Spanish Expeditions into Texas, 1689–1768.* Austin: University of Texas Press, 1995. Chapters II & III.
7. Ibid. Chapter IV.
8. Donald E. Chipman and Harriet Denise Joseph. "Louis Juchereau de St. Denis: Canadian Cavalier." *Notable Men and Women of Spanish Texas.* Austin: University of Texas Press, 1999.
9. Domingo Ramon. "Diary of his Expedition into Texas in 1716." *Preliminary Studies of the Texas Catholic Historical Society* (Vol. II, No.5, April 1933).
10. Espinosa. "Diary." 16.
11. Diane H. Corbin. "Angelina." *Legendary Ladies of Texas.* 15–19.
12. Stephen F. Austin. "The Prison Journal of S. F. Austin." *The Quarterly of the Texas State Historical Association* (Vol. II, No.3, Jan. 1899): 185.

13. J. Frank Dobie. "Stories in Texas Place Names," *Straight Texas* (PTFS 13, 1937). Hatboro, PA: Folklore Associates, Inc., 1937. 69–70.
14. J. Frank Dobie. "How the Brazos River Got Its Name," *Legends of Texas* (PTFS 3, 1924). Hatboro, PA: Folklore Associates, Inc., 1964. 211.
15. "Chicken War." *Handbook of Texas.*
16. Eleanor Claire Buckley. "The Aguayo Expedition into Texas and Louisiana, 1719–1722." *The Quarterly of the Texas State Historical Association* ([Vol. 15, No.1, July 1911): 25–28.
17. J. Frank Dobie. "The Marques de Aguayo's Vengeance." *I'll Tell You a Tale. 117–123.*
18. Joseph F. Combs. "The Legend of the Lady in Blue." *Legends of the Pineys.* San Antonio: The Naylor Company, 1965.

Consuelo Samarripa

THE PASSAGE OF SCOTLAND'S FOUR/
EL PASAJE DE LOS CUATRO DE ESCOCIA

by Consuelo L. Samarripa

De lejos, muy lejos de aqui, far from the land of the Gaelic accent, came the vessels across the challenging waters of the Atlantic to America's different ports of entry. The vessels carried immigrants whose uncharted destinies would be remembered for many generations *en la tierra de el nopa, de el mesquite,* and mammoth trees draped with Spanish moss. We, *Tejanos,* just like them, have had our own fight for freedom and liberty. We will remember the passage of Scotland's four, *el pasaje de los cuatro de Escocia.*

Pues quiza algunos Tejanos le llamavan Valentine. Most often he was called Richard W. Ballentine (1814–1836).[1] The surname Ballantyne is from Sept of the Clan Campbell; their Argyll motto is *"Ne obliviscaris,"* Roman Latin meaning "Forget not." Ballentine was a twenty-two-year-old Scottish lad whose family had established residency in Marengo County, Alabama. He was recruited to serve with "The Mobile Greys" for Texas.[2] Some Greys traveled by land and others by sea. In December 1835, the schooner named *Santiago* left the port of New Orleans, Louisiana.[3] It carried fifteen recruits on her manifest; among them was Richard W. Ballentine. On his journey, he befriended a young aristocrat named Cleveland K. Simmons (1815–1836) from Charleston, South Carolina—born and raised. On December 9, 1835, they drafted, dated, declared, and documented they would defend Texas at the expense of their lives, liberties, and fortunes.[4] So, the journey brought Ballentine, a rifleman, to San Antonio de Bexar.

David L. Wilson (1807–1836) was also born in Scotland. His surname is a Sept of the Gunn Clan; their motto is *"Aut pax aut bellum,"* Roman Latin meaning "Either peace or war," *paz o guerra.* He had established residency in Nacogdoches, Texas. He was the son of James and Susanna Wesley Wilson and his wife's name was Ophelia. It has been speculated that David L. Wilson was perhaps a volunteer recruited by Captain Philip Dimmitt (1801–1841).[5] While Dimmitt's travels included journeys to San Antonio de Bexar, it appears his travels did not include Nacogdoches.[6] Thomas J. Rusk (1803–1857) lived in Nacogdoches, where David L. Wilson resided. Rusk organized volunteers in Nacogdoches, then traveled to assist Stephen F. Austin at Gonzales. Rusk then led the army of volunteers to San Antonio de Bexar. The volunteers remained at their new duty station, while Rusk returned to Nacogdoches. I believe that David L. Wilson was a member of the militia organized by Thomas J. Rusk. Thus, I believe Wilson came to San Antonio de Bexar.[7]

Isaac Robinson (1808–1836), like David L. Wilson, came from the Sept of the Gunn Clan. He arrived at the port of New Orleans, Louisiana, and was immediately recruited for service. He didn't have time to establish residency; he was sent to the battlefield at San Antonio de Bexar. After the battle at Bexar, he had earned the rank of Fourth Sergeant and 640 acres. Robinson served in NCO Company of Captain William R. Carey's (1806–1836) artillery company. It would be in NCO Company that the fourth Scotsman would be found.

The fourth Scotland native was a bagpiper. He had established residency in Nacogdoches, which is currently known as one of the oldest historic towns in Texas. But, back then it was known as a hometown of smugglers, gamblers, and other characters lacking angelic natures, just the kind of town for the jaunty Scotsman called John McGregor, Tartan from the Gregor Clan, the clan also known as "The Children of the Mist." He had earned the rank of Second Sergeant after the battle at San Antonio de Bexar. The Scotsman was very dedicated to his bagpipes. Epics written speak that even at ten paces, the cat gut groans from the fiddle of the Tennessee politician called Davy Crockett (1786–1836) were no match for the melodic moans from John McGregor's bagpipes of Scotland. If there were any references to "Scottie," I dare say it probably would have been John McGregor.

The four Scotsmen's journeys had brought them to the Texas Revolution. They, like the rest of the men behind the walls of the old Spanish mission at San Antonio de Bexar, had already seen *la bandera roja,* hoisted to the top of *la Igleisa de San Fernando.* The flag was the Mexican symbol meaning "No quarter, no surrender, no mercy." The thunderous response came from the old Spanish mission. Colonel William Barret Travis (1809–1836) had ordered the firing of the cannon called the 18-pounder. The shot sailed more than eight hundred years away and missed its target, but defiantly made its point! So, the men had time to think twice with regard to their beliefs and their destinies. On the predawn hours of March 6, 1836, Generalissmo Antonio Lopez de Santa Anna ordered the bugler to trumpet the blood curdling *"El Deguello." Paso por paso,* step by step, the Mexican soldiers marched to their orders.

It is customary for armies to rally behind a flag. Legends have it that several flags were flown within the walls of the Alamo. There was the flag made of *verde, blanco, y colorado,* a green, white and red flag with the year 1824 on its center strip; some men rallied behind the flag of the Mexican Constitution of 1824. There was another flag, of the same colors: *verde, blanco, y colorado,* and on the middle white stripe there were two golden stars, *duos estrellas de oro. Una estrella representa el estado de Coahuila, el estado de donde mis abuelos nacieron.* One star represented the State of Coahuila, the state where my grandparents were born. The second star represented *Tejas;* that is where I was born. But the legendary flag, whose presence was archived, was an azure blue with gold fringe. Bold black letters spelled "First Company of Texan" at the top; at the bottom the phrase continues with "Volunteers! From New Orleans." The center of the flag had a flying eagle; in his beak was a ribbon that carried the words "God & Liberty," also in black letters.

The New Orleans Greys were sometimes referred to as the "Invincibles." It was their banner that was hoisted to the top of the long barracks where the artillerymen were quartered. The Invincibles' banner snapped in the March wind as the Mexican *soldados* stormed the Alamo. Several hours later more than one hundred eighty men lay silenced beneath a fight for liberty. The Invincibles' banner also lay in the rubble. *La familia* de Jose Gregorio Esparza claimed his body and buried him nearby at *Campo Santo.* But the remaining *Tejanos'* bodies were indiscriminately tossed with their *compadres* in the fires that burned after the battle. We, as *Tejanos,* will remember that—*de lejos, muy lejos de aqui,* far from the land of the Gaelic accent came the vessels that brought *nuestros compadres.* We will remember: Private Richard W. Ballentine, Rifleman; Private David L. Wilson, Rifleman; Fourth Sergeant Isaac Robinson, Artilleryman; and Second Sergeant John McGregor, Artilleryman, and also known as the Bagpiper. By some genealogy origins, the meaning of the McGregor name is "a storyteller."

Thus, we will remember the passage of Scotland's four, *el pasaje de los cuatro de Escocia.*

ENDNOTES

1. In most references, R. W. Ballentine's name has been spelled with the letter "i" instead of the letter "y," generally spelled Ballantyne. The Sept of the Clan Campbell is one of the oldest surnames in the Highlands.
2. James Butler Bonham (2/20/1807–3/6/1836) is credited for helping organize volunteers for service in Texas at Mobile, Alabama. The color of their uniforms was reflected in the name, "Mobile Greys." The other volunteers from Alabama were referenced as the Red Rovers. Captain [Dr.] Jack Shackleford's Company of Red Rovers from Alabama would be massacred at Goliad on March 27, 1836.
3. Walter Lord. *A Time to Stand,* (University of Lincoln and London Press, 1978), 55. "The little group that boarded the *Santiago* on December 7 was typical." Lord lists December 7, 1935 as the date of departure. Dates of departure conflict.
4. Bill Groneman. *Alamo Defenders, A Genealogy: The People and Their Works* (Austin, Tx: Eakin Press, 1990). "Richard W. Ballentine embarked for Texas on *12/9/1835* aboard the schooner *Santiago,* as did Alamo Defender Cleveland K. Simmons. His name is sometimes listed as 'R. W. Valentine.'" 11. Confusion over the name is perhaps due to a typographical error in the statement, "He traveled to Texas in January 1836 aboard the schooner *Santiago,* along with defender Richard W. Ballentine." 100. Groneman's *Notes Part II: Their Words* includes documented contents and is noted as, " Richard W. Ballen-

tine, Cleveland K. Simmons et al. on board the *Santiago, 12/09/1835.*"
135. Regarding the dates and events conflict, I resolved that these two defenders departed New Orleans in December and the documented pledge was drafted while on board on December 9, 1935.
5. Captain Philip Dimmitt's name has also been spelled as Philip Dimitt.
6. I have made this statement, based on the resources of this paper's bibliography.
7. "Rusk, Thomas Jefferson." The Handbook of Texas Online. *http://www.tsha.utexas.edu/handbook/online/articles/view/RR/fru16. html* [Accessed Sat Nov 24 1:00:56 US/Central 2001]. "He organized volunteers from Nacogdoches and hastened to Gonzales, where his men joined Stephen F. Austin's army in preventing the Mexicans from seizing their cannon. They proceeded to San Antonio, but Rusk left the army before the siege of Bexar. "I have for the first time documented my analogy, which does, indeed, challenge previous speculations, and now may add to another debated issue in history."

BIBLIOGRAPHY

The Clan Campbell. DISCscribe Ltd, 1998, Genealogy via Internet.
The Clan, "The Clan Finder." *http://www.tartans.com.*
"Dimmit, Phillip." *The Handbook of Texas Online,* s.v. *http://www.tsha .utexas.edu/handbook/online/articles/view/DD/fdi19.html* [Accessed Sat Nov 24 0:47:45 US/Central 2001].
Groneman, Bill. *Alamo Defenders, A Genealogy: The People and Their Words.* Austin: Eakin Press, 1990.
Lind, Michael. *The Alamo, An Epic.* Boston, New York: Houghton Mifflin Company, 1997.
Lord, Walter. *A Time to Stand.* Reprinted by Lincoln and London, University of Nebraska Press, 1978.
"Mobile Grays." *The Handbook of Texas Online,* s.v. *http://www.tsha .utexas.edu/handbook/online/articles/view/MM/qjm3.html* [Accessed Fri Nov 23 13:18:17 DS/Central 2001].
"The Mobile Greys." *http://home.att.net/~wnbonham/mobile.htm.*
"New Orleans Greys." *The Handbook of Texas Online,* s.v. *http:// www.tsha.utexas.edu/handbook/online/articles/view/NN/qjn2.html* [Accessed Fri Nov 23 14:26:49 US/Central 2001].
"Rusk, Thomas Jefferson." *The Handbook of Texas Online,* s.v. *http:// www.tsha.utexas.edu/handbook/online/articles/view/RR/fru16.html* [Accessed Sat Nov 24 1:00:56 DS/Central2001].
Thomas J. Rusk (1803–1857). *http://www.lsjunction.com/people/rusk .htm.*

(Row 1) George T. McCannon   Alice Jane McCannon
(Row 2) Ernest P. Mollenauer   Julia E. Mollenauer
(Row 3) George Elmer McCannon   Mary Louise McCannon

GONE TO (SOUTH) TEXAS

by Janet McCannon Simonds

The lore of the nineteenth century Texas frontier includes many stories of pioneers leaving their homes in the North to seek new homes in Texas, and of their difficult journeys and more difficult lives after arrival. Regardless of the motivation, it took great courage to leave the known—families, friends, homes, businesses, and their very ways of life—for the unknown, which was often full of discomfort and privation. This pioneer spirit and courage, however, did not stop at the end of the nineteenth century. In the early twentieth century, vast areas of Texas were yet unsettled, and there were still people in the northern United States with the same courage, adventurous spirit, and desire to make a new start that characterized their predecessors. The Rio Grande Valley of Texas was one of those last twentieth-century frontiers, and a destination of many such pioneers.

The area of South Texas between the Rio Grande and Nueces Rivers was for many years after the Texas Revolution a contested area called the Nueces Strip, maintaining a virtual dual nationality even after the 1836 Texas Revolution when Mexican President Santa Anna was forced to cede all area north of the Rio Grande. In the 1840s, ranchers in Matamoros, Mexico, grazed their cattle in the area north of the river, near present-day Brownsville, and Mexican outlaws raided ranches in the area, driving the stolen cattle across the river to Mexico.[1] Three years after Texas' annexation to the United States, the 1848 Treaty of Guadalupe-Hidalgo, following the Mexican War, again declared the Rio Grande River as the official boundary between Texas and Mexico, but little or nothing changed on the ground. The Nueces Strip remained an area of contention and banditry well into the twentieth century.

In the southern-most tip of this untamed strip, the fertile delta area of the Rio Grande River, lies the area known as the Rio

Grande Valley, which includes the present-day counties of Hidalgo, Cameron, Willacy, and Starr. Although the Texas Rangers, under the leadership of Captain Leander McNelly, had cleared out most of the large bandit gangs in the 1870s, the Rangers, and even the Army, were still frequently called in after the turn of the century to suppress banditry in the area. Albert Hughes, who came from Indiana to the Valley with his family in 1915, at the age of thirteen, told of his experience in a 1960s interview:

> We made the trip by train. After leaving Kingsville, the lights within the train were turned out and armed guards sat at the windows. We realized the full meaning of that precaution when we reached Lyford about ten o'clock that night and found two companies of the 26th Infantry camped in our hotel yard and two bandits chained to a mesquite tree. We spent the night in the hotel and went on to the ranch the next day; an armed guard rode on the wagon carrying our luggage.[2]

He went on to tell of a neighbor being killed from ambush by bandits. After the family fled, the bandits burned their house. The area would remain a wild and dangerous place until economic growth in the nation began to effect changes in the 1920s and '30s.

In the early decades of the twentieth century, the United States was rapidly becoming urbanized. This, coupled with the advent of World War I, brought an increased demand and rising prices for agricultural products. Although the Valley had been used primarily for cattle ranching through the turn of the twentieth century, the great cattle drives were over, and beef prices were down. Mild winters, rich soil, and available irrigation water from the Rio Grande made the Valley an ideal farming area. By 1908, the citrus fruit industry had been launched in the Valley, and by 1929 there were an estimated five million citrus trees in the Valley, plus numerous commercial farms producing vegetables.[3] Banks and land developers in the northern United States began to see the Valley area as a potential land bonanza, and they started to buy up land and promote it in the North. They cleared the land of the scrubby mesquite and cactus, laid out town sites, and marked off farming tracts. One of the major land developers, W. A. Harding, bought 53,000 acres of Valley land in the 1920s. J. E. Wilkins, who was contracted to clear the land, recalled in a 1960s interview that he hired a total of 10,000 men, with a payroll of $75,000 every two weeks, and finished the clearing in two years and one month. (Every pay day he had two foremen with sawed-off shotguns and a sheriff and a Ranger with Winchesters to guard the payroll.)[4]

The developers ran special excursion trains to bring potential buyers to the area. "Land parties" of potential buyers were treated to (usually) three days of luxurious accommodations in "Club Houses," where they were entertained and served exotic meals with fish and shrimp from the Gulf of Mexico. They were driven in groups in large touring cars to see the property. The developers worked hard at making the property attractive. They began building canals to move river water to the farms. They built roads and lined them with palm trees from Mexico. The Harding and Gill Land Company even showed some 40-acre blocks already cleared and planted in citrus trees.[5] In the early 1920s, as many as 200 land-seekers a day were being brought into the Brownsville area.[6] However, the Valley was mostly still untamed, raw land. E. G. Pinkston, at one time a Field Superintendent for the Harding and Gill Land Company, told of the area where he lived and worked:

> Monte Alto had only about 25 acres cleared when I came here in 1928. No roads were paved or even graded. It was a busy place during working hours with about 250 laborers at work; but after working hours, it was a very lonely place to live. No entertainment was available, and most of the laborers had no means of transportation. When it rained, the roads were totally impassable because all had lagoons at one place or another. When these lagoons were full of water, not even a tractor could

get through. The brush was full of deer, *javelina* and rattlesnakes. Those snakes were large and abundant. In the summer time, employees often killed 50 to 75 rattlesnakes a day in the normal operation of their jobs.[7]

The Valley was in need of adventurous, hard-working families—pioneers—to turn it into the paradise the developers envisioned, the "Magic Valley" that it came to be called in the second half of the twentieth century.

The George T. McCannon family, from Ames, Iowa, and the Ernest P. Mollenauer family, from Canonsburg, Pennsylvania—my grandparents—were two of the brave pioneer families that helped settle this semi-tropical new frontier of Texas. Here are the stories of their pioneering experiences.

THE McCANNONS

George T. McCannon (1867–1949) was a third-generation American whose great-grandfather came to America from Ireland in the 1790s. In 1910, George T. sold his 200-acre farm near Numa, Iowa, and moved his wife Alice and four children to Ames, so the older two children could go to college there. In 1911, a fifth child, George Elmer (my father) was born and, for a while anyway, enjoyed all the attention of his four older siblings. Soon, however, the siblings finished college, married, joined the Army, or otherwise had gone their separate ways. In 1920, when "Elmer" was nine, George T., attracted by bank and land company advertisements and encouraged by his father Daniel Sylvester McCannon, who had relocated to Katy (near Houston) in 1912, decided to look into the land deals being offered in the Rio Grande Valley.

George T., Alice, and Elmer traveled by train to Houston, where they visited with Daniel Sylvester and his second wife, and then took the "Excursion Train" to Harlingen, in the Rio Grande Valley. There they were met by representatives of the land developers and were put up in a large hotel/boarding house in Harlingen, while they looked at various parcels of land. George T. bought forty acres of land south and west of the little village called Santa Maria in Cameron County, only about a mile-and-a-half from the Rio Grande River. After returning to Iowa to sell their property there, they came back to the Valley and began the task of clearing the land and preparing it for farming.

Although the Valley lies in the river delta and the soil is rich, good farm land, the area is hot, and at that time was shaded only by twisty, thorny mesquite brush, and littered with prickly pear and other cacti. Several of the families who had bought land got together and helped one another clear the land and build houses and barns. The women and children lived in a boarding house in town. The men camped out in tents on the land, where George T. said they ate mostly boiled pinto beans and Mexican tortillas, both of which could be easily cooked over a camp fire. They got regular, home-cooked meals only when they came into town on Saturday

George T., Elmer, and Alice Jane at home near Santa Maria, 1923

afternoons for the weekends. Building supplies and bulk food-stuffs, stored in great warehouses, were available in Harlingen. Staple foods like flour, beans, coffee, and bacon could be obtained from a small proprietary store in the area.

The McCannon farm took shape and maintained the family well in the following years. There was a small house and a barn and garage. George T., in his late 50s now, farmed the land—on a much smaller scale than the original farm near Numa. He kept a few cattle for meat and milk, plus pigs and chickens. On the acreage, George T. and Alice had a kitchen garden, and grew corn and cotton as cash crops. New friendships were established, and family visited from Iowa and California. Visitors were always taken to the special places—Mexico, the piers at Port Isabel, or the pretty beaches at Boca Chica, near the mouth of the river. (There was no bridge to Padre Island at this time; it was inhabited mainly by birds and sand crabs.)

The Anglo residents in and near Santa Maria established a small English-speaking community school which Elmer attended. He

George T., Alice, two visiting daughters, and neighbors pick up supplies at the warehouse, 1923

Elmer with his sister Myrtle visiting from California, 1923

rode his horse in the chaparral with his Anglo and Mexican friends, and learned to speak Spanish like a Mexican. The Depression of the '30s had little effect on the McCannons; their small farm sustained them. However, after high school, with jobs hard to find, Elmer (now called "Mac" by his friends) enlisted in the Civil Conservation Corps in 1933, at Fort Brown in Brownsville, Texas. He was assigned to the "Tree Army," where he worked with crews cutting fire lanes in the forests near San Augustine and Center, Texas. Mac and his friends hitched rides into Nacogdoches for a little recreation on their time off. After his discharge in 1934, he worked for a time in San Antonio, and returned to the Valley in 1936. There, in 1938, he met and married another child of a Valley pioneer family, Mary Louise Mollenauer.[8]

THE MOLLENAUERS

Ernest P. Mollenauer (1878–1958), the third child of a first generation German-American father and a German immigrant mother, was born in Pennsylvania. His mother did not speak English, and she required the children to speak German at home until they were sixteen years old. After finishing high school and working at various jobs, Ernest P. went to Pittsburgh and enlisted in the United States Marine Corps in January 1902. That September he sailed to Panama, where he was sent ashore at Colon to guard a railroad. In January 1903, he was sent to the Philippines as part of the occupation army. He attained the rank of sergeant before he was discharged from the Marine Corps in January 1906, and returned to Pennsylvania.[9] After the war, he joined his brothers in a company they called The Mollenauer Brothers, laying oil pipelines all over the eastern part of the United States. While laying pipelines in West Virginia, he met and married Julia Parthenia Ellis in Milton, West Virginia, in 1908. They returned to Pennsylvania, where they established their home on a mortgaged 112-acre farm six miles south of Canonsburg. There they reared eight children. They worked hard on the farm, selling their produce, milk, and eggs in the local community.

Mary (my mother) was the seventh of the eight Mollenauer children. She and the other children were required to work long hours doing chores on the farm, but had a barrel of fun as well. At family gatherings in later years, Mary and her siblings would tell the many (by now, iconic) family stories of life on the farm in Pennsylvania. Among the tales of how hard they had to work digging potatoes and such, they told of swiping the best peaches or strawberries (which their dad would have sold) and sneaking cream from the spring house to dip them in. They told of walking to school in snow so deep the smaller children had to walk behind the bigger children who "plowed" a path for them, and rolling snowballs down the hill—the ever-growing snowball hitting the neighbor's rail fence at the bottom so hard that the rails went flying into the air. They told how the girls avoided their mother's wrath by raising their skirts and sliding down the snowy slopes on their underpants on the way home from school (so they didn't ruin their skirts). And they told how their father always knew when they had been swimming in the horse trough, because the horses would rear and refuse to drink the water. The horses got especially skittish after the kids had blown up toads with oat straws and floated them in the trough, an incident which earned the irrepressible kids one of many "skinnings" they received.

In 1927, Ernest P., suffering from "catarrh" (recurring bronchial problems probably left over from malaria contracted in the Philippines), needed a change of climate. Responding to an advertising campaign by one of the banks, he and Julia and the baby, Dorothy, took the "land excursion train" trip to Texas' Rio Grande Valley to see what it might offer. They paid a nominal fee for the trip, and were treated to luxury accommodations, including exotic foods from the Gulf of Mexico. Julia said they were served shrimp, but she didn't like those "little balls of lard." They bought forty acres six miles east of Edinburg, near the San Carlos community in Hidalgo County, and returned to Pennsylvania to prepare for the move.

The following year, Ernest P. returned to the Valley and partially cleared the land for the house and the citrus orchard. Then, in August of 1929, according to family lore, Ernest P. and Julia sold the farm, auctioned off most of their earthly possessions—save a bed, a dresser, and some kitchen and farm implements—and packed up the family and went to Texas. The youngest child, Dorothy, was three years old; the oldest, Scott, was nineteen when the family set off on the ten-day trip to the Rio Grande Valley of Texas. Scott and Paul (who was seventeen) took turns driving the Model-T Ford touring car carrying the children. Ernest P. drove the Model-T truck piled high with bed, dresser, family clothes, and farm implements. Julia and the baby rode with Ernest P. On the long trip from Pennsylvania, the car trailed the truck. They traveled west through Ohio, Indiana, and Illinois.

On the fourth day, in St. Louis, the touring car got a flat tire. Paul had to pull off on the side of the road to fix the flat, and

Ernest P., in the truck, went on ahead, not realizing that the car had stopped. When the younger children saw their parents drive out of sight, they began to cry and worry that they had lost their mommy and daddy. Paul divided his time between fixing the flat and trying to calm the children down. "Shut Up!" didn't work too well. By the time Ernest P. reached the bridge at the Mississippi River, he realized that the car was not following, and pulled off to the side and stopped. The bridge attendant told him he could not stop there; he must go on across the bridge. Ernest P. told him that a car carrying his children had not yet caught up, and he would stay right there until they arrived. After a while, the car did arrive, and the children were happy to see their parents, and the two Model-Ts crossed the Mississippi River together. They spent the next day resting in Joplin, Missouri, with Ernest P.'s older brother Fred, and were in Texas the following day. After five more days, and about 600 miles of hard, hot driving, they arrived at their property in the Valley.

The Mollenauer family's tent in the mesquite and scrub of the new farm, 1928

This time, there was no welcoming representative or hotel or boarding house for the family to stay in when they arrived. Until they could build their own shelter, there would be only brushy land and bare dirt. They set up two tents, a 14′×15′ Marine hospital tent, and a small 9′×9′ A-wall tent, which were to be their home for the next three months. There was one bed—for Mom and Dad. Mattress tickings were stuffed with corn shucks for the kids to sleep on. The older girls, ages fourteen and fifteen, hated this new life. The younger children found it a great adventure—young Ernest's hatchet was handy for chopping up the ever-present water moccasins and rattlesnakes. All suffered from the heat and sand sores and fleas. The family kept a cow and chickens and a horse to pull the great wooden farm wagon. The children attended the county school in Edinburg, catching the bus at five o'clock in the morning and getting home late in the afternoon.

Ernest P. and the boys built a barn and animal pens, and what was ostensibly to be a garage for the farm equipment but would serve as a temporary house, just until a real house could be built. Instead of the big two-story house they had in Pennsylvania—the house with the big kitchen (with the cold cellar where they stored food, and the big dry attic where they dried and threshed white navy beans), the house with a parlor (where they put up the Christmas tree every year), the house with four bedrooms upstairs and one downstairs—the family now had a garage to live in. In this long, low building, a 10′×20′ room served as kitchen plus dining/living area in one end. A larger adjacent area served as a bedroom for all eight children, with a curtained-off area on the end for Julia and Ernest P. However, they had plans for a better house. They cleared a long lane leading up to the site where the house would be built, and planted ebony trees on each side. (The lane would be used, but the house was never built. When Ernest P. died in 1958, he and Julia were still living in the "garage.")[10]

Ernest P. was a citrus grower. He planted seeds to grow the root stock and grafted on the hybrid grapefruit and orange buds,

A Mollenauer family portrait one year after moving to the Valley, 1929

obtained from other citrus growers, to start his orchard. (The hybrid sweet-tasting oranges and grapefruit we now eat have to be grown on more vigorous root stock.) He planted grapefruit and orange trees for the commercial market and a few lemon and tangerine trees just for the family. Since it would take six years for the trees to bear a good crop, vegetables were grown between the tree rows for income. Working with the Texas Citrus Growers Association, he built concrete canals on two sides of the property to carry irrigation water pumped up through a system of canals from the Rio Grande River. Smudge pots, small ball-shaped oil burners, were placed in the orchards on those unusual nights when temperatures dropped too low, to keep the trees and fruit from freezing. Though there were occasional ruinous freezes, the citrus orchard would thrive in the Valley's rich soil and mild climate, and until the years of the Depression in the '30s, there was a ready market for the fruit.

The Depression was not devastating to the Mollenauers, but it took a toll on the family's resources. Citrus fruit was a luxury the rest of the country could little afford. With the years of reduced income from the orchard, many of Ernest P.'s dreams would never be realized. But the family was strong, and the Mollenauer children had learned to be hard-working and confident in their own abilities. They would grow up to embrace their new home state, and would achieve their own successes in Texas and elsewhere. Three boys would serve in the armed services in WWII, and two children would earn degrees from Pan American College, in Edinburg. Mary Mollenauer had finished two years of college when she met George Elmer (Mac) McCannon. (The story goes that she was dating Mac and a sailor at the same time, until on one visit Mac told her that if the sailor was there the next time he came, he would not be coming back. She got rid of the sailor.) Mary and Mac married on June 2, 1938, joining the two Texas pioneer families for all time.

Mac worked as a mechanic for several employers until 1953, when he opened his own repair garage and moved the family to Monte Alto, where Mary and Mac lived for the rest of their lives. After raising their three children, Mary finished her college degree and taught English in Valley high schools until she retired in 1985. George, Raymond, and I—Mary and Mac's first-generation Texan children—grew up in the Rio Grande Valley of Texas. As we were growing up in the '40s and '50s, we saw no indication that our pioneer grandparents had any regrets about their move to the Valley. Though they had had some hard times, those hard times were always followed by better ones. After WWII, their fortunes revived along with the rest of the country; after all, they had the pioneer attitude of courage, hard work, and a strong belief that they could do what they set out to do.

We learned those traits too, and made our own memories in the security and love of our extended family. We fed the chickens and gathered the eggs for Grandma; we climbed up the cow stall onto the barn roof to pick buckets full of mulberries, and we played house or Cowboys and Indians under Grandpa's grapefruit trees. We heard many times the stories of our two families' pioneering days and took pride and delight in our heritage. We also— much like the early settlers of the eastern United States—had early lessons in eclectic cultures and tolerance, for we lived among a multitude of immigrants. The population of the four-county area of the Rio Grande Valley had grown rapidly in the first half of the twentieth century. Because of its proximity to Mexico, many immigrants came from there; many others were families who had migrated to the Valley from diverse parts of the United States. Many of these families, like ours, had traveled to the Valley—as pioneers—early in the twentieth century, while the area was still covered with mesquite and cactus.

ENDNOTES

1. *Handbook of Texas Online.* s.v. "Cameron County." *http://www.tsha
.utexas.edu/handbook/online/articles/CC/hcc4.html*   (accessed December 5, 2006).
2. Mary R. Pharis. "The History of Monte Alto." A paper prepared for an American History class at Pan American College. Edinburg, Texas. 1969. 1.
3. *Handbook of Texas Online.* s.v. "Agriculture." *http://www.tsha.utexas
.edu/handbook/online/articles/AA/ama1.html* (accessed December 5, 2006).
4. Pharis. 2–3.
5. Pharis. 6.
6. *Handbook of Texas Online.* s.v. "Cameron County." *http://www
.tsha.utexas.edu/handbook/online/articles/CC/hcc4.html*   (accessed December 5, 2006).

7. Pharis. 6.
8. Dates and details for the McCannon family were taken from documents, photos, newspaper clippings, genealogical records, and interviews with George Elmer McCannon in the 1980s and 1990s.
9. From the Journal of E. P. Mollenauer, written between January 31, 1902, and February 10, 1906, while he was in the U.S. Marine Corps.
10. Dates and details for the Mollenauer family were taken from documents, photos, genealogical records, and personal reminiscences written by Edna Mollenauer Coleman (fourth child) and Ina Mollenauer Pollard (sixth child) in the 1980s and early 1990s.

William Riley Marchman and Fannie Franks Marchman on their front porch, Grand Saline, Texas

FANNIE MARCHMAN'S JOURNEY FROM ATLANTA, GEORGIA TO JEFFERSON, TEXAS—BY RAILROAD, STEAMBOAT, AND HORSE AND WAGON, IN 1869 AND BEYOND

by Ellen Pearson

Fannie Franks was born to Amanda and George Fowler on Amanda's mother's plantation, near Holly Springs, Mississippi, on the 19th day of September, 1851. One year after the family returned to their own home in Holly Springs, George Franks went to New York City to buy goods for his store. He died there of pneumonia. Fannie and her mother moved back to the plantation. Fannie's mother died when she was three years old. Fannie's only memories of her mother were, first, after the little girl had got into a hive of bees, looking up at a mirror and seeing her mother searching her "light curls" for the remaining bees and, second, of Amanda's sister taking Fannie to her mother's bed, when she was dying. Amanda's brother, Mitchell Fowler, and his wife took the girl to a suburb of Atlanta, Georgia, and raised her graciously and generously.

Fannie met her husband-to-be, William Riley Marchman, at her school, called Pantherville, ten miles from Atlanta. "Mr. Marchman," as Fannie always referred to him, rode horseback to the school to visit his brother-in-law, James Harmon, who was principal of the school. Mr. Marchman asked the teacher to pick him a sweetheart, and Fannie was the one selected. When W. R. Marchman visited Fannie, he told her he was going to the Army and wanted to see her on his return. She refused to kiss him across the garden gate, and he left with her uncle to fight in the American Civil War. Her uncle never returned and was never accounted for. Fannie, her aunt, and the aunt's three children survived the burning of Atlanta and the incursion of the Yankees with remarkable ingenuity and stoicism. That is another story.

Fannie wrote her Life Story in the early 1940s, stating, "I will be 91 years old September, 1942." Fannie's account of her travel to Texas begins when Mr. Marchman returned from the War. The bulk of this account is in Fannie's own lucid and colorful words. Strangely, Fannie never mentions her husband's death in 1923:

> The war is over, things are left sad and desolate, but Mr. Marchman had returned and was visiting me every opportunity, so we were married November 24, 1868. He had a mother and sister, with four children, this sister's husband came to Jefferson, Texas to locate a home for us. His name was James T. Harmon.
>
> We left Atlanta February 6, 1869, Mr. Marchman's mother, a sister, the four children and Mr. Marchman and I, and a bird dog that belonged to the brother-in-law. We all boarded an emigrant train with well filled baskets of chicken, ham, and everything good to eat. The coach had a stove in it, and they gave us permission to make coffee. We rode this train to Mobile, Alabama, where we took a boat. We were not on this boat many hours until we boarded another train, and rode to Lake Pontchartrain. This boat took us to a six mile train that carried us into New Orleans. We had a letter from J. T. Harmon, Jefferson, Texas, telling us to leave New Orleans on the Mittie Stephens, a large side-wheel steamer. The Mittie Stephens was at the wharf, but one of the children was very sick. We had to call a doctor. He advised us not to move that child, so the Mittie Stephens left us in New Orleans.
>
> As soon as we could leave we took a stern-wheel steamer, Era No. 9. When we arrived at Shreveport the hull of the Mittie Stephens was still burning, and there were sixty-five [*sic*] lives lost,

and they were dragging the dead bodies out of the lake, a sight that I shall never forget.

On February 8–14, 2004, Archie P. McDonald wrote a piece entitled "The Mittie Stephens Disaster" in his syndicated column, published in over 40 East Texas newspapers. The subtitle of the article reads, "On February 12, 1869, a fire burned her to the waterline in Caddo Lake." McDonald writes:

> Robert Fulton won the technological race to find a way to utilize steam power for transportation when he successfully sailed the Clermont on the Hudson River 1807. He did not solve another problem: how to make such travel safe.
>
> When we remember steamboat accidents, most of us think about boiler explosions, which resulted from excessive pressure or faulty equipment, or both. But the boiler was working well on the side-wheeler "Mittie Stephens" on February 12, 1869, and did not explode: instead, a fire burned her to the waterline in Caddo Lake near the Texas-Louisiana border.
>
> Steamboats became pervasive on America's inland waters during the first half of the nineteenth century. Moving passengers and cargo over water was also slower. But with only animal powered wagons, and after 1837 the "iron horse" railroads as competitors, steamboats proliferated and their owners prospered. Still, there was danger on the water.
>
> "Mittie Stephens" came out of a shipyard in Madison, Indiana, in 1863, in time to be a part of the effort to preserve the Union. She served as a naval packet for a year, but after the failure of the Red River Campaign in 1864 she was sold. Civilian owners used her on the Missouri River and then

stationed her in New Orleans. In 1866, "Mittie Stephens" began regular roundtrips between New Orleans and Jefferson, Texas, via the Mississippi and Red rivers and Cypress Bayou. Her last voyage began on February 5, 1869. Seven nights later, "Mittie Stephens" steamed on Caddo Lake near her destination with 107 passengers and crew, plus cargo, which included hay stacked on deck. Sparks from a torch basket located on the bow to illuminate the ship blew in the wind to the dry hay, ignited, and a conflagration resulted.

The helmsmen steered for shore but the ship "grounded." That meant that passengers might have saved themselves by jumping overboard and wading to shore. But the side-mounted paddle-wheel kept turning in an effort to force the ship on to shore, and many who leapt overboard were sucked into the wheel. Sixty-one people perished.

"Mittie Stephens" burned to the water line, though parts of her, including the bell, and some machinery, were salvaged. Her remains reminded those who visit the lake of the danger that await those who move upon the waters well into the twentieth century.[1]

Archie McDonald refers to the "failure of the Red River Campaign." This Union Campaign had two major goals: to secure cotton for northern textile mills, and to end any hope of the French intervening through Texas. Textile mills in many northern states were closing for lack of cotton, causing widespread unemployment. Northwest Louisiana and East Texas were believed to be teeming with stockpiled cotton. President Lincoln believed it was imperative that the Union regain control of Texas to discourage the French from making inroads. The campaign, focused near Shreveport, involved Union land forces, as well as a fifty-eight-ship flotilla, including twenty-three gunboats, thirteen of them ironclads. The Confederates had been expecting an invasion but, unbeknownst to them, were tactically unprepared to face it. Nevertheless, the South claimed a major victory, in great part because the Red River was at a twenty-year low, and Union boats constantly ran aground on sandbars.[2]

The *Mittie Stephens,* during this time, had been illegally seized by Union forces, which used her to carry dispatches, troops, and supplies for the Red River Campaign. During peacetime, she was used on the Mississippi and later became a New Orleans to Jefferson packet. In fact, on her ill-fated voyage in February 1869, she was carrying, in addition to passengers, "a government consignment of hay, gunpowder, and a $100,000 payroll for troops in Jefferson."[3] These provisions, notably the hay but also the gunpowder and paper money, surely added flame to the fire, which burned her to the waterline.

Fannie Marchman, eighteen years of age and mercifully unaware of the stormy history of the steamboat whose unhappy misadventures led to her fiery end, continues with her account:

> We finally arrived at Jefferson after a ten days journey. Mr. Harmon had rented a large farm with cabins on it from emigrants, and a large two-story hewed log house, situated sixteen miles from Jefferson. Mr. Harmon met us with a large carriage, with two fine horses hitched to it, and a wagon to take trunks, baggage, etc. We rode this sixteen miles in a short time. This house had a large fireplace. The men put rocks in this fireplace for andirons, to lay the wood on, built a fire, and we made coffee, broiled meat, etc., were enjoying a very good meal: when those rocks got real hot they began to explode like they were loaded with powder, and threw pieces all over the room.
>
> Mr. Harmon remained on this farm for several years, but Mr. Marchman got work in a shoe store in Jefferson, so we moved there, bought a half acre

lot and built a nice cottage home, set out a fine orchard of different kinds of fruit.

We lived on this place until after all three of the boys, Riley, Oscar and Orville, were born.

About four years after we moved into our new home the Texas & Pacific Railroad was built. Jefferson had many stores fronting on the wharf, and I have seen as many as ten steamboats at that wharf at one time to carry off cattle, cotton, hides, and tallow, and all kinds of produce that was raised in Texas, and they were there to bring goods to the merchants in Jefferson. Jefferson is situated on a bayou that was made navigable by the aid of a dredge boat run by the Government.

Jefferson was a thriving city with street cars and horse drawn cabs, good schools and churches, and many factories manufacturing different articles. One was the first artificial ice that was ever invented and made in an ice factory, by Scott & Boyd. There were hundreds of wagons drawn by oxen that hauled produce to the boats to be shipped out of Texas.

Observations made by Fannie Marchman in her early twenties, recounted seventy years later, are corroborated by history. Her impeccable typing on two-holed, lined, (now yellowed) loose leaf notebook paper has almost no errors. She documented the life of the times in which she lived and, without realizing it, revealed her lively, practical approach to living in those times. She also understood the significance of the various modes of transportation essential to the growth and vitality of the state of Texas and the nation.

In his description of Jefferson, Texas, Christopher Long described efforts in the late 1840s to clear Big Cypress Swamp for navigation. According to Long, following the clearing of the swamp, steamboats were regularly traveling from Jefferson to Shreveport and New Orleans, transporting cotton, produce, manufactured goods, and other supplies, including the materials and

Aunt.

My mother had fifteen brothers and sisters, including three half brothers. She had a sister with two boys Wafer and Bud Boring. Bud married Fannie Whitlow, a school mate of mine, and they had a daughter, Bessie Boring Gardner, living in Decatur, Georgia, and I correspond with her. Wafer Boring had a son, Rev. Will Boring, a fine Methodist Preacher.

I am the only living first Cousin that I know anything about in the Fowler family. I will be 91 years old September, 1942.

The war is over, things are left sad and desolate, but Mr. Marchman had returned and was visiting me every opportunity, so we were married November 24th, 1868. He had a mother and sister, with four children, this sister's husband came to Jefferson, Texas, to locate a home for us. His name was James T. Harmon.

We left Atlanta February 6, 1869, Mr. Marchman's mother, a sister, the four children and Mr. Marchman and I, and a bird dog that belonged to the brother-in-law. We all boarded an emigrant train with well filled baskets of chicken, ham, and everything good to eat. The coach had a stove in it, and they gave us permission to make coffee. We rode this train to Mobile, Alabama, where we took a boat. We were not on this boat many

-14-

A page from Fannie Marchman's personal account

furnishings needed for the many new homes being constructed in the burgeoning Texas city. "By the late 1840s Jefferson had emerged as the leading commercial distribution center of Northeast Texas and the state's leading inland port."[4] Construction of a railroad line, linking the town to Shreveport and Marshall, began in 1860, but it was disrupted by the Civil War. After the war, the town's economy quickly recovered. In 1867, Jefferson became the first town in Texas to use natural gas for artificial lighting purposes, and ice was first manufactured on a commercial scale there in 1868. By 1870, Jefferson had a population of 4,180 and was the sixth largest city in Texas. "Between 1867 and 1870 trade grew from $3 million to $8 million, and in the late 1860s more than 75,000 bales of cotton were being shipped annually."[5]

Long notes that in 1873 two events occurred that eventually ended Jefferson's significance as a transportation hub. "The first was the destruction of the Red River Raft, a natural dam on the river above Shreveport. In November of 1873, nitroglycerin charges were used to remove the last portion of the raft, which had previously made the upper section of the river unnavigable. The demolition of the raft reopened the main course of the river but significantly lowered the water level of the surrounding lakes and streams, making the trip to Jefferson difficult, particularly in times of drought."[6] The Red River Raft was essentially a 100 mile log jam. The water backed up by the raft gradually formed Caddo Lake and wetlands on the border between Texas and Louisiana. These wetlands, referred to by Fannie Marchman as "a bayou," comprised three areas: the Little Cypress, Big Cypress, and Black Cypress bayous, which are said to be the largest cypress forest in the world.[7]

The alteration of the waterways was only part of Jefferson's problems. Long states, "Even more important to Jefferson's decline was the completion of the Texas and Pacific Railway from Texarkana to Marshall, which bypassed Jefferson. Although another line of the Texas and Pacific reached Jefferson the following year, the development of rail commerce and the rise of Marshall, Dallas, and other important rail cities brought an end to Jefferson's golden age as a commercial and shipping center."[8]

Geological and man-made hydrologic changes notwithstanding, Fannie Marchman continued to make note of the small moments and continuities of her life. It seems that her travels across the great expanse of Texas, and the years that passed one

Fannie Marchman in 1891

after the other, could not sever the connections Fannie Marchman made during her lifetime:

> Dr. O. M. Marchman, Jr. [Fannie's grandson] is Captain in the Army at Kelly Field and does special eye work in the Sam Houston Hospital. His wife is with the Red Cross, studying First Aid. They are a happy couple and doing fine. The teacher asked a member of her class to explain the circulation of blood through the body. Her answer was "The circulation of blood through the body, had to go down one leg and up the other." But she did not explain how the blood got from one foot to the other. Well, I am getting off of my subject, and I must go back to Jefferson.

There were thousands of long horn cattle in Texas and all kinds of wild game. In the Bend where Harmon lived there were deer, wild turkeys, streams full of fish and wild pigeons by the thousand, so many of them would light on one limb and break it off with their weight.

Mr. Marchman and I used to often visit his mother and sister on that large farm, where there were several cabins filled with emigrants from Alabama and Georgia. The brother-in-law, Mr. Harmon, would rig us up horses, and we would ride to Jim's Bayou, several miles, and catch Goggle Eye perch as fast as we would drop our hook in. There were many wild hogs in that country, and a man and family named Stratford killed the hogs and made kegs of lard. Mrs. Stratford told us to bring the fish and she would fry them for us. Her children's names were Boots, Tildy, Sug, Hun and Towhead. We had a couple with us, and Mrs. Stratford filled her iron skillet with lard, mixed meal and salt together, rolled the fish in it and fried them whole. Let me tell you that we all enjoyed fresh fish.

Fannie goes on, jumping between the past and the present, always engaging, and always thoughtful of her family, its travels, and how they affected Texas' progress and prosperity:

When this T&P Railroad was built it carried the produce by Jefferson on to other points, so then people began moving, selling their houses for a song to Negroes or any one that would buy them. We sold our lovely little home, with flowers, fruits and every convenience that we could get at that time, for $250.00. We followed the T&P Railroad to Mineola, where we lived until the boys were grown. Riley, my oldest son, had a business in Lindale, Smith County, for years. Oscar, my second son, studied medicine, went to Grand Saline, practiced there a few years, then moved to Dallas, where has had an office since 1906. He had two children, Dr. O. M. Marchman, Jr., of Kelly Field, and Mrs. Horace Nash, of New York. He is still having more work than he can do, and is looking well after all these years.

R. G. Marchman moved to Waxahachie, has two children, a son, Laurens, and a daughter, Mrs. Gene Williams, and two grandchildren, and Dr. Marchman's daughter has a little girl, Martha Louise, so he too is a grandfather. My youngest son, Orville Marchman went to Wichita Falls about 1908. He built a hotel, and I named it "The Marchman." He passed away three years ago. His name is on a monument on the Capital grounds in Austin as one of the builders of Texas. His wife still runs the hotel with the help of a nephew, Morgan Gillum. That hotel is brimming full of people all the time.

My eldest son and family live in Waxahachie, forty miles from Dallas, a nice road, and they come over almost every Sunday afternoon.

Dr. Marchman and his wife live on Live Oak Street, so I am left without children in my home, but they all except two grandchildren that are too far away come to see me every Sunday eve.

I employ a lady to live with me, thought it best not to break up, as I cannot have many more years to live, as I have already lived on twenty-one years borrowed time, so I guess I will remain in my home, surrounded by flowers, shrubs, etc. I have two hundred rose bushes; all were in bloom and a

**Fannie Marchman's Queen's Wreath Vine,
November 1934**

perfect picture. We had a hail last Wednesday that knocked them all off the bushes, but they will bloom again.

Fannie Marchman died on January 1, 1943. Her epitaph in a cemetery in Ft. Worth, Texas, reads: "She was a kind and affectionate wife, a fond mother, and a friend to all."

ENDNOTES

1. Archie P. McDonald. "The Mittie Stephens Disaster." *http://www.texasscapes.com/AllThingsHistorical/Mittie-Stephens-* . . . Feb. 8–14, 2004.
2. Tyger. "The Red River Campaign: March–May, 1864." *http://www.civilwarhome.com/tigerredriver.htm* Feb. 14, 2002.
3. Shelley Lang. "The *Mittie Stephens:* A Sidewheel Steamboat on the Inland Rivers, 1863–1869." *http:anthropology.tamu.edu/t_naut.htm* August, 1986.
4. Christopher Long. "Jefferson, Texas." *http://www.tsha.utexas.edu/handbook/online/articles/JJ/hgj2.html* Feb. 23, 2005.
5. Ibid.
6. Ibid.
7. "Caddo Lake." *http://en.wikipedia.org/wiki/Caddo_Lake.*
8. Long.

Walter Henry Burton—age 18, 1888

WALTER HENRY BURTON'S RIDE—BELL COUNTY TO JUAREZ, MEXICO IN 1888

by James Burton Kelly

Walter Henry Burton was the first of seven sons born to John Henry Martin Burton Jr. and Cynthia Priscilla Pass Burton. He was my maternal grandfather. He stood about 5′ 7″ tall and probably weighed 150 pounds—boots, hat, longjohns and all. But to me, he was a giant of a man, from my first recollection of him until the day he was buried in the Cleburne cemetery following a fatal automobile accident at age 76.

I could and hopefully will write a lot more about his life and the stories he told me when I was a young boy and spent all of my summers and holidays on the family farm and ranch six miles southwest of Cleburne in Johnson County, Texas. This story is about his two trips horseback from Bell County, Texas, to Juarez, Mexico, to visit and work for his maternal grandfather Lafayette Pass in 1888.

Walter Burton's children called him "Dad" and his grandchildren called him Daddy Burton. When I was very young, Daddy Burton had an old paint horse named Tony that he kept for his grandchildren, miscellaneous nieces and nephews, and friends' children to ride for amusement. I remember riding Tony when he was about 25 years old and I was about three years old. (My sister insists I was more like four years old, but who knows?)

One summer day when I was six (I remember it was the year I started to school), Daddy Burton and I drove some cows from the "back pasture" to the milking barn and I was riding old Tony. It was only about a mile but it seemed like a long ride at the time.

After we put the cows in the lot, we walked the horses over to the barn and horse lot to unsaddle them and give them some oats. Daddy Burton unsaddled old Greg (his big dapple-grey gelding) while I watched, and then he unsaddled Tony. I was not big enough to reach the girth and pull the saddle off without help. While I was watching this unsaddling, I commented, "It sure was a long ride from the back pasture to the cow pens." I remember he stopped the unsaddling, looked at me with a smile and said, "Why son, that's a short ride. When I was a young man I rode a horse from my home in Bell County to see my grandfather in Mexico." I said, "How far was that, Daddy Burton?" to which he replied "About 600 miles as the crow flies."

"How old were you?" I asked. "Oh, I was 18 the first time. I went out there twice. I rode the train home the second time." I can't tell you the impression this made on me and how I was amazed at this revelation. To ride a horse by yourself for this distance was mind boggling to me at the time, and still is for that matter. The more I learned about this trip the more excited I became to learn more. It seemed that he had other things to do that afternoon and was not too interested in telling me the whole story at the time. I did ask him how he found the way and he said, "Oh, there were roads I could follow."

During the following nine years, before his death, we had a number of conversations about this great journey from his home in the Blackland Prairies of Central Texas, across the Edwards Plateau and into the Chihuahua Desert of West Texas and northern Mexico. In hindsight, there were dozens of questions I should have asked but didn't. A lot of the story I have had to flesh out from the history of that time and the area. You are certainly welcome to use your imagination and fill in the blanks of the questions I didn't ask.

Let's first go back to the mid-1800s and review a little history of the times and of our family just to set the stage for this story.

At the outbreak of hostilities that was to become the War Between the States in 1861, our branch of the Burtons lived in Benton County, Alabama, where they had moved from Chesterfield County, Virginia, in the late 1830s. Walter's father, John Henry Martin Burton Jr., joined the army of the Confederate States of America on December 5, 1863, at Talladega, Alabama. He was 15½ years old. He became a private in Company B, Lockhart's Battalion, Alabama Exempts, which later became the 1st Regiment, Alabama Infantry. He was captured by Union forces on April 9, 1865, at Blakely, Alabama, and sent to the Federal Prisoner of War Camp at Ship Island, Mississippi. He was repatriated from Ship Island, Mississippi, to Vicksburg, Mississippi, May 1, 1865, and paroled at Camp Townsend May 6, 1865. He was discharged from the Confederate Army in the summer of 1865.

Having lost everything in the war, the family moved to the Canehill community in Washington County, Arkansas. There he met and married Cynthia Priscilla Pass on March 23, 1869.

In April of 1870 Walter Henry Burton was born. While we don't know what year the family moved from Arkansas to Texas, we do know that their second son, Arthur Thomas Burton, was born in August 1872, in Arkansas, and that their third son Charles was born in January 1875, in Texas.

When they got to Texas, my great-grandfather, John Henry Martin Burton Jr., traded two wagonloads of apples he had brought from Arkansas for a cotton farm in the Little River community of Bell County. The family no doubt ran a typical family farm of that era, and their seven sons were an important part of the labor required for such an operation.

In the meantime, back in Arkansas, Cynthia Priscilla Pass Burton's mother had died and her father, Lafayette Pass, moved to Juarez, Mexico, just across the Rio Grande River from El Paso, Texas, where he opened a mercantile store. He later married a Mexican woman. Probably at the invitation of his grandfather, Walter Burton decided to leave home and go to Juarez and work for his grandfather. I don't know how he came to decide this, but I presume his mother had been in touch with her father and there had been correspondence between them. Walter, being the oldest son, was probably the first to have inclinations to be out on his own. No doubt he was curious to know his grandfather and felt it would be a great adventure to make the trip and work and live in a foreign country. Surely a lot of preparations were necessary to make the trip, including the clothes to take and food and other necessities to carry along, as well as how to find his way. The family probably didn't have a lot of cash money, but he probably didn't need much until he got to Juarez, either.

As I mentioned, in our first conversation, Daddy Burton told me that on his second trip he rode the train home. I have given a lot of thought to this in the last few years. I wondered if at the time of his first trip the railroad had not been "built through" between El Paso and Central Texas, if he didn't have the money for the fare, or if he just wanted to ride horseback to Juarez for the adventure.

I have researched the history of the railroad and learned that passenger service was available. Remember that his first trip was in 1888. I have found two dates. One report said the Texas and New Orleans Railroad had been built through from Houston to San Antonio in 1879 and from San Antonio to El Paso in 1881. Another report said the Southern Pacific Railroad completed the Sunset Limited route on January 12, 1883. It is obvious at the time of his trip in 1888, he had the option to ride the train. Why didn't he? I wish I had asked.

Another concern would have been hostile Indians. The Comanche Indians were still raiding to some extent across the route he had to follow. And he had to go through the heart of the Apache area of Texas to reach El Paso. He might have crossed the well-known Comanche Trail twice. That trail crossed the Pecos River at about Horsehead Crossing where it went south to Comanche Springs near Ft. Stockton. Here it forked and one trail went on south and crossed the Rio Grande at Boquillas and one at Presidio. Most of the Comanches were on reservations in the Oklahoma Territory by the late 1870s. However, Molly Nicholson Burton, Walter's wife and my grandmother, told me a story of the Comanches when she was a young woman in the mid to late 1880s. She said she was living with her parents and sisters on the northwest side of Austin. On a number of occasions in the evening her father would blow out all of the lamps and make everyone lie on the floor because he suspected Indians were around the house. She said on several occasions they could see the Indians walking by the windows backlighted by the moon. None ever broke into their house but some of the neighboring farms were robbed. She heard her father and other men say they were Comanches and a few were caught and sent to jail or the reservations. She said they were a sad-looking people that were poor, half-starved and desperate enough to beg or steal whatever they needed to exist. She remembered being terribly frightened, but felt sorry for them in many ways.

Most of the last large band of Apache Indians, the Lipans, were wiped out by Col. Ranald S. Mackenzie of the U.S. Army in 1873. The survivors were moved to the Mescalero Apache reservation in New Mexico. Apparently a few bands remained in southwest Texas until 1905 when the last of the Lipan Apaches wandered in to the Mescalero reservation, according to the *New Handbook of Texas*. I never thought to ask Daddy Burton about the Indian situation.

I have no idea of the route he took on these trips. While he told me there were roads he could follow, we can only speculate what route he took. At that time there were army forts and camps on routes across West Texas which offered travelers some protection from the Comanches and Apaches. One route he could have followed was to have gone northwest from Bell County and joined the fort-protected route from Fort Worth to Abilene, Pecos, Fort Stockton, and on to El Paso. The other army-protected route would have been to travel south to San Antonio and then turn west through Brackettville, Del Rio, Langtry, Fort Davis and El Paso. There were several more forts and outposts on both of these routes. All of these forts were active in 1888.

It is quite possible that he followed some of the routes of the stagecoaches that had been in existence. Most of the stagecoach companies had gone out of business by the time of his trips due to the railroads coming in. But there were a few still working and the old routes were well known. He could have gone west from his home on the Little River to Lampasas, Brady and San Angelo or Ft. Concho, all towns that were well established in 1888. From there a logical route would have been southwest to Ft. Stockton and hit the main fort road from San Antonio to El Paso. I am not sure the actual route is important to the story.

I asked him one time where he stayed and how he ate on the trip. He told me that usually he stayed at ranches. They were all hospitable and welcomed him to stay as long as he liked and they fed him very well. When he left they usually packed food for him to eat on the trail. He said they were all anxious to see someone from the central part of the state and to have the latest news. Many of them offered him a job if he would stay on, but he was intent on reaching his destination and seeing his grandfather whom he probably had not seen since he was two or three years old. I have a picture of him at this stage of his life and I can tell you without prejudice, he was a very attractive young man. Many people have said I look very much like him. Some of the ranchers would suggest friends further down the road where he might stop. As you can see, most of what I know about his trip is a mixture of what he told me and what I could find out about the history of those days. And I know even less of what went on while he was in Juarez with his grandfather. I do know he worked in the store and learned to speak pretty good Spanish. I heard him tell the story several times that at some point later in life, he could not get workers for the cotton harvest one year and he went to south Texas and hired Mexican laborers. They came from south Texas to Johnson County in wooden railroad boxcars. He was selected to go on this mission by other farmers in the community because he could speak Spanish. He also was the interpreter while they were in the area working.

When he returned from the first trip and made the second trip is also only guesswork on my part. It must have been fairly soon because he was back for good and married my grandmother, Molly Nicholson, on December 23, 1890. She also told me in later years how well he could speak Spanish. Some years after Daddy Burton's death my grandmother told me that Grandpa Pass had sent his Mexican wife back to Central Texas to stay with them for a while. She had her daughter with her. I can't remember why she came, but it seems it had to do some way with an illness in the family.

He never told me how the train ran from El Paso on his second trip home. One route could have been the Southern Pacific from El Paso to San Antonio and then from San Antonio north to Temple. The railroad was also open on the northern route that went from El Paso northeast through Ft. Stockton, Pecos, Abilene, and Ft. Worth. From there he would have gone south to Temple or Belton.

I have told you most everything I know about how Daddy Burton got to Juarez and back, but what about the time he spent there?

Daddy Burton only told me that his Grandfather Lafayette owned a "mercantile" store. He did not elaborate on specifically what that meant or what the store specialized in, if anything. It could have been a general store that handled a lot of different things, but one day I did ask him what a mercantile store was and he said, "Oh, they sell a little of this and a little of that." One can imagine that restrictions on crossing the border 100 years ago were somewhat less than today, and no doubt the store may have had customers on both sides of the Rio Grande.

Where did he live and what was his relationship with his grand-father? I assume that the relationship was good or he wouldn't have been permitted to return for the second trip. I also think if it had not been a pleasant experience he would not have told me or at least would have been more reluctant to talk about it, which he certainly wasn't. He returned to marry Molly Nicholson and start his own life as a farmer and rancher. His parents and younger brothers moved to Johnson County in November of 1891. In January 1892, he and his wife of just a year moved on to Johnson County to join the rest of the family. Here they bought a small farm and started their family.

From as early as I can remember, as soon as school was out in June, my mother drove me the 400 miles from our home in south Texas near Sinton to spend the entire summer with Mother and Daddy Burton on the ranch southwest of Cleburne. She came back and got me just before school started in September. As a little boy I thought this was wonderful and that Mom did this so I would get to know my grandparents. As I grew older and had my own chil-dren I wondered if it wasn't an easy way to get a free baby-sitter for the summer. I have so many great memories of living with them in

Walter Henry Burton—age 74, circa 1944

the summers. I followed Daddy Burton around the place like a
puppy dog, either on foot, on horseback, or riding in his new 1937
Chevy pickup. In retrospect, he really put up with a lot just to
accommodate me. As I got a little older he taught me how to drive
a team of mules pulling a wagon, how to care for your horse and
how to milk a cow—but never let me drive that new Chevy pickup.

We got up before daylight and before breakfast he tuned his old Philco radio in to station WBAP in Ft. Worth for the 6:00 A.M. news and farm report. Unlike most country men of his time, he didn't particularly like hot biscuits for breakfast, but preferred light bread toast. I remember when we finally got electricity at the ranch in about 1938 my grandmother tried to make toast in the new electric stove. She was never able to master this appliance and invariably would burn the toast. I can tell you it wasn't thrown out. She scraped the burn off with a knife and we ate it. I don't think she ever got used to making toast in that stove, but didn't give up. I never heard her use profanity but she said some pretty terrible things she would like to do with that stove. On several occasions Daddy Burton would say to me, "Come on Son, breakfast is ready. I hear your grandmother scraping the toast." My wife is still amazed that I can eat burned toast.

The first summer I missed going to the ranch was the summer of my fifteenth birthday. The oil company my dad worked for hired many of us as roustabout laborers to earn some money for school or whatever. That was the summer Daddy Burton was killed in a car wreck at age 76. He could still catch that big old dapple-grey gelding of his and ride him. That horse wouldn't let anybody else catch him let alone ride him—including me or any hands that worked on the place. About a year after Daddy Burton's death, my older brother who had taken over the ranch was able to catch the horse and ride him. I think that old horse understood the succession of rights. Three summers later when I had my eighteenth birthday, I thought a lot about Daddy Burton's ride to Juarez and I thought to myself, my god, I wouldn't think of trying that now in 1949 let alone in 1888.

Photo courtesy of Skip Clark Collection

THE GALLOPING GOURMET; OR, THE CHUCK WAGON COOK AND HIS CRAFT

by John O. West

The trail drive of the American cowboy is well known to the reading and viewing public of the entire world, thanks to the influence of television and movies and their enormous capacity for education. As is also well known, unfortunately Hollywood is not always careful with its facts—indeed, a new folklore might well be said to have developed because of the public media's part in the passing on of information and mis-information. Such is the nature of oral transmission itself; one might recall: one old cowpoke remembers singing to the cattle to keep them calm; another points out that the average cowboy's voice was far from soothing, and his songs might well have precipitated (rather than averted) a stampede. Of course, with the dulcet tones of Gene Autry and the Sons of the Pioneers as evidence, the popular view is of the romantic persuasion, as is much of the lore of the American cowboy.

Usually overlooked are the factual matters of the cowboy cook and his rolling kitchen. Of course, "everybody" knows that chuck wagon cooks are genially irascible—"as techy as a wagon cook" goes the old saying.[1] George "Gabby" Hayes of the Western movies of the '40s is an excellent model; and all Western movie buffs know that a chuck wagon looks pretty much like an ordinary covered wagon with a pregnant tailgate. But that's about as much as most folks know. The day-to-day routine of the cook gets him up hours before breakfast to rustle grub for a bunch of unruly, and often unappreciative, cowpokes. Then there is the day-long battle to keep ahead of the herd, arriving at pre-designated meal-stops with enough time to spare to put together a meal that would stick to the ribs. But all that is a largely unsung epic!

The portions that have been sung are all part of the past, recorded reminiscences of cowboys and bean-artists that have long since gone up the Long Trail. Still, from those memories a pretty clear picture can be drawn of the lore of the chuck wagon cook. Frank S. Hastings, veteran manager of the SMS ranch, wrote that "a Ranch in its entirety is known as an 'Outfit,' and yet in a general way the word 'Outfit' suggests the wagon outfit, which does the cow-work and lives in the open from April 15th when work begins, to December 1st, when it ends."[2] Thus, for three-quarters of a year the chuck wagon was home for a dozen or so cow punchers, and the cook was the center thereof. The cowhands stuck pretty close to camp: "They rarely leave the wagon a night," says Hastings, "and as a result of close association an interchange of wit or 'josh,' as it is called, has sprung up. There is nothing like the chuck wagon josh in any other phase of life, and it is almost impossible to describe. . . . It is very funny, very keen and very direct."[3]

Jack Thorp, Easterner-turned-cowboy who wrote *Songs of the Cowboys*,[4] among other works, described "A Chuck Wagon Supper" for the New Mexico Federal Writers Project of WPA days. Apparently never before published, it gives a clear picture of a bygone scene:

> A chuck wagon arrives at Milagro Springs. The cook, who has been driving, hollers "whoa, mule," to the team of four which has been pulling the load. Getting off the seat he throws down the lines, and calls to the horse wrangler, who is with the *remuda* of saddle horses following the wagon, to "gobble them up," meaning to unhitch the team and turn them into the *remuda*.
>
> The cook now digs a pit behind the chuck wagon, so when a fire is built, wind will not blow sparks over the camp and the punchers surrounding it. The chuck wagon is always stopped with the wagon tongue facing the wind; this is done so that the fire will be protected by wagon and chuck box. The horse wrangler, with rope down, drags wood for the fire. The many rolls of bedding are thrown

off the wagon, and the cook brings forth his irons. Two of them are some four feet long, sharpened at one end, and with an eye in the other end. The third is a half-inch bar of iron some six feet long. Once he has driven the two sharpened irons into the ground above the pit, the long iron is slipped through the eyes of the two iron uprights; this completes the pot-rack, or stove. Cosi, as the cook is usually called—which is an abbreviation of the Spanish word *cocinero*—hangs a half dozen or so S hooks of iron, some six inches long, on the suspended bar, and to these are hooked coffeepot, stew pots, and kettles for hot water.

The rear end of the wagon contains the chuck box, which is securely fastened to the wagon box proper. The chuck box cover, or lid, swings down on hinges, making a table for Cosi to mix his bread and cut his meat upon, and make anything which may suit his fancy. (There are several dishes whose names cannot be found in any dictionary, so consequently not knowing how to spell them, I omit.) There is an unwritten law that no cow puncher may ride his horse on the windward side of the chuck box or fire, or Cosi is liable to run him off with a pot-hook or axe. This breach of manners would be committed only by some green hand, or "cotton-picker," as Cosi would probably call him. This rule is made so no trash or dirt will be stirred up and blown into the skillets.

The *cocinero*, now having his fire built, with a pot-hook in hand—an iron rod some three feet long with a hook bent in its end—lifts the heavy Dutch bake oven lid by its loop and places it on the fire, then the oven itself, and places it on top of the lid to heat. These ovens are skillets about eight inches in depth and some two feet across, generally, but they come in all sizes, being used for baking bread and cooking meat, stew, potatoes, and so forth. The coffee pot is of galvanized iron, holding from three to five gallons, and hanging on the pot-rack full of hot coffee for whoever may pass. Sometimes a pudding is made of dried bread, raisins, sugar, water, and a little grease, also nutmeg and spices; this is placed in a Dutch oven, and cooked until the top is brown. This is the usual cow-camp meal, but if there is no beef in the wagon, beans and chili are substituted.

Then Cosi, in a huge bread pan, begins to mix his dough. After filling the pan about half-full with flour, he adds sour dough, poured out of a jar or tin bucket which is always carried along, adds salt, soda, and lard or warm grease, working all together into a dough, which presently will become second-story biscuits. After the dough has been kneaded, he covers it over, and for a few minutes lets it "raise." A quarter of beef is taken from the wagon, where it has been wrapped in canvas to keep it cool. Slices are cut off and placed in one of the Dutch ovens, into which grease—preferably tallow—has been put. The lid is laid on, and with a shovel red hot coals are placed on top. While this is cooking, another skillet is filled with sliced potatoes, and given the same treatment as the meat. Now the bread is molded into biscuits, and put into another Dutch oven. These biscuits are softer than those made with baking powder, and as each is patted out, it is dropped into hot grease and turned over. These biscuits are then put in the bake-oven, tight together until the bottom of the container is full. Now comes the success or failure of the operation. The secret is to keep the Dutch oven at just the right heat, adding or taking off the right amount of hot coals, from underneath the oven or on top of the lid. If everything goes right, you may be assured of the best hot biscuits in the world.

Along in the evening, as the men are through with the day's roundup or drive, tired horses are turned into the *remuda,* and Cosi hollers, "Come and get it or I'll throw it out." The punchers in their chaps, boots, and spurs flock to the chuck wagon, and out of the drawer get knives, forks, and spoons, and off the lid of the chuck box take plates and cups that Cosi has laid out. They then go to the different bake ovens and fill their plates, which like the cups are made of tin; the knives, spoons, and forks are of iron or composition. Lots of banter usually passes between the punchers and Cosi, though he generally gives as good as he receives. Plates filled, the boys sit around on the different rolls of bedding, the wagon tongue, or with crossed legs either squatting on the ground or with their packs against a wagon wheel. Of course, there is no tablecloth on the chuck-box lid, but it is usually scrubbed clean enough for the purpose of eating—though no one uses it.

As the boys finish their meal, plates, cups, knives, forks, and spoons are thrown into a large dishpan placed on the ground underneath the chuck-box lid. If some luckless puncher should place his "eating tools" on top of the lid, he would be sure to be bawled out by Cosi. All the eating tools, when washed, are put on shelves or in drawers of the chuck-box, while the heavy Dutch ovens and such are put into a box bolted underneath the wagon bed at its rear end.

This is the real chuck wagon and way of eating as found in New Mexico, though some Northern outfits have a different lay. From the Cimarron

River north, as far as grass grows, many outfits have quite elaborate lays. Those that have a large tent or tarp spread over the wagon and extending out on both sides are generally called by real punchers "Pullman outfits," and old hands will tell you that they use them so that the punchers won't get sunburned, and usually add "bless their little hearts," also explaining, with very straight faces, that these Pullman boys usually wear white shirts, and are obliged to shave and shine their boots every morning before starting work.[5]

A photograph in *From the Pecos to the Powder* shows a chuck wagon with an iron cook-stove plus a tarpaulin shelter[6]—obviously a Pullman outfit—and a description in the same work tells how the stove is chained on behind, with poles extending behind and rawhide thongs holding the whole thing secure.[7] The famous chuck wagon races engaged in annually at the Calgary and other Canadian rodeos began, says Cliff Claggett, in cooperative roundups when cooks actually raced to get the best locations to set up their campsites; further, in the present-day races, an outrider has to hoist a stove onto the rear of the wagon to start the race.[8] But in chuck wagon races filmed at the Calgary Stampede for the Academy Award-winning Disney movie *Hacksaw,* the outrider loaded a trunk onto the back of the wagon, rather than a stove.[9]

The original chuck wagon, according to tradition, was created by pioneer cowman Charles Goodnight, who took a "government wagon" and had it altered, replacing the wooden axles with iron ones, and adding the chuck box at the rear.[10] The chuck box was widely copied, says Ramon Adams: two to three feet deep and four feet high, it had shelves and drawers covered by the hinged lid. The inside thus resembled a kitchen cabinet, holding some supplies, pots, and simple medical nostrums—including horse liniment for man or beast. With sideboards added to the wagon bed, there was room for sacks of beans and flour, and canned goods.[11]

Photo courtesy of Skip Clark Collection

Not to be forgotten is the "possum belly" or "cooney" (from Spanish *cuna,* cradle), where firewood was carried, or, in treeless areas, "prairie coal"—cow or buffalo chips.[12] It was simply a cowhide stretched beneath the wagon while still green, and filled with rocks to stretch it.

Of course, there was no such thing as a school for cooking for cowboys nor soldiers nor lumberjacks—they just grew. Jack Flynt remembers how his dad, Holbert W. Flynt, back about the turn of the century, got "elevated" to such a position: "They were building the old Orient railroad, down near Alpine, Texas, and Dad was a teamster, running a six-mule scraper. One day the assistant cook didn't show, and somebody had heard Dad tell about how he had learned to barbecue goats from *his* dad—so they put Dad to work as assistant cook. Later, when the cook quit, Dad got the job. Wasn't but about nineteen, but he handled the job for quite a while. He'd boil a hundred pound sack of potatoes at a time, in a 55 gallon drum!"[13]

That railroad crew was lucky, judging by the oft-told tale of the amateur cowboy cook. A version I picked up from a contestant at a rodeo in Odessa, Texas, in 1960 tells of the outfit whose cook had been run off by the sheriff, and no replacement was at hand. So, the foreman had the hands draw straws, and the short straw-drawer was elected cook, to serve 'til somebody complained. Well, nobody complained for a good while, and Cosi wasn't too happy in his job—so he started getting careless; but nobody dared complain, since whoever complained had to take the job himself. Finally he got desperate, and dumped a double handful of salt into the beans and served 'em up. One of the boys took a mouthful and nearly strangled. "By God," he hollered, "them's the saltiest beans I ever et!" About then he noticed the cook starting to take off his apron. "But that's jest the way I like 'em!" he concluded.

Both the tradition of using substitute cooks and a host of stories arising out of it, "all of them almost too old to bear repeating," are mentioned in *Come and Get It.*[14] I have often been told the same tale—except that the extra ingredient is usually cow manure—a detail that links it with the lumberjack's story found by Barre Toelken in Maine in 1954—both as an oral tale and in the form of a ballad, where the cook-against-his-will served up what should have gotten him fired:

> One by one the boys turned green,
> Their eyeballs rolled to and fro;
> Then one guy hollered as he sank to the floor
> "My God, that's moose-turd pie!
> [Shouted] Good, though!"[15]

Frequently, the chuck wagon cook was a stove-up cowboy who could no longer handle regular range chores, but he soon became master of his small, vital kingdom, guarding it jealously from any encroachments. Even the owner of the cattle was expected to stay out of the sixty-foot circle surrounding the wagon.[16] Range etiquette required that a horseman slow his steed when nearing the cook wagon, to avoid stirring up dust—or the cook's temper. The body of the wagon, as Jack Thorp noted, usually carried bedrolls for the hands, but the rest of the rig was the cook's domain. One old timer recalled a double killing that arose out of a cowboy's brashness:

> French and a fellow named Hinton got into it over Hinton digging into the chuck box, which was against Frenchy's rule, as it was with any good cooky. They did not want the waddies messing up the chuck box. Hinton seemed to get a kick out of seeing Frenchy get riled. . . . Frenchy never refused to give any one a handout, but Hinton insisted upon helping himself. The evening that the fight took place, Hinton walked past Frenchy and dove into the chuck box. Frenchy went after Hinton with a carving-knife and Hinton drew his gun. The cooky kept going into Hinton slashing with his knife and Hinton kept backing away shooting all the while, trying to get away from the knife, but Frenchy never hesitated . . . finally he drove the knife into Hinton's breast and they both went to the ground and died a few minutes after.[17]

The huge coffeepot was the first item to go on the cook's fire when it was built, and generally the last to come off when breaking camp. "Around chuck wagons," says Francis Fugate, "early Westerners renewed their energies with coffee, the aromatic brew that 'quickens the spirit, and makes the heart lightsome.' Chances are that Arbuckles' was the brand in all those coffeepots. In fact, the use of the Arbuckle Bros. coffee was so widespread that its brand name came to be synonymous with the word 'coffee'. . . ."[18] The cook (strongly supported by the cowhands) believed in making it stout: "A recipe went the rounds from ranch to ranch, confided by cooks to greenhorn hands: 'You take two pounds of Arbuckles', put in enough water to wet it down, then you boil it for two hours. After that, you throw in a horseshoe. If the shoe sinks, the coffee ain't ready.' "[19] One of the reasons the brand was so popular was the premiums used by John Arbuckle to stimulate sales—and thereby hangs a chuck cook trick: a stick of sugar candy included in each bag lightened the cook's load. "If a cook wanted the next day's supply of coffee ground, he would call out, 'Who wants the candy?' and get a rash of volunteers to turn the crank on the coffee grinder, which was inevitably fastened to the side of the chuck wagon."[20]

One of the proofs of the existence of a folk group is a shared language—and the chuck wagon scene had its share of useful terms, far beyond those already cited herein. Jack Thorp, in a list he termed "not finished," recorded a number of these for the New Mexico Federal Writers Project:

Air tights	canned goods
Biscuit-shooter	a waitress
Chuck	food of any kind
Dough-gods	biscuits
Dough-wrangler	cook
Feed-trough	to eat at a table
Fluff-duffs	fancy food
Frijoles	beans
Gouch hooks	irons to lift the heavy lids of cooking vessels
Lick	syrup (or a salt lick)[21]

Salt pork went by " 'sow belly,' 'hog side,' 'sow bosom,' and 'pig's vest with buttons.' Bacon was often sarcastically referred to as 'fried chicken,' 'chuck wagon chicken,' and 'Kansas City fish.' It was not used to a great extent, because it became rancid in the heat and anyway the cowman preferred fresh meat."[22] Of course, there were names for particular dishes—son-of-a-gun stew, for example, which was also called by its more natural, less polite name. Ramon Adams says it was made of practically everything the cook had at hand, excepting "horns, hoof, and hide." And perhaps the name came from the first cowboy who tasted it, and hollered "Sono-fabitch, but that's good." But Adams also notes the tendency for

Postcard courtesy of Skip Clark Collection

an outfit to call the dish by the name of some enemy—"a subtle way of calling him names which one dared not do to his face."[23]

The good chuck wagon cook learned to make do with whatever he had. A mixture of sorghum and bacon grease was a substitute for butter, for example,[24] and it was a mighty poor cook who couldn't spice up the usual menu, which was always strong on "meat and whistle-berries [beans]."[25] Dried apples and raisins were staples on many wagons, and they served to make pies—one item cowboys dearly loved. Cosi would roll out his dough with a beer bottle, put it in a greased pie pan and add the previously stewed fruit, then cover it with another layer of dough—with the steam escaping through the outfit's brand cut in the crust![26] "Spotted pup"—raisin and rice pudding—did pretty well, especially with sugar and cream (when it was available), but as a steady diet it could produce mutiny![27] "Some cooks were expert at making vinegar pies," reports Ramon Adams, concocted of a combination of vinegar, water, fat, and flour, all turned onto a layer of dough in a pie pan, and then covered, cobbler style, with criss-crossed strips of dough and baked.[28] And then there was "pooch"—tomatoes, stewed with left-over biscuits and a little sugar—that cowboys enjoyed as much as dessert.[29] Rather than pack a lunch, a hand would carry a can or two of tomatoes to tide him over if he was going to be gone over the meal hour; they served as both food and drink.[30]

Another side of the grouchy cook—the very one who died defending his turf in the story above—is presented by John Baker:

> The belly-cheater on the Holt outfit was a fellow called Frenchy, a top cooky. He was one of them fellows that took enjoyment out of satisfying the waddies' tapeworm. Frenchy was always pulling some tricks on us waddies and we enjoyed his tricks, because he always made up for the tricks by extra efforts in cooking some dish we hankered after. He could make some of the best puddings I ever shoved into my mouth. One day at supper we were all about done eating and Frenchy said: "If you dam skunks wait a second I'll give you some pudding. It is a little late getting done." Of course we all waited and he pulled a beauty out of the oven. We all dived into it and took big gobs into our mouths. We then started to make funny faces. What he had done was to use salt instead of sugar when he made it and that pudding tasted like hell. We all began to sputter and spit to clean our mouths. He then pulled a good pudding on us and that sure was a peach. We had forgot that the day was April 1. He would use red pepper on us in some dishes we hankered after, also cotton in biscuits, but we knew something extra was coming up to follow.[31]

The cowboys often cussed the chuck and the cook, and called him names like Vinegar Jim, and Bilious Bill, and Dirty Dave—not to mention some less polite handles.[32] But on a dry drive, when the cowboys were working the clock around to keep the steers moving north, the cook kept open house all night long, with food and Arbuckles' to keep the waddies going; he knew that hardship was easier to bear if the hands were well fed.[33] And on more normal nights, when the cook had put a lighted lantern on the tip of the wagon tongue to guide the night crews back to the outfit, and pointed it towards the North Star to provide bearings for the next day's drive,[34] it was easy to remember that the wagon was home, and the chuck wagon cook—ugly and irascible though he might be—was in some ways the heart and soul of the outfit. Jack Thorp said a bunch when he wrote, "when it came to serving up ample and good-tasting food under unfavorable conditions, I never saw anybody to beat the average cow-camp cook."[35] Without him the roundup, the trail drive, and the cattle industry could never have been—and even with the distortions of fact that Hollywood provides, his lore lingers on, relic of a bygone day.

Endnotes

1. Ramon F. Adams. *Come and Get It: The Story of the Old Cowboy Cook.* Norman: University of Oklahoma Press, 1952. 5.
2. Frank S. Hastings. "Some Glimpses into Ranch Life." History of Grazing in Texas, Division VI, Part A, Steps Toward Stability and Conservation, Texas Writers Project, Barker History Center, The University of Texas at Austin. Unpaginated.
3. Ibid.
4. N. Howard Thorp. *Songs of the Cowboys.* Estancia, New Mexico: News Print Shop, 1908.
5. N. Howard Thorp. "A Chuck Wagon Supper." File 5, Division 4, Folio 3, Folder 5, New Mexico Writers Projects, History Library, Museum of New Mexico, Santa Fe, New Mexico. (The bread, raisin, and sugar pudding is essentially *capirotada,* a traditional Mexican delicacy served during Lent; Lucina L. Fischer, interview with the author, El Paso, Texas, 12 December 1984.)
6. Bob Kennon, as told to Ramon W. Adams. *From the Pecos to the Powder: A Cowboy's Autobiography.* Norman: University of Oklahoma Press, 1965. 36.
7. Ibid. 82–83.
8. Glenn Ohrlin. *The Hell-Bound Train: A Cowboy Songbook.* Urbana: University of Illinois Press, 1973. 213.
9. Larry Lansburgh, Producer/Director. *Hacksaw.* Walt Disney Productions, 1971.

10. J. Evetts Haley. *Charles Goodnight: Cowman and Plainsman*. Boston: Houghton Mifflin, 1936. 121, qtd. in Adams, 11.
11. Adams. 12–13.
12. Ibid. 14–15.
13. Jack Flynt. Interview with the author, El Paso, Texas, 23 November, 1984.
14. Adams. 155–156.
15. J. Barre Toelken. *The Dynamics of Folklore*. Boston: Houghton Mifflin, 1979. 66–67, 179–180.
16. Adams. 5–6.
17. John J. Baker. "Ft. Worth Texas Narrative." Fort Worth History Notes, Folder 68: Interviews, Texas Writers Project, Barker History Center, The University of Texas at Austin, 26856–26857.
18. Francis L. Fugate. "Arbuckles': The Coffee That Won the West." *American West* 21, No. 1. January–February 1984. 61.
19. Ibid. 62.
20. Ibid. 63.
21. N. Howard Thorp. "Cowland Glossary." File 5, Division 4, Folio 3, Folder 6, New Mexico Writers Project, History Library, Museum of New Mexico, Santa Fe, New Mexico.
22. Adams. 111.
23. Ibid. 91–92.
24. Ibid. 116.
25. Baker. 26830.
26. Adams. 103–104.
27. Kennon/Adams. 87.
28. Adams. 105.
29. Ibid. 111.
30. Ibid. 110.
31. Baker. 26855.
32. Kennon/Adams. 82–87.
33. Andy Adams. *The Log of a Cowboy: A Narrative of the Old Trail Days*. Boston: Houghton Mifflin, 1903, 1931. 60.
34. Ramon Adams. 154.
35. N. Howard Thorp, in collaboration with Neil M. Clark. *Pardner of the Wind*. Caldwell, Idaho: Caxton Printers, 1945. 270.

BIBLIOGRAPHY

Adams, Andy. *The Log of a Cowboy: A Narrative of the Old Trail Days*. 1903. Boston: Houghton Mifflin, 1931.
Adams, Ramon F. *Come and Get It: The Story of the Old Cowboy Cook*. Norman: University of Oklahoma Press, 1952.

Baker, John J. "Ft. Worth Texas Narrative." Fort Worth History Notes. Texas Writers Project. Barker History Center, The University of Texas at Austin, Austin, Texas.

Fugate, Frances L. "Arbuckles': The Coffee That Won the West." *American West,* 21, No. 1 (January/February 1984) 61–68.

Haley, J. Evetts. *Charles Goodnight: Cowman and Plainsman.* Boston: Houghton Mifflin, 1936.

Hastings, Frank S. "Some Glimpses into Ranch Life." History of Grazing in Texas. Texas Writers Project. Barker History Center. The University of Texas at Austin, Austin, Texas.

Kennon, Bob, as told to Ramon W. Adams. *From the Pecos to the Powder: A Cowboy's Autobiography.* Norman: University of Oklahoma Press, 1965.

Lansburgh, Larry, Producer/Director. *Hacksaw.* Tab Hunter, Susan Bracken, George Barrows, and Russ McCubbin. Walt Disney Productions, 1971.

Ohrlin, Glenn. *The Hell-Bound Train: A Cowboy Songbook.* Urbana: University of Illinois Press, 1973.

Thorp, N. Howard. "Cowland Glossary." New Mexico Writers Project. History Library, Museum of New Mexico, Santa Fe, New Mexico.

———. "A Chuck Wagon Supper." New Mexico Writers Project. History Library, Museum of New Mexico, Santa Fe, New Mexico.

———. *Songs of the Cowboys.* Estancia, New Mexico: News Print Shop, 1908.

Thorp, N. Howard, in collaboration with Neil M. Clark. *Pardner of the Wind.* Caldwell, Idaho: Caxton Printers, 1945.

Toelken, J. Barre. *The Dynamics of Folklore.* Boston: Houghton Mifflin, 1979.

W.C. Jameson

THE LANGUAGE OF THE TRAIL DRIVERS: AN EXAMINATION OF THE ORIGIN AND DIFFUSION OF AN INDUSTRY-ORIENTED VOCABULARY

by W. C. Jameson

INTRODUCTION

There exist in this country, and quite likely throughout the world, numerous examples of industry-oriented vocabularies. It can be argued, for instance, that the defense industry in the United States has a unique vocabulary oriented toward specific goals and projects. The baseball and football industries, both professional and collegiate, have their own specific vocabularies and terminology. Even academicians, depending on their specific areas of concentration, have a jargon peculiar to their interests and professional activities.

The vocabulary addressed herein is associated with the ranching and livestock industry as it evolved and thrived in South-Central Texas from the late 1830s to approximately the mid-1880s, a vocabulary which, in much the same form, is still in use today.

Several aspects of this vocabulary beg discussion. One critical element is concerned with how it came into existence as a result of the juxtapositioning of certain critical events and several different cultures. Another relates to the diffusion processes involved in disseminating the vocabulary throughout a portion of the United States and even the world—a diffusion process which has gone through at least two phases and, to some limited extent, continues today. Finally, some comments will be offered relative to the endurance of this vocabulary and what specific factors might have enabled it to remain in use for well over a century, even though the trail drives and the specific cattle ranching operations of the last century no longer exist.

CULTURAL MIX

Prior to Anglo settlement in the central and southern parts of Texas, the region was minimally populated by scattered tribes of Native Americans and a few Spanish friars and associated followers who entered the area to establish missions and, in part, to deliver Christianity to the Indians. Among other things, the missionaries encouraged agricultural pursuits, particularly cattle husbandry. In order to accomplish this goal, the church leaders brought with them hundreds of the durable Moorish cattle from Spain, animals that were the predecessors of the Texas longhorns.

During the 1830s, a different type of settler began moving into Texas—Europeans other than the Peninsular variety. As a result of the impetus provided by the establishment of the Austin, Dewitt, and other colonies in central and north-central Texas, many Europeans, mostly Germans and Czechs, sailed from the old country to begin a new life in this new land. In addition, in 1835 a promotional booklet entitled "Guide to Texas Emigration" was compiled by one David Woodman and distributed throughout much of the eastern United States, enticing many to consider a move to Texas to take advantage of the abundance of available land, gentle climate, natural resources, and the numerous "wild" cattle living in the dense brush.

These new arrivals settled into the established colonies and, logically, undertook farming and ranching. Before long, these new citizens of Texas began gathering up many of the feral longhorns left over from the Spanish missionary farms and ranches, and using them for barter as well as for beef. As the ranches evolved and prospered, an obvious need for qualified handlers of both bovine and equine livestock was generated. It became well-known very quickly that the Mexican *vaqueros* from south of the Rio Grande were among the continent's most expert horsemen and cattlemen, and many of them were lured north of the Rio Grande to work on the new Anglo-operated cattle ranches.

As more and more settlers arrived in this part of Texas, a growing labor force evolved. Many of the newcomers secured jobs on the area cattle ranches and immediately began learning the herding and livestock techniques of the Mexicans. Represented in this new wave of migrants to Texas were Upper and Lower South Anglos, some Blacks, and even a few Cajuns from southern Louisiana. These were joined by a small number of Comanche and Kiowa Indians from the Texas and Oklahoma plains, themselves highly skilled horsemen.

It has been observed that during this era the Mexican *vaqueros* clearly dominated relative to livestock handling and horsemanship skills, and they soon became a major influence on techniques used. It is understandable, then, how easy it was for much of their livestock-oriented language to be incorporated into the rapidly expanding terminology associated with the ranching industry.

There was a strong Anglo influence on the growing vocabulary, but the dominance of the Spanish language was apparent. Much of the Mexican terminology was misunderstood and mispronounced by the Anglos, Blacks, Indians, and Cajuns, and there eventually evolved a kind of *linqua franca* unique to this specific geographic region that became, in effect, a hearth area relative to the development and evolution of the vocabulary.

For example, the word "lariat," a common word for a rope, is still used today. The word is derived from the Spanish *la riata,* meaning a rope used for roping horses and cattle. The word "buckaroo," generally used to identify a young cowboy, comes from the Spanish *vaquero. Vaca* means cow, and a *vaquero* is one who works with cows. A *caballero* is one who works with *caballos,* or horses. A "hackamore" is a rope halter and comes from the Spanish *jaquima,* which means the same thing.

The term "mustang" is derived from the Spanish *mesteño,* which in turn comes from the word *mesta,* which means "a group of stock raisers." The horses that escaped from a range controlled by the *mesta* were called *mesteños.* The suffix *–eño* means "belonging to." A man who chased the mustangs was called a *mesteñero,* or, in the Anglicized version, a mustanger. The term "mustang," which is normally associated with wild horses, originally referred to cattle.

Diffusion

Around the mid-1860s, Texas ranchers began to notice that the prices paid for beef in New York and other eastern markets ranged from twenty-five to thirty-five cents per pound, considerably higher than local rates. The cattlemen wanted to take advantage of this new market, but the problem was how to get the cattle currently residing on the South-Central Texas ranges to the prime beef-consuming centers in the east. The nearest railheads were hundreds of miles away, so the trail drive was employed to deliver the cattle to the railroads, which in turn would transport them to the viable markets in the east.

The concept of the trail drive was neither new nor unique to this particular situation. In fact, trail drives had been utilized many times in the American South, the Middle Atlantic States, and even in Europe long before they were ever perceived as a process for getting Texas cattle to the northern railheads.

Exclusive of some early deliveries of cattle to the New Orleans market, the first serious trail drives to emanate from the South-Central Texas region journeyed northward to railheads at Abilene and Dodge City, Kansas, as well as other places in Colorado and Nebraska, and involved thousands of head of cattle and sometimes dozens of cowhands. Some of the more famous cattle trails include the Chisholm, the Goodnight-Loving, the Western, and the Shawnee.

The trail drives employed many of the ranch hands who worked on the Texas ranches, and as the drives moved northward, these cowhands carried with them the elements of that unique cultural package that evolved from working with the cattle: the herding and roping techniques; the mode of dress; and, of course, the vocabulary. Despite what is seen in movies and on television, or read in novels, many of the early trail drivers were Mexicans, Blacks, and even Indians.

The trail drives brought hundreds of cowhands to new and different parts of the country. At trail's end, as well as at various points along the way, many of them encountered opportunities not available to them in Texas—occasions to work on one of the many growing cattle ranches in the area, as well as chances to start their

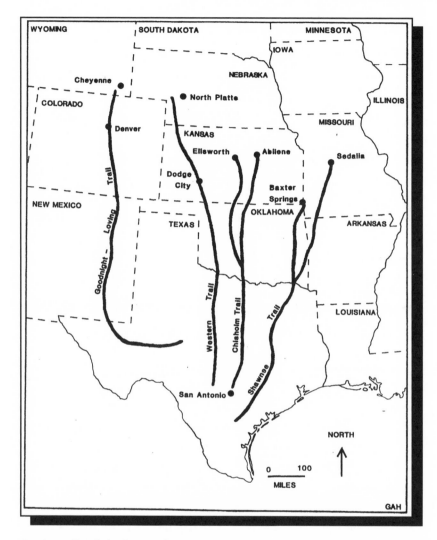

Cattle trails of the late 19th Century

own stock-raising operation. Consequently, many of the cowboys remained to ply their trade and apply their skills. Virtually all of them continued to use and perpetuate the industry-oriented vocabulary that evolved earlier in South-Central Texas. In this manner, the vocabulary, as well as the herding methodology, were diffused into areas outside of the hearth area of the so-called "diamond" region of Texas. This new area of diffusion is herein referred to as the "cattle-drive shed."

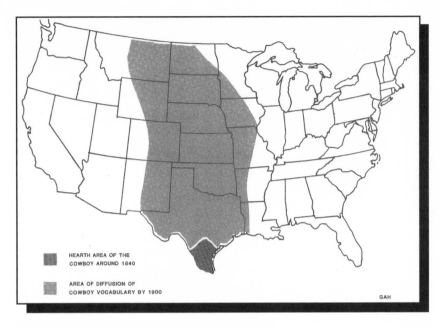

HEARTH AREA OF THE
COWBOY AROUND 1840

AREA OF DIFFUSION OF
COWBOY VOCABULARY BY 1900

GAH

The "spread" of the cowboy and his language

Around the mid-1880s, the trail drives began to slow down and were soon to cease altogether. When they finally did stop, the effective diffusion of this specialized vocabulary slowed down along with it. Even though there was some leakage through and across the natural barriers of the Rocky Mountains and the Mississippi River, the vocabulary, with some exceptions, was largely confined to the shed area. One major exception was Southern California, which experienced a parallel evolution of language use, derived primarily from the *vaqueros* who came north from the Mexican state of Sonora.

There followed a period of relative dormancy until the 1930s. At that time two things occurred on the American cultural front which further stimulated diffusion of the language: Western movies and the growing commercialization of rodeo. The western movie captured the fascination of the American public in the late 1930s and throughout much of the 1940s like nothing ever had before, and because so many of the original western movie actors and extras had been real-life cowhands, much of the original trail drive and ranching vocabulary was incorporated into the films which were shown coast to coast and even in Europe. As a result of the appeal of the early manly western heroes and the popular action-adventure pace of their films, many people outside of the original diffusion area (the cattle drive shed) were exposed to the vocabulary, and the American language was becoming spiced with words like "buckaroo," mustang, and "whoopie ti-yi-yo," even though many people had neither the vaguest idea of the origin of those words and phrases nor even, in many cases, what they actually meant.

The popularization of rodeo also helped diffuse the trail drive vocabulary, although with a somewhat more limited efficiency. Most of the early rodeo participants were commonly ranch hands that possessed exceptional livestock-handling skills like roping and riding, and some of them discovered they could earn a good living utilizing these skills via competitive sport. Because of the acceptance of the cowboy image through popular films and an increasing number of western novels, it was a relatively easy thing for the "new" sport of rodeo to make significant inroads into the American culture. Rodeo is at the same time an athletic competition, which strongly appeals to most Americans, as well as a legitimate descendant of the wild west show and Mexican *charreadas*. The subsequent sophisticated commercialization of rodeo created growing markets for the sport, and by the end of the 1930s they were even playing in Madison Square Garden.

CONCLUSION

The American cowboy which is, in fact, the Texas cowboy, has been a remarkably enduring icon for well over a century. Along with this powerful image, other iconic elements, both real and imagined, include the cowboy's implied ruggedness, his sense for justice, his mode of dress, and, of course, his vocabulary.

Thus, via film, television, novel, and rodeo, the diffusion of this special industry-oriented vocabulary was effective and relatively rapid, and the language itself was and is quite enduring. Even today, most of the original terminology employed by the early cowhands is still used in much the same manner that it was over a century ago.

THE MODERN

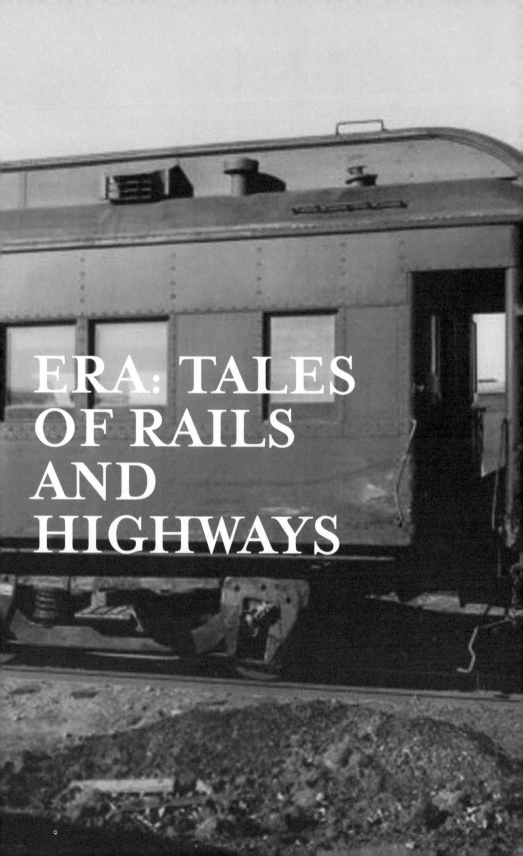

ERA: TALES OF RAILS AND HIGHWAYS

The Durango and Silverton train

RAIL REMEMBRANCES: THE TRAIN IN FOLK MEMORY AND IMAGINATION

by L. Patrick Hughes

—~—

> If you've ever heard the whistle of a fast freight train beat-
> ing out a beautiful tune,
> If you've ever seen the cold on the railroad tracks shining
> in the silvery moon,
> If you've ever felt a locomotive shake the ground then I
> know you don't need to be told,
> Why I'm goin' down to the railroad tracks to watch them
> lonesome boxcars roll.
>
> Butch Hancock, "Boxcars"

Without question, the coming of the railroads was one of the most revolutionarily transformative events in the history of the United States and the American people. Seen as a prerequisite to both the conquest of the Far West and the realization of the national goal of industrialization, privately owned and operated railroad companies received financial subsidization from government at all levels in the form of land grants, loans, and tax incentives. The faster, cheaper, and more reliable transportation the railroads represented resulted in the subjugation of the Native American, the settlement of the Great Plains, and the exploitation of the region's cornucopia of raw materials and natural resources. Gold and silver, bison and longhorns, grain and cotton flowed outward as settlers and manufactured goods from far beyond the horizon flooded in. Silver rails connected factories with consumers and the city with the countryside.

Demographically, America changed as well. Cities sprung into being from nothingness on sites that had served as construction camps. Towns bypassed by the lines shriveled up and disappeared as residents fled for locations that had won rail service. In the long run, the roads transformed frontier outposts such as Dallas and

Fort Worth into great inland transportation hubs and bustling metropolises. Capable of heretofore unheard-of speeds of twenty, thirty, and more miles an hour, the railroads in a figurative sense shrank the world. The physical isolation of Americans one from another became a thing of the past as the frontier vanished and a more modern age began.

The golden age of the railroads has, of course, long since passed. In the aftermath of World War II, millions of American travelers, taking advantage of the new interstate system of super-highways, abandoned trains for private automobiles. Jet airliners winging coast-to-coast at speeds bordering on the supersonic siphoned off most of the rest. Denied its profitable passenger base, the industry refocused, restructured, and resigned itself to the hauling of freight. Amtrak's meager offerings notwithstanding, those of a new century wishing to experience their grandfather's "magic carpet ride" must avail themselves of tourist attractions such as the Texas State Railroad, the Cumbres and Toltec, or the Durango and Silverton excursion trains. In the words of Texas tunesmith Steve Fromholz, for most Americans "the train just don't stop here anymore."

While the railroads are today but a shadow of their former selves, no form of transportation has had a more profound and enduring impact upon folk memory and imagination as expressed in the songs of the people. Compositions featuring boats and planes are few and far between. Automobiles enjoyed a heyday in popular music when, in the early-to-mid sixties, postwar baby boomers simultaneously reached the age of dating and driving. The shelf life of tunes such as "Little Deuce Coupe," "409," and "Hey Little Cobra," however, proved exceedingly brief—atop the charts one day, unheard thereafter. Railroad songs, by contrast, have been one of the most enduring topics in the music of the people, most particularly in the fields of country, folk, and the blues.

Perhaps it was the sights and sounds of the gargantuan mechanical beast that first produced Americans' fascination with the "iron horse." Whether standing still or in motion, steam-powered locomotives belching smoke and cinders were an awesome sight to behold for young and old alike. The sounds were no less impressive. The chug of the exhaust, the clatter of the side-rods, the soothing clickity-clack of the wheels on the rail joints, and the blast of the lonesome whistle rolling for miles across the countryside all left an indelible imprint on the memory. While grown-ups, forced by society's norms to behave as adults, fought to hide their inner glee at the sight of a train, children faced no such encumbrance. Their unbridled pleasure manifested itself in numerous ways: counting passing freight cars at every grade crossing, inducing engineers to acknowledge their presence with a toot of the engine whistle, and placing coins on the rails to be flattened as thin as a sheet of paper. If the truth be told, parents enabled and took vicarious enjoyment in all such rituals. They also passed along to each succeeding generation their fascination with and love of trains in song.

Legendary trains of fact and fiction represent a major subset of the larger genre. Examples are numerous: Steve Goodman's "The City of New Orleans," Ervin T. Rouse's "Orange Blossom Special," and Huddie Ledbetter's "Rock Island Line" are but three. None, however, is rooted deeper in public memory than "Wabash Cannonball." An imaginary train running "from the great Atlantic Ocean to the wide Pacific shore," it had been a staple of rural musicians' repertoire for a full four decades before being copyrighted by A. P. Carter in the latter twenties. It was, however, Roy Acuff's 1936 recording that transformed the song into an American standard. So popular was the Vocalion release that the Wabash system sought to capitalize on the hit recording, renaming its Detroit-to-St. Louis express "The Cannonball." Rail executives must have thanked their lucky stars decade after decade each time Acuff called upon WSM's Grand Ole Opry audience to "listen to the jingle, the rumble, and the roar" of the mythical train.

Composers and musicians from the beginning found rail tragedies a veritable goldmine of new material. Early train travel was risky, with derailments and collisions all too common occurrences. For engineers, firemen, brakemen, and other employees, the danger was ever-present and death a very real possibility.

Leycester Hughes of San Antonio was but one of countless fatalities. The grandfather I never knew perished when two International and Great Northern trains met head-on six miles north of Jewett, Texas, in 1930.

In death, other railroaders found immortality in song. Blamed not for the foolhardiness that most often led them prematurely to their maker, engineers trying to "bring 'er in on time" are almost always lionized. Such was the case with Casey Jones in 1900. Inheriting an Illinois Central locomotive out of Memphis running two hours behind schedule, he'd made up all but two minutes before crashing into a stalled freight outside Vaughn, Mississippi. He lives on, however, in "The Ballad of Casey Jones," performed through the years by artists as varied as Gid Tanner and His Skillet Lickers on the one hand and the Grateful Dead on the other.

Perhaps Jones shares cab duties on the glory train with Joseph Broady. Commemorated in "Wreck of the Old 97," Broady was piloting a late-running mail train out of Monroe, Virginia, in September 1903 when tragedy struck:

> He was goin' down the grade making 90 miles an hour,
> When his whistle broke into a scream,
> They found him in the wreck with his hand on the throttle,
> Scalded to death by the steam.

Had it not been for David George's ballad and recorded performances by Vernon Dalhart, Mac Wiseman, Johnny Cash, and others across the decades, perhaps Broady would have been yet another statistic. The song and, more importantly, its resonance with Americans of the twentieth century ensured that his leap off a curved trestle that September day would remain an enduring part of folk memory.

Fueled by wanderlust, a certain breed of American had roamed the nation since its very inception. The advent of the train, however, allowed such individuals the ability to travel further, faster, and more widely than ever before. Some simply enjoyed the lifestyle. Others took to the rails only when economic circumstances left them no alternative. The freight-hopping hobo in search of work and sustenance was never more prevalent than in the thirties at the depths of the Great Depression. It comes as no surprise then that he is a major theme of the era's musical record. Harry McClintock's "Big Rock Candy Mountain," Woody Guthrie's "East Texas Red," and Waldo O'Neal's "Hobo Bill's Last Ride" are but three examples. Jimmie Rodgers, the "Singing Brakeman" from Meridian, Mississippi, left perhaps the most evocative remembrance of the stranded hobo's plight in "Waitin' for a Train." In those years of want and despair, countless numbers of Texans had personally witnessed those such as Rogers' itinerant alongside railroad tracks "a thousand miles away from home, sleepin' in the rain."

In a day and time when trains were ever-present and all-important, they served as powerful symbols for all of life's major events. As such, they proliferate in the music of the people. At times, the next train out of town represented escape from trouble, most often love gone bad. The trip for some was mournful, an act of despair. Clarence Ashly's scorned lover in "Dark Holler," for instance, saw "a freight train farther on down the line" as his only relief from the pain of rejection and a lifetime of loneliness. Those of whom Hank Snow wrote and sang in compositions such as "I'm Movin' On" and "The Golden Rocket" evidenced a more resilient attitude in matters of the heart. Their means of conveyance—the symbol of their freedom—nonetheless remained the same: "that big eight wheeler rollin' down the track." Hank's expression of joy at liberation literally explodes from lyrics such as these:

> Hear that lonesome whistle blow
> That's your clue and by now you know
> That I got another true love a-waitin' in Tennessee
> This midnight special's a-burnin' the rail
> So woman don't try to follow my trail
> This Golden Rocket's gonna roll my blues away.

Freedom for some quite often appeared unattainable for others. To unfortunates such as Huddie Ledbetter, incarcerated at the

Central State Prison Farm outside Sugar Land, Texas, in the early twenties, the passing train represented everything they'd lost and might never regain. Leadbelly's nightly prayers for freedom found musical expression in the oft-recorded masterpiece titled the "Midnight Special." Hank Williams' inmate in "(I Heard That) Lonesome Whistle" knew the wait would be a long one: "I'll be locked here in this cell till my body's just a shell and my hair turns whiter than snow." For many Americans, however, the third verse of Johnny Cash's classic "Folsom Prison Blues" is the ultimate rendering of a prisoner's agony at the sight or sound of a train:

> I bet there's rich folks eatin' in some fancy dining car
> They're prob'ly drinkin' coffee and smoking big cigars
> Well I know I had it comin', I know I can't be free
> But those people keep a'movin' and that's what
>   tortures me.

A devotee of trains, "The Man in Black" utilized the metaphor in an entirely different manner in "Hey Porter." Written as his Air Force tour in Germany drew to a close in 1954, Cash recalled years later the song's genesis: "I used a train as a vehicle in my mind to take me back home and counting off the miles and minutes till I could get home. . . . My excitement about coming back to Dixie was just about as alive as it appears in the song." It is a lyrical exultation that succeeds beyond measure:

> Hey Porter, Hey Porter, would you tell me the time?
> How much longer will it be till we cross that Mason-
>   Dixon line?
> When we hit Dixie would you tell the engineer to slow it
>   down?
> Or better still just stop the train 'cause I wanna look
>   around.

Composers across the years have also found in the train a symbol for life and death, good and evil, salvation and damnation. The

Carter Family, for instance, warned sinners in the 1930s to get their business right because "there's a little black train a'comin' [and] it may be here tonight." As Josh Turner's hit release of "Long Black Train" in 2005 makes clear, the idiom has lost none of its effectiveness. Turner warns listeners to hew to the straight and narrow in the following manner:

> I said cling to the father and his holy name
> And don't go riding on that long black train
> Yeah, watch out brother for that long black train
> That Devil's driving that long black train.

Conversely, a long-time favorite of believers is titled "Mountain Railway." Dating from the 1890s, it reminds the faithful that:

> Life is like a mountain railway, with an engineer that's
>   brave,
> We must make the run successful, from the cradle to the
>   grave,
> Heed the curves, the fills, the tunnels, never falter, never
>   quail,
> Keep your hand upon the throttle and your eye upon the
>   rail.

Alas, the golden age of trains has long since passed into history. Passenger depots of old stand abandoned and forlorn in communities of all sizes across Texas and the nation. They represent, along with the occasional steam locomotive permanently displayed in some city park, deteriorating reminders of times past. Our forebearers' "magic carpet ride" nonetheless remains not only alive but vibrant in folk memory and imagination if our music is any indicator. Having touched our lives in so many different ways, songwriters and performers utilize the image of the train to invoke joy and sorrow, good and evil, freedom and its loss, as well as life and death. The train of song, unrestrained by the laws of physics, regularly carries us back through time and space to treasured moments with loved ones long since gone. Through lyrics such as those of Fred Moore in "What a Ways We've Come," it even has the ability to carry individuals like me back to moments we missed but wish we could have shared:

> When I was a wee lad my granddad would take me out on
> the C & O;
> When a locomotive on a fast freight exploded by he'd hold
> me up and yell: "Boy, there she goes!"
> Big wheels turning, side rods churning, the noise always
> made me cry;
> I'd hold Granddaddy tight 'til the train went out of sight
> and he'd take me in his lap and dry my eyes.

Wabash Cannonball (P. Carter)

From the great Atlantic Ocean to the wide Pacific shore
From the queen of flowing mountains to the southern belt by
the shore
She's mighty tall and handsome and known quite well by all
She's the combination on the Wabash Cannonball.

She came down from Birmingham one cold December day
As she rolled into the station, you could hear all the people say
"There's a girl from Tennessee, she's long and she's tall
She came down from Birmingham on the Wabash Cannonball."

Chorus:
> Listen to the jingle, the rumble and the roar
> As she glides along the woodland through the hills
> and by the shore
> Hear the mighty rush of the engine; hear the lone
> some hobo's squall
> We're traveling through the jungles on the Wabash
> Cannonball.

Our eastern states are dandy, so the people always say
From New York to Saint Louis and Chicago by the way
From the hills of Minnesota where the rippling waters fall
No changes can be taken on the Wabash Cannonball.

Here's to Daddy Claxton, may his name forever stand
And always be remembered 'round the courts of Alabam'
His earthly race is over, and the curtains 'round him fall
We'll carry him home to victory on the Wabash Cannonball.

(Repeat Chorus)

Jan Epton Seale

SAFE IN THE ARMS OF TRAINMEN

by Jan Epton Seale

⌐—◦—¬

She was Lana Turner and I was Hedy Lamarr when the train went by. The rest of the time, we splashed about, with hopes of getting properly wet in her twelve-inch-deep concrete swimming pool, née watering trough. The pool was at the foot of her long sloping backyard, a kind distance from her mother's ears but not out of sight of a watchful eye from the kitchen window.

We were seven and eight years old, my friend Priscilla and I, both very white dishwater blondes growing up in that small North Texas town. Our suits were not Barbie bikinis, no spandex, no Day-Glo colors. They were one-piece, colored burnt orange or royal blue, held up by a tie around our necks sometimes defaulting to allow an innocuous nipple to ride over the rim of the décolletage.

But already we were trying out our skills as "glamour pusses." When that first woof-woof came drifting down the tracks, we stopped what we were doing and prepared for the passage of the Katy some few yards away. We dipped our hair in the water and slicked it back, stood up and patted our soggy suits, clamored out of the water and perched, one on each of the back corners of the pool, like a couple of Acropolis porch maidens. Though we didn't know to suck in our bellies, the rest of us was ready—bony little feet angled, one knee provocatively bent, one hand on a hip, the other couching a head tossed back wantonly.

When the train finally made the California Street crossing, blasting full away at its stiff warning, and proceeded north, parallel to Lindsay Street, the click of the rails drowning out any other reality, we began to giggle like crazy.

For we were doing something forbidden. We held our poses for the engineer and his assistant, sitting high up with their blue caps and red neckerchiefs in the cab of the engine. Yes, we wanted their eyes to pry, to think us beautiful candidates for true love, always, of course, just beyond reach. And sometimes we did indeed seduce them. Sometimes they would flirt back—or so we thought—with a couple of friendly riffs on the whistle as they charged on down the track.

Then came the challenge of the people in the passenger cars. Now our hand on the hip was assigned to wave, condescendingly, of course, like a pretty beauty queen, not giving over too much heart or heat.

After the heads in the windows blurred by, we'd hop from our posts, traverse the cockleburs to the edge of the track bed, and stand rapt, counting, always counting, as though our lives depended on the correct number. The rattling, dizzying cars holding "c" things—coal, cattle, cotton, chemicals, construction—sped past us. We screamed the count into the chaos, glad for momentary relief of inhibitions imposed on us as nice little girls.

Then we'd sense a slackening of the din and prepare ourselves for the caboose man. Was he the lowest in the hierarchy? Did he have official duties? We never knew what his job was, except to stand holding the back railing, surveying the receding scene and waving to us.

With him, we ladies of innuendo, we scandalous vamps turned virtuous, our ruse was over. To be sure, we had had about all the excitement we could manage. So we stood, hoarse and shivering now, a little pigeon-toed and pot-bellied, waving our sweet little hands to this uncle of a fellow, this last chance at daring contact with men.

About that same time in my life, there were two other safe men at the scene of a train. On the shoulders of my father, in the summer of 1948, I see the only president I have ever seen, before or since, in person. Harry S. Truman is on his famous whistlestop tour, barnstorming the country, standing where the cabooseman usually stands. This time it's called "the rear platform" and it's flag-draped.

Leaning forward, I yell into my father's ear, "He waved at me." My hands grip the crown of his head, my starting-to-be-long legs yoke his Old Spice neck.

"That's nice," he murmurs upward, "but pipe down."

"No, you don't understand," I say urgently, this time cupping his chin in my hand in a play for full attention. "He looked at *me, me!*"

"Oh, all right," my gentle father says quietly. "Yes, I think I saw him do that."

And I wiggle a little, satisfied. For what more could a train ask, than to bring a girl's father and her president into perfect narcissistic alignment for her?

Another time, just before I drift off. My mother and I are going somewhere on a Pullman. The porter, tall and pure black, with pink palms that my blue eyes cannot quit staring at, has boosted me into an upper berth. Strange, he's done it so aseptically that it's as though he's not even touched me. Still, I lie there honored, flattered, feeling delicate and rich. Then he's said, "Goodnight, little lady," and drawn the curtains, taking my brown oxfords off somewhere to be shined like a princess's before morning.

The scene is a far cry from my maternal grandmother, Dora Pearl Bell, riding the train from Tupelo, Mississippi, to Clarksville, Texas, in 1895, as a seven-year-old. The family had had a hard winter, with nothing to eat but sowbelly and beans, and her father determined to give it a go in Texas. The womenfolk and children were in the passenger car, up front, while the men and boys were two cars back, with the cattle and household goods. If they kept the windows closed, the air was suffocating with body odors and tobacco, as well as stifling hot in the southern humidity. With the windows open, the wood-burning engine belched ashes and cinder on them.

I do not think my grandmother had any train flirtations. I hope she had safe men on her train.

By the time I knew of trains, I knew of the dangers of men. So why do the trainmen, all of them, chug in and out of my memory as such wholesome personages? For one thing, they were public figures, to be trusted like policemen and postmen. They wore uniforms; they had hats. And they were kind to us kiddies, parasites forever waving alongside their tracks. They thrilled us with their whistles, and most of the time they bothered to raise their big worn hands to return our greetings. We could prance, preen, flirt, try all our instinctual wiles on them, and there was no chance they would stop the engines and come down to "get us," whatever that might mean.

And they had power. They operated those screaming, blasting behemoths up and down the land, dragging miles of cars, in a display of muscle that was so far from the domain of girl dreams that it seemed, at the least, the job of Assistant God.

And what of the other men in my life, hubbed around the memory of trains? The gentlemanly black porter, with more elegance than salary; my father, allowing his daughter up on his shoulders after a long wait on the brick-inlaid depot yard, to afford her a glimpse of a president he roundly disliked—the same Harry S. Truman on his presidential tour who waved at *me,* just an ordinary American girl. Gosh!

They were all, all of them, honorable trainmen.

The mysterious caboose man. *Photo by J. F. Curry, from the Dane Williams Collection*

Photo by J. F. Curry, from the Dane Williams Collection

TALES OF THE RAILS

by Charlie Oden

～

[These tales of the rails come from the T&NO (SP) Railroad. Friends told some of them to me. The rest are from personal knowledge.—*Oden*]

WE'RE ON FIRE!

252 miles in 252 minutes. That was the schedule of the Sunbeams, No. 13 and No. 14, when the Southern Pacific Railroad began running streamlined passenger trains between Dallas and Houston in 1936. The streamlined cars were swank, uptown. The coaches had comfortable seats instead of the old padded benches. There was a dining car with real white linen tablecloths and napkins. Passengers enjoyed dining from quality crystal, china, and a real silver service that had silver coffeepots. Chefs in tall white caps prepared the food and waiters in white jackets served it.

Passengers rode in comfort in a big windowed observation car and watched the cars on the highways and cattle in pastures. Romances bloomed there during the 252-minute travel time in World War II. The door was located right over the wheels, and when the door opened, passengers heard the busy clickety clack of wheels on rail joints.

No one delayed these trains. Superintendent Tom Spence was inflexible on that point, and several persons learned their lessons the hard way—in their pocketbooks. Mr. Spence fired them for periods of thirty or sixty days. No. 13's schedule was 4:45 P.M. from Grand Central Station in Houston, so around 3:00 P.M. dispatchers began placing freight trains so they couldn't get in the way of those varnished cars. For some crews, this might mean two hours at a blind siding waiting until No. 13 was gone. Others might get a break. To the crews it was like drawing the black beans or the white beans.

Houston-bound Sunbeam No. 14 at Ennis passenger station. *Photo by J. F. Curry, from the Dane Williams Collection*

And so it came to pass that on a day in 1944, Jack Morgan, a heads-up conductor, and Leon Kruse, one of the best hogheads on the Division, were on Extra 777 East, a freight train of about fifty empty tank cars going from Humble Oil and Refining Co. in Bayonne, New Jersey, to Humble Oil in Baytown, Texas. Right behind the engine was a lone box car loaded with wooden window sashes.

When I came to work second shift at Hearne that day, Extra 777 East was stopping at Hempstead at the water tank, which was close by the train order office. As soon as the train stopped, Jack Morgan, the "brains" (as conductors are called) trotted from the caboose to the train order office to see if the new orders would be a white bean. Sure enough, the new order gave the Extra East an additional thirty minutes to go all the way to Eureka Tower. This meant that if the crew would hustle, they could go all the way home, and, be it ever so humble, there's no place like home.

When the train left the water tank, Jack Morgan had the order and was on the engine, standing on the steel apron of the water tank and right behind Leon Kruse, the engineer. Both men must have been grinning over this favorable turn of events. By golly, they were going to have their feet under their tables at home come dinnertime that evening!

As they left town, Leon Kruse was busy getting the engine up to speed. Here the "Tallow pot," fireman J. R. Lewis, was playing a key role because he was the one who was creating the steam the hoghead had to have to get the speed needed to make Eureka Tower for the varnished cars. They were like the baseball player on second who gets an unlooked-for-break and runs for home plate as fast as his legs can carry him.

Lewis was using all of his skills to heat the boiler to its maximum steam pressure of 210 pounds as quickly as possible. He sat on the cushioned top of a tool box facing an array of gauges and handles. He was watching the water gauge and the steam pressure gauge. He was spraying fuel against the boiler crown sheets with a firing valve that combines the thick oil with steam and makes it burn like gasoline, all the while injecting water into the boiler as needed so that the roaring flames could turn it into the steam that the Mike engine needed to respond to the engineer's demands.

Leon Kruse also faced an array of gauges, including the water, steam, and air gauges. The throttle and whistle cord were overhead. He was operating an air-actuated device whose function is roughly that of the stick shift transmission in a truck. His skill in getting up speed was in knowing when to shift gears up or down to the best advantage. The engineer and fireman were giving that Mike engine their best, and the Mike engine was giving them back its best. Both the head shack (brakeman riding the engine) and the rear brakeman were intently watching the empty tank cars in the train to detect any hot boxes or dragging brake beams that might endanger the train. It was teamwork at its best.

786 "Mike" engine (MK-5) pulling the "Hill Country Flyer." *Photo by J. Parker Lamb, Courtesy of ASTA and Dr. Robert W. Schoen*

From Prairie View, six miles east of Hempstead, to Hockley was the fastest track between Dallas and Houston, and you can bet your boots Leon Kruse took full advantage of that. Going by Hockley he "had 'em in the wind"—that is, they were really sailing. I heard the Cypress annunciator buzz shortly thereafter. The men were going home for dinner.

At Hot Wells, which is just past the side track at Cypress, a loaded gasoline truck drove into the 777 and exploded, sending a ball of orange flame over the engine and severely burning Jack, Leon, the fireman, and the head brakeman. Someone at Cypress drove the suffering Jack Morgan back to the side track where the dispatcher's telephone was located. I heard a popping sound in the phone and answered. Jack was stammering and crying as he said to me, "We're afire! We need help!" and told me about the accident. The operator at Eureka Tower broke in and said that an ambulance was on its way.

I was stunned, but recalled that Jack held a live running order. I said, "Jack, I've got to annul your running order." He replied, "Hell, man! Don't you understand? I can't copy an order. The flesh of my hands is sticking to the phone now!"

It was a long time before the men got back to work, and the Houston terminal forces took charge of the railroad.

Back to Hot Wells: There was no crew on the train. Right behind the engine the lone box car loaded with wooden window sashes was burning. The empty tank cars were next to the box car. Someone told me later that a man in the uniform of one of the armed forces was among the spectators. He uncoupled the burning car and the engine and moved them a safe distance away. No one knew him, and he never identified himself. To this day, he remains the unknown and unsung hero of the tragedy of the Extra 777 East.

I have talked at some length to two retired locomotive engineers who assure me that this part about the unknown hero is utterly impossible because the engine would have been too hot, the air brake hoses would have been melted, and, because of the way in which air brakes operate, it is simply not possible for the hero part to happen. So what does this mean? It means that a genuine folk tale has been attached to an otherwise true story. It happens all the time. I have read that journalists watch to prevent this from happening in their writings, but despite their care, some folk tales are published as being true anyway.

He Dropped Her in the Corner

If someone suddenly accelerated the engine in his car, he might tell you that he "put the pedal to the metal," and you would understand what he meant. If the engineer of a steam engine wanted to express to you that he had suddenly accelerated his engine, he would say that he had "dropped her in the corner."

Vernon Willis, head brakeman, and Albert Williams, rear brakeman, No. 257. *Photo by J. F. Curry, from the Dane Williams Collection*

About three or four o'clock one morning, No. 257 was operating from Ennis to Denison and at the time had only about a half-dozen cars. Vernon Willis was head brakeman and rode the engine.

Everything was wet. It had been raining for about a week. Water stood in the fields, streamed down the ditches, ran in the branches and creeks, and flooded the rivers, filling them over their banks. Inside the cab of No. 257 the flames in the firebox were flashing, making shadows that jiggled about. The headlight's full candlepower was thrusting its super beam through the darkness, revealing what was ahead. The rest of the world was black, very black.

The train was crossing the bridge over the East Fork of the Trinity River near McKinney when Harry Tolar, the engineer, called Vernon over to his side and said, "Take a look at that." The front of the engine was plowing through the water as if it were the prow of a ship. Water was running over the bridge!

Vernon replied, "There might not be a bridge under us for long." Tolar dropped her in the corner, and the train rocketed forward to safety.

And the river? It was just like "That Old Man River"—it just kept rolling, it just kept flooding along, and it washed out that bridge. Five days passed before the line was open again.

HOGHEADS AT THE PEARLY GATES

Two EsPee locomotive engineers died and went to Heaven. Unfortunately, they found themselves standing in a line before the Pearly Gates. The line was long and moved very slowly. It was enough to try the patience of Job.

As they were commenting on how slowly the line was moving, they noticed a little man with a sun visor on his head and sleeve garters on his arms walking by. An ink pen was in his right hand, and a carefully rolled train sheet was tucked under his left arm. He walked past the entire line and right into Heaven.

H. C. Dinkens, train dispatcher, Ennis. *Photo by J. F. Curry, from the Dane Williams Collection*

This angered the engineers. How dare a dispatcher run around them? (A "run around" in railroading is a humiliating experience for the crew. It is strongly resented by the crew and causes a loss of earnings.) As the two waited their turn he was all they could talk about. When they finally reached Saint Peter, they wanted to know why he let the dispatcher run around them in line. Saint Peter told them that he had done no such thing. Both of them swore that he did. As the argument went back and forth, one of the engineers saw him, the little man with the sun visor and sleeve garters. A train sheet was still tucked under one arm.

Seeing the man the engineers pointed out, Saint Peter said, "Oh him? That's no train dispatcher, that's God. He just thinks he's a train dispatcher."

Photo by J. F. Curry, from the Dane Williams Collection

Newton Gaines, 1929. *Photo courtesy of TCU Special Collections*

THE FORD EPIGRAM

by Newton Gaines

A unique form of American folk-lore is the Ford epigram. It may be defined as a short saying, witticism, epithet, or slogan written on the side, fender, cowl, hood—indeed anywhere on the "Model T" Ford.[1] Although truly folk-lore, its first notable characteristic is that it is written, a characteristic which it shares, I believe, only with the disreputable writing on walls and fences. Another characteristic is that it is a by-product of a mechanical triumph. This distinction it shares with the railroad song. It happened that one Henry Ford and his engineers developed a gasoline engine that lasted longer than the body of the car it propelled. When the sad appearance of the family Ford caused Dad to buy a new machine, perhaps graduating to a Chevrolet or Buick, the son of the family fell natural heir to the old "Model T" to do with as he liked.

He could do but little with it, though, for his purse was flat. A coat of enamel or Duco was out of the question. A sufficient quantity of either would cost too much at one time. As it stood, the old Ford was impossible, even for a young fellow. It didn't look good, and it didn't look entirely disreputable. The latter state, provided that the demoralization was complete, was greatly to be preferred to obscure mediocrity. To accomplish utter disreputableness then, the young fellow began to devise all manner of witty epigrams and to embellish every conceivable portion of his Ford with them.

Never did any form of lore spread more rapidly than Ford slogans. They outran the cars on which they were painted. A young Texan, for instance, drove his emblazoned "flivver" up to Chicago or New York. Upon this occasion he was inspired to unusual originality—or effort at it—by the excitement incident to his getting ready for the trip. He added new quips to the ole ones, and started gaily forth. In every village through which he passed his wit was duly admired and his slogans quickly adopted by other young owners of old Fords.

The foregoing account explains in part why this body of lore is not the product of "knitters and sitters in the sun," but is rather an expression of a very lively American youth. Young people in all parts of the United States contributed about equally to the Ford epigram, and so rapid was its diffusion that the folk-lore became even more uniform throughout the country than our American language.

The youngsters today are moving (or have moved) on to other interests. The much-used epigrams have become trite, and Dad's old cast-off "Model T" is wearing out, even in the motor. Modern youth, flaming or otherwise, finds no fun in pushing worn-out cars up hills. Soon this evanescent product of youthful inventiveness may disappear and be largely forgotten. Far less numerous now than formerly are dilapidated cars covered with epigrams.[2] But the future of fads and crazes cannot be foretold with confidence. They come and they go and, like "these bones" they may rise again.

I applied the word *inventiveness* to the creative power of youths who compose Ford epigrams. But they are, as B. A. Botkin has pointed out, largely adaptations from any and all available sources, the more modern the better. No copyright law protects the inventor or original adapter, and less ingenious or more imitative owners of rambling wrecks appropriate his gems with heartbreaking speed. Like slang, they soon become public property, and trite, and many have gone or are going to the scrap heap, along with the junk which they adorn, now "Henry's made a lady out of Lizzie." The Ford jokes, too, have changed. A typical "Model T" joke concerned the conversation of a Ford and a mule on a country road.

"Who are you?" asked the mule.

"I am an automobile," answered the Ford. "Who are you?"

"I am a horse," the mule replied.

A "Model A" joke used to run something like this: The driver of a Cadillac was making about fifty miles an hour when a new Ford passed him so fast that he seemed to be standing still. The Ford owner, however, stopped his new car a little farther up the road and hailed the Cadillac owner.

"Are you familiar with the standard gear shift, Mister?"

"Why, yes," replied the Cadillac owner.

"Then will you please show me how to get this thing out of first gear?"

But back to the Ford epigrams. Every young man who owned a "Model T" had to name it. On, near, or attached to the radiators were such signs as "Little Go-Creep," "Leaping Lena," "Galloping Snail," "King Tut's Chariot," "Puddle Jumper," "Public Enemy No.1," "American Tragedy," "Gimme Room," and "Mah Junk." Then there was "Lousy Lizzie," alliterative and inelegant, derived from "road louse," a name which Americans sometimes applied to the "Model T," and which the Mexicans approximated in the epithet "la cucaracha." In April 1928, an enterprising young Fort Worthian sold to adolescent Ford owners many well-painted placards bearing the name "Rolls Ruff." "Willys-Night-Out" and "Asthma" were other names. A T.C.U. sophomore named his machine "A Chemical Disturbance." Lindbergh's achievement accounts for the name "The Spirit of St. Vitus." Among the earliest of the Ford labels were "Baby Lincoln" and "Lincoln Pup," the latter printed on a placard I saw hanging on a new Ford in 1921—no doubt a bit of advertising by the Ford Motor Company.

The noisy, temperamental engine of the Ford came in for its full share of epigrams, which were usually written on the hood. Among them were "This can't go on forever," "That isn't a knock—that's static," "Just knocking along," "Sick cylinders—all five of them," "Stop, look, but don't listen," "So's your old man," "Boiler Room—Keep Out," "Born 1900, Died many times," and "Twin Two" (in imitation of "Twin Fours" and "Twin Sixes"). "Seventy degrees inside—and then some" was suggested by the signs on air-cooled theatres and barber shops. "Baby, here's your rattle," or a variant such as "40 rattles but no button," was one of the most appropriate inscriptions for the hood. The most famous of all Ford epigrams, "I do not choose to run," appeared in the summer of 1927 soon after President Coolidge's ambiguous pronouncement.

"This side up," placed on the cowl, was intended as instructions to Mother Nature in case the driver turned a corner too fast.

"Windshield" might be written on the cowl when the glass itself was missing. "100 percent A Merry Can" was at times inscribed on the cowl, and sometimes nearer the radiator, as the name of the car. This slogan will probably be revived, now that subversive activities are being uncovered.

A "plus" sign on the left-hand fender and a "minus" sign on the right-hand fender of one student's car gave cabalistic road rules to approaching motorists. On the false door "Fire Exit" or "Ladies' Entrance" might often be seen, or "Use can opener, insert here, cut along dotted line." "Howdy, folks! We're from Texas, the land where men are men and women are governors," and "Pardon us—Ma did" were popular for wandering Texas cars at the height of Mrs. Ferguson's administration. "This car, like true love, never runs smooth" and "I repair automobiles—fix Fords" were sometimes telescoped to read "True Love," which might serve as the name of the car. Brake-conscious veterans of road accidents gave these "sage advices": "To save breaks, use brakes," "Common sense now or prayers later," and "You'll soon be cold if your brakes don't hold." Humorists longing for free perpetual motion labeled the gasoline tank: "Put in only one gallon at a time; I'm trying to wean her."

The rather thin sheet iron of the body of the "Model T," as well as the cheap enamel used in painting it, accounts for many epigrams. "Use no hooks," "Beauty is only tin deep," "The tin you love to touch," "Fishy body," "The spirit is willing but the body is weak," "If Noah had lived three weeks longer, he'd have seen me," "Don't laugh, girls; you'd look like hell too without paint," "Don't laugh; you may be old yourself some day," "Tin-tin-tin," "Strike matches here," and "Thanks—I'd rather walk," were widely popular.

Perhaps the hankering after flirtation produced these inscriptions: "Chase me, chickens; I'm young and full of corn," "Ladies only," "Get in, peaches; here's your can," "Hot cha cha," "Boop boop a doop," "Thanks for the buggy ride," "Good pick-up; four dames in one hour," "40 gals to the gallon," "Chicken, here's your coop," "Papa's Chicken Coop," "God's Gift to the Women," and "Don't rush me, girls."

Near the running boards were written "Watch your step," "Stumble Inn," "Girls Step Inn," or "Board of Education." A student whom I knew, in decorating his car for the home trip in June, varied this last sign to read "Bored of Education." He was. Springs, wheels, or worn-out tires account for signs testifying "Honest weight—no springs," "Danger—10,000 jolts," "Broken Arches," "Dis squeals," "Four wheels—no brakes" "Four wheels—all tired," and "Tacks Collector."

Almost anywhere on the decadent "Model T" could be found some of the following: "We don't need any top; this car covered by mortgages," "Fresh Air Taxi," "Sun Parlor," "Sun Tan Special," "Ten more payments and she's ours," "Tiz for tired feet," "Beauty in every jar," "Leap in and limp out," "Pray as you enter," "She ain't what she used to be," "A wreck, but nobody killed," "An Accident Ready to Happen," "Do laugh; I was once the property of a Detroit millionaire," "rattles before it strikes," "Rambling Wreck," "Henry's Wild Lady," "Henry's Brainstorm," "Oh Henry," "O. Henry; I tell no tales," "99 per cent static," "Almost human." When the warping of the body of the "Model T" caused a door to stick shut, it might be marked "Closed—A Sign of Progress"—perhaps a borrowing from the State Highway Department. If a door would not close, it was marked "Open at all hours."

The rear surface of the "Model T" offered much space for epigrams. Here might be found: "To pass right, pass left," "Hit me easy; I'm a nervous wreck," "Detour" (with an arrow pointing to the left), "Coward, don't hit me in the back," "Don't scratch my back," "My rear is no bumper," "If you must bump me, use your head," "Don't rush me, Big Boy," "A rear tackle preferred," "Don't crowd; this is no streetcar," "School children—drive slow," "Danger ahead—soft shoulders, curves," "If you hit this car, you have gone too far," "Whoa up," "If you can read this, you are too damn close," "Excuse my dust," "Three days in this makes one weak," "Grumble Seat," "Look out—I may do something foolish," or "Follow me for parts."

If a Society for the Preservation of Decency in Ford Epigrams was ever organized, I have never heard of it. But some epigrams have been viewed with alarm. A former instructor at a university in Iowa informs me that about 1926 certain students were expelled for the use of two coconuts at the rear of a Ford with the legend "You can't call me Lizzie any more." The following may or may not merit expulsion: a rude picture of a tomcat running very fast, and inscribed "Seven miles to a dirt road," "Girls who smoke may put their butts inside," "Constipated—can't pass a thing," "Experienced women wanted," "Mayflower—the boat she came across in," "I'm old but I still get hot," (next to the engine). The *Fort Worth Star-Telegram* of May 1, 1929, contained an article which read in part: "Police Wednesday were busy trying to find a charge to place against youth who drive automobiles on which are written obscene lines and words." The officers were of the opinion that the charge of "public nuisance" or "exposure of obscene language" might serve their need.

Enterprising manufacturers of toys have not overlooked the opportunity to make a novelty that has sold in great numbers—a tiny tin model of a Ford car provided with eccentric wheels and a spring motor, and covered with epigrams selected by the manufacturer. The following are transcribed from two toy "Tin Lizzies" bought from Montgomery Ward about March 1929: "Barnum wuz right," "Spirit of Detroit," "Mrs. Often" (on the hood), "Love 'em and leave 'em," "Hotsie Totsie," "Rolls-Nice," "Rolls-Woice," "Leap Year—girls, leap in," "Lizzie of the Valley," "Car under construction; ride at your own risk," "Flappers' Special," "Don't hit me; I'm old," "Another Mistake," "4 everything breaks," "Not a coffin a car," "Here we are—and how."

The qualities that make the Ford epigram unique in folk-lore are these: first, it is a written lore; second, it is the by-product of a mechanical triumph; third, unlike the usual types of lore, it spread very fast; fourth, it is nearly uniform throughout the country: and fifth, it is purely the product of youthful minds.

ENDNOTES

1. This paper in substantially the present form, was read on April 19, 1929, at Fort Worth, before the annual meeting of the Texas Folk-Lore Society. A few sentences have been added here and there. Vivian Richardson had a full-page article on "flivver" labels in the *Dallas Morning News* for April 25, 1926. Since then other folk-lorists have been at work in the same field, notably B. A. Botkin, of the University of Oklahoma, whose excellent articles "The Lore of the Lizzie Label" and "Anthology of Lizzie Labels" appeared in American Speech for December 1930, and October 1931, respectively. Various newspaper cartoons and comic strips have also focused attention on the subject, especially in the late '20s and early '30s. Certain repetitions in all of these items (including this paper) were inevitable, since Ford epigrams rapidly became standardized throughout the country. It is hoped, however, that my approach will be found somewhat different from those of other writers.

2. For the few remaining ones this inscription might be appropriate: "Blitz-krieged but still doing business."

Photo courtesy of the Southwest Collection, Texas Tech University

WATCH THE FORDS GO BY: THE AUTOMOBILE COMES TO OLD BELL COUNTY

by Kenneth W. Davis

—◆—

Richard Lee Strout and E. B. White gave verbal immortality to Henry Ford's tin lizzie in an essay which once helped freshmen struggling to become literate learn how to string colorful anecdotes together to make sense. Their celebrated essay, "Farewell, My Lovely," focused primarily on the wonder of Ford's inventive genius, the Model T—that vehicle which revolutionized twentieth-century America. In old Bell County, the arrival of mechanized transportation brought Model T Fords, Saxons, Maxwells, Buicks, Cadillacs, and a host of other brands now perished, gone with the exhaust fumes and the dust of unpaved roads. Among these many kinds of automobiles there were some which attained the status of folk objects for their stamina, their contrariness, their comfort, or for their near-epic feats of whatever sort. To a Texas folklorist, the antics of the people who herded these snorting mechanical behemoths over those dirt roads of old Bell County are even more interesting than the legends about good mud cars, fast road cars, splendid courting vehicles, and those which doubled as runabouts hauling feed and seed.

My grandfather, Henry L. Perkins of near Bartlett, was one of the first to own an automobile in Bell County. He started out with a Maxwell, which he kept until Buicks became popular, sometime in the mid-teens or a few years later. Then, he bought the biggest one the Buick agency in Temple could coax from Detroit: a Buick touring car powered by a straight six. The engine was called "the Victory Six," and it generated enough power to propel the heavy car across the mud road between Gooseneck and Schwertner regardless of the depth of the ruts. So great was that Buick's reputation for being able to negotiate those pre-New Deal unpaved roads that the hangers-on and the two barbers in Schwertner regularly waited outside the two-chair shop after big rains to watch my grandfather, a tall man who looked exactly like William Faulkner, come chugging along the Gooseneck Road, his black Buick knocking heroically but never once stalling out. The frame of the car leveled the ground between the ruts. As is often the case among the folk, fortunately, all sorts of stories and several wonderful out-and-out lies grew up about the prowess of Henry Perkins' Buick. One such whopper held that when the Bartlett-Schwertner-Jarrell Railroad Company's only steam engine was on the fritz, the engineer telephoned for Mr. Perkins' Buick to pull the seven or eight heavily loaded boxcars into Bartlett. I know this yarn is a lie, but my grandfather once solemnly assured me that the Buick could have done the job if the need had been great enough.

But the best of the yarns about the coming of motorized transportation to Bell County tell of people learning to drive this new wonder, the automobile. Automobile agencies sprang up everywhere. In the still somewhat small town of Bartlett there were once at least four, perhaps five agencies, as they were called then. Now, the correct term is dealership. These early agencies were concerned with selling cars. They didn't worry much about customer relations such as teaching the new owners how to drive the mechanical wonders sold to people who for years had driven only horses or mules. In one instance of a sale to an uninformed buyer, a comic folk yarn found its genesis.

The Ford agency sold a Model T touring car to a man and his four sons. Not one of these five males had driven even a primitive iron-wheeled tractor. But the dealer told them that driving the car was easy: one lever made it go faster or slower; another device was the brake control. The dealer didn't tell them just which was which, but did get the car pointed toward the Ivichec farm and cranked the motor. Then, the Ivichec men were on their own. With cautious experimentation, old Ligi Ivichec, the family's whiskered patriarch, learned quickly how to steer the device and a bit about speeding up and slowing down. By the time he and his stalwart sons reached their farm east of Bartlett, Old Ligi was as

proud as some Slavic king of old as he herded the smoothly chugging Model T along.

But when he turned into the family's front yard, he realized to
his great terror and embarrassment that he had not the slightest
idea about how to stop his wonderful vehicle. So he slowly circled
the house. By this time, his smiling wife and his six daughters were
all on the veranda waving and laughing and shouting their joy at
the arrival of the long-promised Model T. Old Ligi gravely saluted
them and made yet another turn around the yard. This pattern
kept repeating itself until Ligi feared dark would fall and the cows
wouldn't get milked. So, he had a strategy session with his oldest
son, Tor.

Tor had been through the fifth grade several years earlier and
was considered the family's intellectual. But book learning or no,
Tor was no match for the native cleverness, the horse sense of his
now sweating father. Old Ligi told Tor that when the Model T
slowed down, Tor was to jump off and get the crowbar, a five-foot-
long piece of solid metal tubing used to pry things, dig postholes,
and the like. Then, when Ligi slowed the Model T again, Tor was
to jump back on board. Only that much of the plan was made
known. Tor, ever obedient, did as he was told.

When he was back in the car, Ligi told the heaviest of his sons,
Stanislaus, an enormous hulk of a man, to take the crowbar, crawl
out over the hood to the front of the Model T and on Ligi's signal,
to jam the crowbar into the ground. One does not have to be a
student of physics to guess what happened. The huge young man
positioned himself and the crowbar. Ligi gave the signal, and the
young man sailed through the air as if propelled by some demonic
force. He landed in the silo pit and was only somewhat bruised. In
rage and humiliation, Ligi did the only thing a family patriarch
could: he drove the Model T into one of his magnificently struc-
tured haystacks and the machine stalled out. One account of this
yarn holds that the car stayed there until it rusted to the ground,
but that story is a flat-out lie; I rode in that old Model T when I
was attending first grade at Hackberry School. The car was nearly
twenty-five years old then, but still ran quite well.

Another story about humans and machines in old Bell County involves a lady professor of music at Belton's Mary-Hardin Baylor Female College and Seminary for Women, the oldest institution of higher learning in Texas, chartered by the Republic of Texas in 1845. This lady professor—which is what the old-timers called her—was ahead of her time. She trooped about the country-side with a sketch pad and with some of those funny looking little note-books which are lined so that musical notes can be put in them to make songs and the like. She was a great admirer of what she called the rustic peasant life of Bell County. The truth of the matter was that most of the people weren't peasants; they were just poor, but the academician from Mary-Hardin Baylor enjoyed her illusions and few saw fit to enlighten her.

One fine fall morning when the mists were rising from the Middle Dars Creek just before it leaves the roadside to meander through the old Mazar pasture, this lady professor came upon a curious sight. One of Mr. Mazar's hired hands was trying to crank a reluctant Oldsmobile. The more the man tried, the more the vehicle refused to cooperate. In time, the man began to exhort in some quaintly melodic Slavic dialect whatever gods there were to do something about the situation. The lady professor was fasci-nated with the tonal qualities of the man's ardent prayers to those mysterious European deities. She knew a bit of some of the Slavic languages; she had, after all, attended Southwestern University as well as the mother ship, Baylor-Waco. She whipped out her com-position book and began taking down the sounds, using a combi-nation of phonetics and musical notes. She got the sense of it, she thought.

Finally, the uncooperative Olds opted to spring to fuming life and the hired man drove on. By this time, he was one furious Bohemian, and in his righteous wrath, he gunned the Olds for all it was worth. The car sprang to a terrifying quickness and seemed to take on a life, a purpose all its own. Its driver held to the huge steering wheel, transfixed by fear as the largest of Mr. Mazar's sev-eral haystacks loomed ever closer. In his utter terror, the man began to call more earnestly than before on those Slavic gods who had helped him bring the mechanical monster to life. The lady professor was in an ecstasy: she sketched on her pad and she transcribed on her musical composition book. Now at last, she knew she had the material for the authentic musical folk-epic she felt called to write for production in her choral music classes at Mary-Hardin Baylor.

Just as the Olds began climbing the huge haystack, its fully possessed driver began what seemed a cross between yodeling and Gregorian chant. The lady professor all but expired in her complete delight at seeing and hearing this example of what happens when peasant and machine interact, or as some illiterate moderns would say, "interface." The Olds and its driver disappeared beyond the haystack and were not harmed. The lady professor hurried at a high trot back to her Model T and sped frantically toward Belton and the serenity of Mary-Hardin Baylor, where she spent most of the next two days fleshing out her peasant folk opera as she now styled it. This lady was a true scholar, so when she had finished the piece, she loaded her Model T with provisions and trekked off to the south and the University of Texas—the one in Austin, of course. There she consulted a professor of Slavic Languages to be sure that her work had the ring of authenticity all scholars require of themselves.

The learned don at U.T. sat quietly for a time, then began humming the melodies and trying to figure out the words from the driver of the errant Oldsmobile. The lady professor was pleased; she knew that when music was good, it made people sing and hum and so on. But after a few minutes, the dignified U.T. professor turned red in the face and had a fit of coughing. He sweated some and finally put the manuscript aside and sternly admonished the lady professor from Baylor-Belton to burn all those sheets. The lady was considerably hacked at this turn and demanded an explanation. The U.T. professor reluctantly complied. He told her that what she had transcribed amounted to some of the most vile, filthy, obscene remarks ever to be heard in any language, Slavic, Germanic, or Romance. The lady from Mary-Hardin was appalled, but not convinced until in exasperation the

U.T. professor informed her that the driver of the Oldsmobile had commanded that vehicle to do various anatomical feats which are mechanically impossible for man, beast, or machine. At this, the lady professor left for the return trip to Belton, sadder but wiser.

The arrival of the automobile in old Bell County was important in matters of determining social status. Then, as now, you were what you drove. There were Ford people, Oldsmobile people, Cadillacs, Packards, and so on. In one tale from the early days of motorized transportation in Bell County, there are some familiar folk themes and motifs. The story involves Frederick George Skinner's Cadillac. Freddie George, as he was called for short, up and married into Temple society. He married into a lumberyard family whose name I won't divulge here. At any rate, his bride was a yuppie before the term was even dreamt of; she was a social climber of the first class. She agreed to move to Bartlett and live on Skinner's Hill, the more or less ancestral home of the Skinner clan, only if Freddie George would plumb the house for running water and install all the conveniences. The Skinner house thus became one of the first to have indoor facilities. And the rich young bride demanded the best automobile in the county so that she could get over to the Austin-Temple Highway, which was already graveled then—how modern can things be? On that fancy highway, she could roar along to Temple to attend bridge parties, high teas, and whatever else rich women do in their spare time to keep from being bored or whatever.

Freddie George was a good business man and farmer, and some said that when he died years later, he still had nine cents of the first dime he ever earned, but for his beloved bride, he shelled out whatever it took to get the best Cadillac the agency in Waco could provide. He hated to spend that much money and determined at once to do everything possible to make that Cadillac last forever. From his father, Big Freddie George, he learned the valuable lesson of applying Red-Top Axle Grease to keep moving parts on machinery from wearing out. So, on the way home from Waco, he stopped off in Holland at the Mewhinney Merchantile Company—everything from the cradle to the grave was their motto: they had a mortuary as well as a dry goods department which sold baby clothes and diapers. At this old-time emporium, he bought four cans of Red-Top Axle Grease. He hurried home.

When he reached the freshly painted plank gate at the bottom of Skinner's Hill, he was a contented man. Few people in the county could afford plank gates; most had to be content with barbed wire (bob war) gates. And he had the Cadillac his beloved desired. And he had Red-Top Axle grease to keep that Cadillac young forever. What more could a man want? That night after supper, he cranked up the generator plant and turned on the lights in the newly constructed garage, the home for the Cadillac. He got out the Red-Top Axle grease and applied it lovingly and diligently everywhere there was any kind of friction possible. He even greased the brakes thoroughly. Very thoroughly indeed.

The next day was Sunday, and in honor of the arrival of the new Cadillac, Freddie George promised his bride they would drive all the way to Temple to attend divine services at the Episcopal Church, his bride's spiritual home. She somehow found the deep-water Baptists, the Campbellites, and the local Methodists a bit lacking. The bride was overjoyed; she would in an hour or so arrive at Temple's beautiful Episcopal Church in what was surely the finest motorized chariot in the county. Her pride was boundless in that car, her new dress, and even in Freddie George.

Freddie George turned the ignition and Mr. Charles Kettering's happiest invention, the electric starter, brought the mighty engine to life. Down Skinner's Hill Freddie George and bride began. And when he applied the brakes to stop for the opening of the gates, nothing happened. The heavy car gained more and more speed and with a great flourish of broken headlamps, twisted bumpers, and bent fenders, the massive vehicle hastened toward the deep ditch across the road from the ruined gate, and then into the shallows of the Middle Dars Creek. Had the lady professor been there to transcribe the dialectical variants in true folkloric-linguistic fashion, she might have earned a chair at Harvard. Neighbors a quarter of a mile away heard the pride of Temple society swear like a field-hand, and soon Freddie George answered

Don't grease *every* moving part

her in kind. It was a grand day for swearing. Some commentators argued that the event "served them high-toned Skinners right for being so uppity."

A final instance of the interaction of man and machine in old Bell County is one which also illustrates how the coming of the automobile enriched folk speech as well as folkways. Max Beyer lived east of Bartlett and was a frugal man. When he decided to buy a car, he took down a shoebox full of twenty-dollar bills and walked three miles into town to the Buick agency. There he pondered the merits of three cars in the showroom before picking a sporty roadster. He paid cash, but demanded a few lessons. He had heard of what happened to Ligi Ivichec. The salesman obliged. Max drove out of the show room toward home confident that he knew all there was to know. But Max was a bit deaf and felt that he had to hear the motor before it was ready for him to let out on the clutch—as the folk put it. He would gun the motor of the Buick until the car literally vibrated all over. Then, as today's youth say, he dug out in a cloud of blue fumes, spewing gravel and dust. On a clear day, the men who worked at Crook Rosenbalm's Gulf Station said they could hear Max when he left home—some two miles away. Of course, he had to have a new clutch put in about every three months, but he didn't mind. He took a sort of pleasure from revving up the motor, then burning rubber, as we say today.

In every small town, as all of us Texas folklorists know, the elders consider it their bounden duty to train the rising generation in the ways they should go. Long after Max Beyer was gunning chariots through the Pearly Gates, the local mechanic employed a phrase which Mr. Beyer contributed to the folk patois of that part of old Bell County. When I first learned how to aim a somewhat rickety 1936 Ford V8 over the ten graveled roads of Bell County, the local mechanic, by then an elder in his congregation, sincerely admonished me not "to go pulling no Max Beyer." By that he meant I wasn't to dig out, burn rubber, gun the engine, and thus wear out the clutch.

Today's youth, who for the most part drive vehicles with automatic transmissions, power steering, fog lights, rabbit hunting spots, and four wheel capacity will never know what it is to "pull a Max Beyer." Now, in the shank end of my fifth decade, I still hear that pious mechanic's serious admonition whenever I am tempted to roar across an intersection with my left foot longing for the comforting stresses a straining clutch provided when I was driving a '36 Ford V8. Digging out with an automatic transmission just isn't the same.

The Granberry family at the beach, 1941

DRIVING ACROSS TEXAS AT THIRTY-FIVE MILES PER HOUR

by Jean Granberry Schnitz

Progress. That's what they call it. True, travel is easier and faster than it was when I was a child, but trips across Texas are not what they were during the 1930s and 1940s. Expressways and interstate highways now speed travelers to their destinations. The wonderful little towns, the cities full of amazing sights, the courthouses, many with matching small-scale jails—all are by-passed by modern transportation systems. Gone are stop lights and bumpy roads, but not hot, dusty afternoons and freezing mornings. We just don't notice the outside weather as much now that the windows are tightly closed!

Imagine having no radio or tape deck or CD player or television to bombard the vehicle with sound! Modern children cannot imagine dashing across Texas at thirty-five miles an hour—or less. How long would a mere six-hundred-mile trip take at that speed? It would require seventeen hours of driving, plus time for meals, fuel, and other stops. Seventeen hours strapped into a child safety seat would be pure torture! Despite the long hours, I wouldn't take anything for the experiences my family had during such trips. Boring? Not with my parents along!

The first long car trip I remember was in 1936 when I was five years old. My brother, Billy Granberry, was two. My family was moving from Spur, Texas, to Victoria, Texas, where my dad, Dewey L. Granberry, was taking a job as Manager of the Victoria Chamber of Commerce. My mother, Lena Belle Scudder Granberry, was a teacher of piano and an accomplished musician. I don't remember much about that particular trip except that we got to Victoria after dark on a very cold night. We checked into a bleak little hotel room. Both Billy and I had terrible earaches, probably as a result of the change in altitude. Dad went out, found some "sweet oil" and heated it on the radiator in our room. After the oil was poured into our ears, we were able to sleep.

Also in 1936, my family made a trip by train from near Victoria to Dallas for the Texas Centennial celebration. Though I was only five years old, I clearly remember being in the audience of a stage production with bright lights, vivid colors, and beautiful music. I also remember seeing fireworks and being carried through the crowd on Dad's shoulders. We boarded the train in the early evening and arrived in Dallas the next morning. I remember the swaying of the Pullman cars that made it easy to sleep all of the way to Dallas and back. I wanted to run up and down the aisles but Daddy put a stop to that! That was one of the few trips we made by train instead of the family car.

Most of my family's trips were for short distances, such as between Victoria (where we lived) and Sinton to visit my Grandmother Della Granberry and Uncle Elton, Aunt Mary Granberry, and three cousins. The most memorable part of those shorter trips for my brother and me was the way we spent the last hour on the road—peering into the distance to get a glimpse of Sinton's water tower so we could be the first to shout and chant, "I see Sinton, I see Sinton. . . ."

Most of the long trips my family made were between Victoria (near the coast of the Gulf of Mexico) and Abilene or Slaton in West Texas, depending on where my grandparents were living at the time. Slaton is on the outskirts of Lubbock on the Staked Plains. Winter or summer, we left during the early morning hours, well before daylight. The reasons for early leaving were several: (1) to get as far as possible before the hot day made the car uncomfortable; (2) to get as far as possible before the children woke up; (3) to get through San Antonio before rush hour; and (4) to get to the destination before it got late, requiring us to wake up the entire household we were visiting. It was out of the question to stay overnight in a motel or hotel.

I remember a Hudson sedan of uncertain vintage, but Dad had bought it second-hand sometime during the 1930s. It was pretty basic and probably pretty rickety, though, because the windows didn't always work and there were flimsy floorboards. There was no heater, air conditioner, or radio. We later acquired a brand new 1940 Chevrolet sedan, which was driven for many years because civilian passenger cars were not manufactured again until after World War II.

The reasons for traveling at thirty-five miles per hour were also numerous: (1) the speed limit during many of those years was thirty-five; (2) our car was unable to go faster than that anyhow; and, most important, (3) Mama got a headache and white knuckles if Dad drove faster. Unfortunately, Mama always got a headache anyway, and the first evening after we arrived somewhere, she had what she called a "sick headache" and lay prone on a bed, white as a sheet, until she recovered.

Necessary travel items included pillows and quilts, a large thermos of coffee for Dad, and a large jar of drinking water for the rest of us—and for the radiator. Mama always packed a picnic lunch for the first meal we ate, usually at mid-morning at a roadside park. We also carried a few snacks of fruit or nuts or cookies. In summer, we rode with the windows wide open. In winter, we closed the windows as tightly as we could, wore coats, mittens and caps, and wrapped up with all the cover we could find.

We always left home in the early morning, except for the one time that Daddy looked at the clock and mistook midnight for 4:00 A.M. By the time he discovered his mistake, the car was loaded and we were ready to go—so go we did! Once we got into the car, Billy and I were usually too excited to go back to sleep right away, even though our parents went to great trouble to get everything ready to leave before they woke us up and carried us to the car. How could we sleep? There were too many interesting animals to see. Skunks were numerous, as were coyotes, armadillos, raccoons, and possums. Only rarely did we see another motor vehicle.

By far the most numerous animals were rabbits—thousands and thousands of rabbits—all along the highways in the middle of the night. They seemed most numerous on the nights when we left the plains coming back toward the coast. There was no way the car could keep from hitting rabbits, and we would shudder and groan when hapless ones went under the wheels of the car. The frequent thumping sound of rabbits being hit continued until daylight. The only way to miss them would have been to stop. They were far too numerous to miss. As far as the eye could see there were rabbits!

Sometimes the trips were related to Christmas, vacations, or other holidays, but other times there were family emergencies such as funerals and illnesses that caused us to travel to Abilene or Slaton. However long we slept, Billy and I always woke up when we got to San Antonio because of the dozens of times the car had to stop for lights and stop signs. It took at least a couple of hours to get through San Antonio during the 1930s and 1940s. (Imagine how long it would take now without expressways!)

We usually started singing about the time we got past San Antonio. The only time Dad ever sang was in the car. His rendition of "The Old Gray Mare" (she ain't what she used to be!) was memorable. We sang many songs of World War I and popular songs, as well as some parodies that were popular at the time. Among our favorite songs was "She'll Be Coming Around the Mountain When She Comes." We all sang lustily and enjoyed making up funny verses about what "she" would be doing when she came. I clearly remember the day when we had been singing that song for a hundred miles. We came upon an old lady riding down the side of the road on a mule. Billy shouted, "There she is!" We laughed about it for the next hundred miles, and we are still laughing.

Another favorite was a parody of "Clementine," which went on endlessly saying,

I found a peanut, found a peanut, found a peanut just now.
I just now found a peanut, found a peanut just now.

Then we sang how we cracked it open, but it was rotten. Then we ate it anyhow, got sick, went to the doctor, died anyway. When

Billy, Jean, and Rascal at home in Victoria, 1941

we went to heaven, we found a peanut and it all started over again. That song was good for nearly a hundred miles, all by itself! (I wrote about the songs we sang during those years in a previous paper.)

Depending on whether our destination was Abilene or Slaton/ Lubbock, we went through Fredericksburg or Junction. There was a particular roadside park on Highway 87 between Comfort and Fredericksburg that was a favorite place for a roadside meal. We could wash our hands in a little spring-fed creek. Our favorite town along the way was Fredericksburg (though our route sometimes went through Junction instead). We always looked forward to seeing the quaint main street and the interesting houses which lined the highway. After Fredericksburg, there were miles and miles of open road, which translated into hours and hours of travel.

At that point, Dad would launch into the most interesting stories I have ever heard. He would keep us entranced for hours with tales of a little boy named Juan and his younger sister, Juanita. Juan and Juanita sometimes got kidnapped by Indians or bandits and had all sorts of fascinating adventures as they traveled with their captors. They always managed to escape, and had further adventures evading their captors while dealing with the elements, making their own tools, and finding food. My most vivid memory of those stories was about the time Juanita found a river. She went down by the water to get a drink from her cupped hands, but she saw the reflection of a mountain lion on a limb right over her head. Juan managed to rescue her by hitting the lion with a big rock or a stick.

Juan and Juanita always got home or got found by their parents about fifteen minutes before we reached our destination. What made the stories so interesting was that the scenery and towns we were traveling through were involved in the stories. Dad would say, "They camped over there by *that* hill." Juan and Juanita got water and fished from whatever stream we were passing. They were with us all the way! They might have looked for help at ranch houses or towns we passed. It seemed very real!

We didn't realize it at the time, but we were also getting a liberal dose of Texas history. Dad was a pretty good historian, having taught history at San Marcos Academy and in the schools of Spur, Texas, between 1925 and 1930. As we passed through the various towns along the way, we also were treated to stories about things that had really happened there, and explanations of why towns, rivers, or counties were named. Historical events were woven into the stories, which went on for hours with me leaning over one of Dad's shoulders and Billy leaning over the other shoulder. (Seat belts? What were they?)

Sometimes we played games. Many were word games, but others involved counting cows or windmills or other such items on the side of the road. We usually carried playing cards, and if the wind from the open windows was not too bad, we played various card games like "Fish" and "Old Maid." We played a number game we called "Buzz." I got tired of that when I decided my little brother was a mathematics wizard. Actually, in this game a number (such as three) was designated. As we counted and came to any number with a three in it (or a multiple of three) instead of saying the number, we said "Buzz." I found out years later that Mama was squeezing his hand when it was time to say, "Buzz"—and he never missed. We also had books to read, but that was not a preferred activity. We'd rather look at the scenery as we went along.

Gas stations were gas stations back then. Engine oil was available and a flat could be repaired. Most stations had a restroom to be used by everybody, but some actually had a separate one for the ladies. Most had a water fountain, and sometimes they sold peanuts, sodas, and/or candy bars (though we rarely bought anything). Stations were not convenience stores as we have come to expect nowadays. Gasoline purchases were cash purchases most of the time.

We always had a picnic for at least one meal, but since we were on the road for so many hours, we always needed to stop for at least one other meal. If Mama had not packed food for another meal, we stopped at a restaurant or small café in some little town along the way. I was grown before I found out that restaurants served anything other than grilled cheese sandwiches or hamburgers. The **only** time we ever ate in restaurants was during trips.

I'll never forget one cold winter morning when we were driving south from Slaton/Lubbock. The roads then were much rougher than they are now, and they were very steep at places like the Cap Rock where the Staked Plains begin and end. As we started down the Cap Rock, Dad said, "Where did that wheel come from?" Mama screamed. Sure enough, the wheel we saw rolling down the highway had come off our car. Since it was a back wheel, Dad managed to get the car stopped without mishap. We watched the wheel roll down the road with Dad in hot pursuit. After what seemed like a long time later, back he came back rolling the errant wheel. Soon we were on our way again. That was the closest we ever came to having an accident (that I know about).

Another time, we left Slaton on a freezing morning in our old Hudson. The number of rabbits set a new world's record. Though all of us were bundled with coats and blankets, we were cold anyway. I counted rabbits through a hole in the blanket barely big enough to see through. Actually, there were too many to count all of them, so I soon tired of that game. There were drafts of cold air coming in around the accelerator, clutch, and brake pedals big enough to cause Dad to have to stop occasionally and walk around outside to get his foot thawed.

I always had great confidence in the integrity of Texas bridges and culverts. Dad occasionally stopped and informed us that he needed to inspect whatever bridge we were near. He and my brother disappeared under the road. When he came back to the car, he always announced that the bridge was quite safe and that there were no problems there. After Daddy and Billy had inspected the bridge, Mama and I inspected it, too. Bridge inspections were necessary, considering how long it took to travel between towns and how rarely fuel stops were needed. There were few public restrooms along the way, and only rarely did another car pass during our bridge inspections.

Sometimes we picked up hitchhikers. We never considered this practice to be dangerous. The years during which we traveled were during the latter part of the Great Depression and during the early years of World War II when the people who were hitchhiking were just plain people who needed a ride somewhere. During the war, the riders were frequently soldiers who were going home or back to war. Our riders always told interesting stories.

Dad drove most of the time. Occasionally, he would decide to take a nap, so Mama drove. That's when our dash across Texas slowed down to below thirty-five miles an hour. Mama did not like to drive that fast. She never liked to drive that fast, EVER. She always drove so slowly that the gears almost needed to be shifted down. Dad got his nap, though, even if we didn't make much progress. Usually, Billy and I decided that was a good time to sleep.

Many roads in those days were paved, but they were narrow and did not have shoulders. There were many railroad crossings and underpasses. Even the main highways still had stop lights and stop signs, especially in the vicinity of towns. The only heavy traffic we ever saw was going through San Antonio. Apparently, the railroads carried goods now carried by truck. What few trucks we saw usually traveled at night. Most were considerably smaller than today's "eighteen wheeler."

Driving across Texas at thirty-five miles per hour is probably gone forever. If we tried it now, we would likely be rear-ended by a big truck! It is still possible, however, to enjoy traveling across Texas on the wonderful modern highways, with conveniences such as rest stops and good signs showing distances and mile markers— and a proliferation of places to eat and stay.

One key to enjoyment of the long, slow trip across Texas was in being aware of the unique beauty of each part of the country through which we traveled. Also, we knew that we could not speed up arrival at our destination; but we were able to savor the joy of being together—laughing, singing, talking. To me, this is the element that is missing in our modern travels. We while away the hours listening to radios or tapes instead of making our own kind of music or telling our own kind of stories. We talk on our cell phones as though we never left home. In our haste to reach the destination, we forget to enjoy the trip!

STILL MOVIN' ON,

ANY WAY
THEY CAN

'48 PA-12 Piper Super Cruiser

HIGH FLYIN' TIMES: ADVENTURES IN A PIPER CUB PA-12 SUPERCRUISER AND A PIPER TRI-PACER

by Barbara Pybas

Our High Flyin' times were good years, the late 1950s and early '60s, a healthy, optimistic, happy era. Even with the Cuban Crisis and Kennedy's death, this ten-year folklore period seemed less complicated and stressful than the ensuing decades of the Vietnam War and national turmoil. Perhaps, to the young, obstacles are undaunting and overcome readily. This account is neither about barnstorming nor acrobatics, but for the pure enjoyment of flying and a good excuse to use it in a farming-ranching operation. DFW Airport was non-existent and the rigid FAA rules not in place; even a radio was not a requirement. VFR (visual flight rules) was sufficient for little planes.

Jay Pybas was bit by the flying bug in his mid-thirties. After returning from World War II Marine Corps service, completing a stint with GI Bill college time and marrying an Oklahoma A&M co-ed, he found his way back to Texas. For ten years he struggled to revive a Red River bottomland farm released by the U.S. Government. This Cooke County area had been used as the infantry and artillery training area for Camp Howze during the war. It had grown to a jungle with disuse but, nevertheless, was fertile and promising. By hard work, stamina and extreme fortitude, in ten years the valley became beautifully productive.

Jay probably needed an outlet, a diversion from the farming operation and being a confined family man (five baby girls in eight years!). Surviving the drought of the '50s, he needed a positive focus. Finally, when the rains came and cattle prices were up, there was time for optimism and enjoyment. He hung around the Gainesville Airport and talked to pilots who kept their light planes there, listening to their tales of adventure and flying times. He

Jordan Ed (Jay) Pybas, 1967

made friends with James Whaley, who had been a flight instructor in World War II. James was back, farming his family farm, working at the airport, and giving flight instructions as well.

Jay asked Whaley, "How much do you get for flight instructions?"

Removing his cigar, the instructor told him, "$2.00 for lessons and $8.00 for plane rental."

What a deal! After a few sessions, Jay figured he could save the cost of plane rental if he owned his own plane. With James' help, he found a '48 PA-12, SuperCruiser for the princely sum of $1,200. What a beautiful little tail-dragger with an extra wide wingspan. It had a 110-horsepower engine and was stick-controlled. The two-place came with another seat behind the pilot. Although there were dual controls, James said he probably would not need to use it. He sat quietly in the back, giving the best advice for flying time, constantly chewing on an unlighted cigar.

Jay was a quick study and even before the required eight hours of instruction, James let him practice slips, stalls, and even a spin or two. Sometimes he would cut the throttle, saying, "Forced landing! Find a place to put 'er down." Jay soon completed his solo and was on his own. He enjoyed the camaraderie with other private pilots who owned small planes at the airport. Soon, he built a shed on the river bottom farm and kept the little plane handy for takeoff and landing, only flying in to Gainesville Airport to refuel.

That fall, Jay bought several hundred steers and placed them on grain pasture near Yukon, Oklahoma. It was a breeze for him to fly up, land on the wheat pasture, and taxi around looking at the steers. He left early one morning and it was rather late evening when he returned.

"How was the flight?" I asked him. He reluctantly told me that he had an engine failure and was forced to a dead-stick landing! He told me:

> I took off with a north wind. Climbing up to 300 or 400 feet the engine started vibrating so bad, I thought it would break the motor mounts. Then it started throwing oil all over the windshield. I took one look and spied a wheat field. It was only a few miles from the airport. I chopped the throttle, sideslipped with no flaps to ease it down and landed on an incline, an uphill landing. I never made a prettier landing, dead-stick and all. I probably didn't roll a hundred yards.
>
> I walked over to the road that runs from Lindsay to Marysville and caught a ride to the airport. I

told James what happened. He frowned and chewed on his cigar. He said, "Well, let's go see about it." We got in his pickup and drove to the wheat field where the plane rested. There was not a scratch on it. He said it was a perfect landing. We took the fence down, lifted up the tail and turned the plane around. We put the tail in the pickup and pulled the plane out on the county road. The wingspans just fit over both lanes. Then we proceeded to pull it all the way to Highway 82. Again, we had to take a fence down along the south end of the airport, and crossed over to the runway.

Well, we opened her up and found out the engine had eat a valve, broke off the top of the jug, and was throwing oil. So I just parked it and started hunting another engine. I studied the Trade-A-Plane catalog and found one that had just been overhauled in Kansas. I drove up there in the family station wagon to get it, the mechanic at the Gainesville Airport installed it, and I was ready to fly again.

Landing in the pasture: Jay Pybas with two of his aunts, 1961

SOLO FLIGHT SURPRISE

Jay's enthusiasm and high adrenalin were contagious. He soon sweet-talked me into taking flying lessons as a backup for when we were flying together. James Whaley agreed to take me as a student. We left the PiperCub at the airport until I was checked out as a student pilot. I had a great summer; a neighboring teenager came to stay with our four little girls while I spent the mornings at the airport and in the air. It was best to fly early before the temperature and updrafts rose, bouncing the little plane around and requiring more concentration.

James put me through the eight-hour requirement for solo. We practiced takeoff and landings, turn and banks, and a stall recovery. I learned every inch of the plane and engine. I read all the controls, especially the altimeter and RPM (revolutions per minute). However, this little plane did not have a radio, so the flights were all VFR (visual flight rules). I had to be knowledgeable about correct flight paths and elevation. I memorized the FAA rules.

James did not tell me in advance that he would solo a student. One beautiful October morning he said, "OK, you're ready." I did all the checks—flaps, prop, engine, fuel—the same as each routine lesson flight. He had no more instructions, and away I flew. What a gorgeous day—fluffy cumulus clouds and a blue sky. I headed out toward the Red River and over our bottom place. The red brown channel snaked its way around two river bends. Perfectly at ease and happy, I practiced the turn and bank and swept down over a neighbor's house. I made a wide perimeter and it took longer than I had anticipated. Heading back for the airport, I circled for the downwind leg and made my final approach. The touch-down was a little bumpy but soon caught and landed smoothly, and I taxied confidently toward the hangar.

As I approached the apron, there was James, chewing on his cigar, with my husband Jay, nervously pushing his hands deep in his pockets. Each seemed to have a somewhat serious, concerned expression. They had expected my solo to be much shorter, and I had given them a few qualms and fearful minutes wondering if I had trouble. I climbed down the step and smiled and waved as they approached. "We were beginning to worry about you," Jay mumbled. But James was nodding, as if approving of my performance.

One bit of information I neglected to tell them before my momentous achievement, was the news that I was pregnant again, for the fifth time. Would they be surprised! However, considering their concern, I decided to save and savor that news for the next trip.

LANDING ON THE LBJ AIRPORT

Jay was first and foremost a cattleman, but incorporated flying into his business ventures. The semen sales representative for Central Ohio Breeders Association (COBA) invited him on a scouting trip to various Hill Country ranches using artificial insemination. Jay had been checking on AI usage for a set of heifers he had recently purchased. Charlie Golightly suggested he meet the COBA plane at the Johnson City airport. Accompanying him were Dr. O. D. Butler, head of the animal science department, and Dr. Tony Sorenson, head of the animal reproduction and physiology research, both of Texas A&M University.

Jay flew down to meet them, flying the PA-12, still on his student license. Breezing along easily with plenty of time, he spotted the Johnson City airport and made a good landing. Suddenly, he was surrounded by Secret Service men, who demanded he hold up his hands as he climbed out of the plane. They interrogated him for his permission to be there. Jay's explanation that he was meeting a COBA plane at the Johnson City airport was ineffective.

"Well, stupid, that is at Fredericksburg," the officer barked at him. "This is the LBJ Airport; don't you read your NOTEMS (Notice to airmen, posted at each airport)?"

Jay tried to tell him that he was a cow pasture pilot and didn't take off from an airport. After frisking him and taking a perfunctory look inside the little plane the security officer chided him angrily, "This airport is closed to private planes. It is a federally regulated facility. Don't you know Lyndon Johnson is the Vice-president of the United States?"

After a few unsettling minutes, thinking he would be taken into custody, Jay was granted permission to take off. Taxiing out and off as quickly as possible, in minutes he landed at Fredericksburg where the COBA Beach Bonanza was waiting. The friends enjoyed a good laugh about Jay dropping in on Lyndon Baines Johnson.

SECOND PLANE: THE PIPER TRI-PACER

Jay was getting more gung-ho about the enjoyment of his flying time and used the business excuse to look for a larger plane. He found a Piper Tri-pacer, a four-place with a tricycle landing gear. It had 150 horses and a radio, OMNI, and a radio direction finder. He was flying to see about cattle in Oklahoma, Arkansas, and sometimes Kansas, finding more projects to justify his new means of travel. It also proved to be a wonderful way to include all his offspring, now *five* little girls.

He proposed a week off, a flying trip to Florida, for just the two of us. How romantic! His mother agreed to stay with the girls even though the baby was only a few months old. We studied the charts and marked our way, filed a flight plan and refueled at Gainesville. The day was bright and sunny and we took turns at the controls. Past Arkansas, the ceiling was really getting low. Landing at Monroe, Louisiana, we waited until the clouds lifted. Flying at a low altitude we followed the Mississippi, viewing the plantation houses and sugar cane fields. What fun! We skirted Lake Ponchartrain.

The New Orleans Airport and the Naval Air Station landing strips were close together. Jay radioed for landing and talked to the tower. He was approved for the downwind leg. "Now proceeding on final approach," Jay told the flight controller.

"I don't see you," he responded. "Uh, oh! Pull up, pull up, you are on the Naval Air Station!" He advised us to go around about three miles for New Orleans. "That's not the first time somebody's tried that landing." He laughed and was very helpful, and we were very relieved.

We hired a taxi, went downtown and registered at the Monteleon Hotel for the first night of our trip. We walked and shopped in the French Quarter, ate oysters at an oyster bar, had Pousse-Café and Hurricane drinks at Pat O'Brien's, spent some time bar-hopping on Bourbon Street, and found ourselves on top of the Roosevelt Hotel for a live broadcast of radio station WWL at 4:00 A.M.

The next morning we decided to call home. Mammy said that the baby had cried all night, and the girls were more than she could handle. Disappointed, we took a taxi back to the airport, arriving home about dark after only a one-night trip. "The best laid plans of mice or men, gang aft aglee"—Bobby Burns.

FLIGHT TO PLAINVIEW FOR PLOW DISKS

Cotton root rot was a problem in the Red River bottom, but with deep plowing it might be eradicated. Jay wanted to put in 300 acres of alfalfa and had hired a dozer track-tractor to pull it. For ultimate success and depth, he needed very heavy plow disks, which were at the plant in Plainview, Texas. Telephoning the manufacturer for the weight of the disks, he felt they could be transported with the Tri-pacer. The plant manager said they would deliver them to the airport by three o'clock.

Jack Jenkins, extension economics specialist from the District 4 office, happened by the ranch. Jay said, "Jack, you want to take a little trip to Plainview? It's about 350 miles. We'll be back by dark." Jack agreed to a pleasant afternoon diversion. The flight to Plainview was smooth and enjoyable. After that it was a downhill experience, one that Jack Jenkins would never forget. He probably asked himself a thousand times, "Why did I ever agree to come with Jay Pybas after hearing some of his bad luck stories?"

The disks were not at the airport by three. After many calls, the delivery came about 5:00. Extra care was necessary to load them into the luggage compartment, roping them securely to prevent any shift in the weight. It was getting dark very soon after takeoff.

Trying the cabin light, Jay found it was not working. He remembered it had needed a fuse. He told Jack to get the flashlight from the map case. "It's not here," Jack told him with a catch in his voice. He was getting a little shook up.

The lights of Wichita Falls were on the horizon. Jay assured him he could follow Highway 82 to Gainesville Airport even though he could not see the compass. But after following the highway for ten or fifteen minutes, without any familiar lights or landmarks, he told Jack, "I think we are going the wrong way." He asked Jack to light a match so that he could see the compass. "My God, we are going south, heading toward Ft. Worth." They were definitely lost.

Trying to make a turn, Jay said he was completely disoriented. Fortunately, the radio was in working order. He finally reached the Wichita Falls controller and told him he was lost but could see lights. The traffic tower told him, "Test your landing lights, keep blinking them and I'll find you." Jack was really getting nervous.

The Wichita Falls Municipal Airport for private planes was also the Sheppard Air Force Base training field. Immediately, they began getting the training planes farther away from the runway. They also cleared and alerted any air traffic. Jay was still circling, hoping to find some place to land. It was pitch dark. He kept blinking the landing lights. Finally, the controller came in, "I see you, now. We'll get you down." He gave the direction and the altitude and how to proceed. Jack, almost in a panic, shook as he held a match to read the altimeter as they began to let down. Suddenly, the big strobe lights of the airfield began shooting up and down the runway, leading them in. What a relief!

After they were settled in, they thought they should call their wives. It was probably difficult for Jack to tell his wife in Denton of his ordeal with a crazy pilot that might have been a sad finish for him. He would not be home that night. Jack must have spread the story around. For years, as Jay ran into other Extension agents and specialists, they'd say, "So, you're the one Jack had the wild, hairy airplane trip that almost got him killed."

FITTING THE WHOLE FAMILY IN THE TRI-PACER—
DESTINATION: MATAGORDA BEACH

Jay's parents had purchased a beachfront house on the peninsula at Matagorda, Texas. Because of severe allergies, his father spent the summers away from any growing broadleaf plants, with only the ocean, sand dunes, and salt grass alleviating his serious skin condition. A small grass landing strip lay behind the line of beach-front cabins. This was ideal for our destination, as the children would tumble out as soon as we landed and race toward their grandparents' special house, high on piers overlooking the surf.

Wrapping up a ranching project or completing an alfalfa hay crop, Jay would say, "Get ready to go to the beach!" Stashing a small amount of luggage under the fuselage, we settled four little girls in the back seat of the Tri-pacer, putting two in each of the two seatbelts. I held the baby on my lap. Gathering the dizzying speed, rushing upwind, lifting up and off the pasture strip, they shivered, squealed and laughed. Soon, though, we were settled on the straight and level.

Jay picked up the mike to file a flight plan. Contacting the Ardmore, Oklahoma, airport he stated, "Departure, Gainesville, 800 hours: destination, Matagorda Peninsula, grass strip; Piper Tripacer 11P; pilot, J. E. Pybas, six passengers."

"Repeat," the controller would say. "How many passengers?" The Tri-pacer was only a four-place plane. He thought there was some mistake; there couldn't be six passengers. "Repeat passengers, again," he insisted.

Jay came in, "One adult, five children, nine months to nine years, all strapped in, not exceeding weight limit!"

One fine Sunday morning, Jay readied the plane for our departure for Matagorda as the rest of us attended an early church service. Quickly, upon our return, we shed our church clothes and rushed to climb aboard. I noticed a neighbor's vehicle coming up the driveway. As they came to a stop, I told my friend, Sue, that we were just leaving, sorry that I could not ask them in.

Sue smiled and said, "I thought you might have forgotten something." I couldn't think what it might be, when suddenly Lou Ann, our four-year-old, came wiggling out of the back seat! "She was asleep on the front pew when you left the church," she laughed. Our daughter, now an OU Pharmacy professor, says (humorously?) she was definitely marked by this experience.

Dad's Last Flight to the Roff Ranch

After dry land farming for thirty years, fighting the elements, my Dad sold out and found a ranch he had always dreamed of in mid-Oklahoma, near the town of Roff. There was outstanding grazing for cattle, generous rainfall, an abundant bluestem hay meadow, good ponds, a lovely two-story home, a fruit orchard, barns and facilities for horses that he had wanted for a long time. It was an oasis. He purchased an outstanding stallion and kept mares for the breeding. Soon there were colts capering in the pasture. Jay and I enjoyed landing on his pastures, bringing the grandchildren for Sunday dinner.

But in 1956, we were all devastated by the diagnosis that Dad had leukemia. He said, "It's just like somebody hitting me in the head with a hammer." However, he continued with his projects and was stoic in staying active and alert. He began his visits to the Oklahoma Medical Research Foundation at Oklahoma City, which focused on treatment for leukemia. "I'm going up for my rejuvenation," he would always say.

The research hospital had only fourteen beds. Sometimes he was required to stay for treatment. There was also a family room for those who could be up and dressed. Jay and I would fly up and land at the Downtown Airpark. Mother picked us up to visit awhile; perhaps we'd play a few games of Pitch, his favorite game.

Beginning with the New Year, 1962, Dad was a resident patient at the Research Foundation, quite ill, but still up and dressed for short periods. By March, spring was on the way. The grass was greening and the trees getting a good leaf. We flew up to see him, arriving about 11:00 A.M. After visiting a few minutes, he surprised us by asking, "Do you suppose we could fly down over the ranch?"

Although it was a chilly morning, the sun was bright. Jay said, "Sure, let's go." We drove through downtown Oklahoma City to the airpark and were soon settled in the Tri-pacer. Mother and I were in the back seat. She was wearing a heavy coat. Dad mustered strength to climb into the front. Somewhat apprehensive but quite joyful, we were glad he seemed eager to make the short flight. The countryside was quite colorful from the air. After twenty minutes, Jay said, "Well, there it is." He pointed as we flew over their house.

"Fly down over the south pasture," Dad told him. "Maybe there are some spring calves down there." Jay swooped down, turned, and banked and slid in for the view. Then he pulled up to circle another pasture.

"There's Joe San in that paddock." Dad was happy to see the stallion. Down we dropped again, making a turn, then leveling out, quite low. Keeping steady, Jay pulled up and circled again.

"Let's see if the meadow is greening up." Dad wanted to see all he could. He was enjoying it thoroughly.

Suddenly Mother said, "Oh, I'm hot!" She pushed her coat off her shoulders. Her face was flushed. "Oh, I'm going to be sick." Quickly, I placed the half-gallon milk carton for her, one we kept in readiness. The entire turning and circling had made her airsick. We turned back toward Oklahoma City, Dad looking closely at the countryside and in quite good shape.

My father was at the Medical Research Foundation from that time on. His flight in March was the last time he saw his beloved ranch. He died May 2, 1962.

Now, in 2007, the decade of this flying account (the mid-1950s and the 1960s) becomes part of true folklore. It cannot be repeated again. It lies before fast-paced technology, exacting governmental regulations, strict national safeguards, and monitoring of each flight activity. The present generation seems to thrive on

Barbara Pybas, 2006

computerized accomplishment and excitement. (Folklore fifty years hence?) Perhaps future generations' focus and requirements will not quell the personal freedoms and exuberance we happily experienced during our "High Flyin' Times."

The author riding in the Hottern Hell Hundred, Wichita Falls, Texas

BACK IN THE SADDLE AGAIN: RIDING THE CHROME-MOLY HORSE

by Lucille Enix

"I'll never complain again," he said in a voice so low it sounded more like a moan. "Now I know the real meaning of pain. I wasn't sure I could get off that horse. I had so many saddle sores."

As the cowboy continued describing his pain, the aftereffects of having ridden 150 miles in a two-day journey from Texas into Oklahoma, he never once mentioned that he'd been riding a chrome-moly horse. Chrome-moly? Yes, chrome-moly. I'm talking about today's cowboy.

For those of you who bemoan the disappearance of the old cowboy, I say, they're still here. They just ride a different kind of horse. My research into this phenomenon began two years ago. I

A chrome-moly cowboy

have since ridden over 5,000 miles of Texas back roads and streets with thousands of others astride chrome-moly mounts. It was here that I first discovered that today's cyclists are yesterday's cowboys. Hear me out before you protest.

As we near the end of this century in a society that now rewards conformity over individuality, individualists still find ways to retain their independence. At the turn of the century, many individualists found solitude in becoming cowboys. Others became explorers who set out on their horses to discover new territory. Both found particular pleasure in sharing an intimacy with the land, its people, and the abundance of nature. Today's fenced-in, paved-over environment inspires corporate farming and cattle raising. Ours is a place hostile to the horse and cowboy. I believe these same individualists have found the bicycle.

Now I'm going to give you some numbers. But I must warn you that the only accurate horseflesh numbers come from those compiled at the turn of the century. That's when statisticians, and other authority types, considered the horse an agricultural commodity. Today horses are no longer considered an agricultural commodity. Horses are considered recreational. Therefore, no one keeps tabs on the overall number of horses or horseback riders. Believe me. I've made telephone calls all across the country. Only horse breeders keep records of their horses.

Here are the best numbers I could get. In 1900, there were 17 million horses. The horse population equaled about half that of the United States. That same year, 1.1 million bicycles were manufactured.[1] Nearly one hundred years later, 83 million people (one-third of our population) ride bicycles.[2] And an estimated 4.9 million people ride horses.[3] For every nostalgic cross-country trail ride that features horse-drawn wagons and drugstore cowboys, there are a dozen groups of bicycle riders pedaling their horses across the country. Another 3,500 chrome-moly cowboys will ride their mounts alone on roads and trails throughout the nation.[4]

There are so many parallels between riders of horses and bicycles that I think you'll find the similarities striking. For example, both riders call their mounts, horses. Both prefer to ride in the open country, to create their own paths through the countryside and to cross the country at their own pace. Both have a keen awareness of their surroundings: the scent in the air, the wind, the lay of the land and especially the hills, temperature variations, and animal life, especially in the form of dogs. They both ride regardless of heat, rain, cold, or high winds. Both engage in a singular, lone activity. Both exhibit an independence not usually seen in others.

Both dread their common enemy: the automobile. The gear used on both mounts shares similar descriptive terms. Both mounts have a saddle, head, stirrups, and carry the rider's goods in saddlebags. Both mounts buck, must be steered from the head, and need to be groomed and put up properly for the night.

Both critters have different breeds. There are three basic chrome-moly mounts. The road mount could be compared to the quarter-horse. Its more slender, high-pressure tires, curved handlebars, and finely-tuned brakes make it more sensitive to touch and ride. It corners rapidly, which sometimes spills its rider. The hybrid has a wider tire, straight handlebars, and a sturdy balance. The hybrid more resembles the cow pony, an everyday work horse that can travel on the road or in the open country. The mountain bike has a smaller wheel, with a fatter tire that has a knobby tread to help it grip the soil. It's probably a cousin to the mustang. Then there are the race horses, those specially bred horses. Hand-built racing bikes are created for such world class riders as Texan Lance Armstrong, who represents the United States in the Tour de France.

Riding a chrome-moly, in fact, is done in much the same way you ride a horse. When your mount starts bucking, you kinda stand up in the stirrups and move with it. If you don't, you can get throwed, just like a bronco rider. Chrome-moly riders, like cowboys of past years, love to sit around the campfire after a hard day's ride and swap stories of courage and extraordinary feats. Some of these stories tell of great escapes.

Remember the stories of all those young men in frontier days who ran away from home by sneaking a horse out of the barn in the dead of night, and riding away never to be found again? This still happens; only chrome-moly stories have a slightly different twist. There is the story of the lone woman found by two cyclists as they crossed the Mojave Desert in their pickup. They had tied down their bikes in the truck's bed. As they neared the woman, they saw clothing flapping out of two shopping bags tied to the back of her bike. When they stopped to offer her a ride, she gratefully accepted. Then she told them that she had been on the road for a week, having taken her son's bicycle to run away from home. She had carefully planned her escape from a husband who had been beating her for years. She had, indeed, stolen away in the dead of night.

Yes, bicycle riders get saddle sores. That woman had plenty of them, plus severe sun and wind burn. She wore none of the peculiar gear chrome-moly riders wear to protect their bodies. Like the cowboys of old, cyclists must protect themselves from the elements. They wear those funny little pants to hold their muscles in place and to quickly disperse sweat. Their helmets can prevent severe head injuries should a crash occur. Gloves not only prevent blisters, but gel padding saves joints from damage caused by the rapid vibration from road surfaces.

Do cowboys find chrome-moly riders a bit strange, or do they recognize them as kindred souls? I think it's some of both. David Lamb, the national correspondent for the *Los Angeles Times,* tells the story of arriving in Dalhart, Texas, having ridden his bicycle cross-country from Washington, D.C., headed toward L.A. He recalled:

> A group of cowboys in Stetsons, jeans and boots eyed me as I leaned my bike against the glass window of a cafe and walked in, feeling quite out of place with my short pants, helmet and sweat-stained jersey. I ordered coffee and a grilled cheese sandwich and, leaving my wallet and glasses on the table, went back outside to buy a newspaper.
>
> "That's a pretty good way to get your money stole, wouldn't you say?" one of them drawled when I returned.

"Back in Washington, D.C., it is," I said, "but I figured in West Texas it's safe."

Later when Lamb tried to pay for lunch, the waitress said the cowboys had taken care of his tab. I think they recognized one of their own.

Do the chrome-moly cowboys ever use their mounts to round up little doggies? Sure. On any given day in any major city in the United States, you'll find police officers riding their mountain (mustang) mounts across their cement prairie, rounding up two-legged doggies. On their days off, they head for the country, just like any other chrome-moly cowboy.

Now when I speak of chrome-moly cowboys, I'm talking about riders of all ages, sizes, and of both sexes. One of the wonderful traits about the chrome-moly mount is that almost anyone can ride the range. Rory McCarthy, a paraplegic, cycled across the country last year and is now on a 12,000-mile ride around the world.[5] Endurance can get you almost anywhere, either on an old horse or a chrome-moly horse. Louise Milner rode 1,200 miles in twenty-seven days through British Columbia, Washington, Idaho, and Montana to celebrate her 69th birthday.[6]

A nephew confessed what happened when his aunt mentioned that she'd like to do a bike ride of 80 miles on her 80th birthday:

> Being the good nephew, I agreed to come along and watch out for her. We began at 6 A.M. and stopped for breakfast at the 16-mile mark. My aunt had packed our breakfast and lunch, including coffee, water and four beers, in her metal basket. We stopped again at the 32-mile mark and my aunt, seeing that I was a bit fatigued, suggested turning back. She also mentioned that she'd already taken the same 80-mile trip earlier in the week. Having gotten this close, I elected to move on. We reached the turnaround after three hours.
>
> On the way back it began to rain and the wind gusted up to 35 mph. With twenty miles left I was

exhausted and fell behind for the rest of the ride. The second half took us seven hard hours.

In the following weeks, while I was licking my wounds, my aunt took another 80-mile ride to a relative's 90th birthday.[7]

Increasingly, you will find people, like this nephew's aunt, riding the back roads and streets of Texas. Texas has the second largest number of bicycle riders (six million) in the United States. That's more bicycle riders in Texas than horseback riders in the United States. Last year Texans bought a half-million new bicycles. That's more new bicycles purchased than new cars.[8]

Now I'm going to give you another of those funny horse numbers. First, no one knows how many horses there are in Texas, much less how many horseback riders. The closest they can come is the approximately 450,000 quarter horses. From these numbers, you can arrive at your own total number of horses in Texas. Some people said 600,000. Others said a million.[9] Take your pick.

We do know that some of the chrome-moly riders are like Johnnye Montgomery of Midland, Texas. When she retired last year, she rode the 2,700-mile perimeter of Texas in fifty-seven days. Not only that, she created her own routes. Other chrome-moly riders follow the 22,000 miles of bicycle routes already mapped. Two different routes run from coast to coast; two routes run north and south along both coasts; and the longest mountain bike route in the world, which reaches from Canada to Mexico along the Continental Divide, has just been completed.[10]

No matter which view of the cowboy you take, we Texans need never fear falling out-of-step with our Western heritage. Texas A&M University can now boast of an aerodynamics laboratory where they test this country's premiere chrome-moly riders. They use wind tunnels to test the latest in racing equipment. And they know which racing stances produce the least wind resistance.

"It strikes me," David Lamb says, "as remarkable that such a simple contraption carried me so far without extracting a single penny for fuel, oil or mechanical repairs. To most Americans, the bicycle is no more than a toy, but as our city streets clog with traffic, it is worth noting that this affordable machine is still the prime source of transportation for the majority of the world's people and remains the most efficient means of self-propulsion ever invented."

If this were 1900, we might be saying that about the horse. I would venture that, fortunately, for us, we're talking about today's chrome-moly rider. Still, the chrome-moly cowboy, like the cowboy and explorer of yesteryear, is generally misunderstood and sometimes resented. Unlike yesterday's cowboy, however, the number of chrome-moly cowboys promises to grow. As the numbers grow, so will the lore and the hoped-for tolerance.

On any given day, but especially on a weekend, you will probably see a group of chrome-moly riders, or a lone rider, pedaling the back roads of Texas. If you listen carefully, as you pass in your automobile, you might hear, "Back in the saddle again, out where a friend is a friend. . . ."

ENDNOTES

1. "Historical Statistics of the U.S." Dallas Public Library government publications.
2. "Injury-Control Recommendations: Bicycle Helmets." U.S. Dept. of Health and Human Services Public Health Services. Atlanta, Georgia, February 17, 1995.
3. American Quarter Horse Association. Telephone interview. Amarillo, TX, 1995.
4. Mike Demnie. Adventure Cycling Association. Telephone interview. Missoula, Montana, 1995.
5. *Adventure Cycling.* May 1995. 19.
6. *Adventure Cycling.* June 1995. 7.
7. *Bicycling.* 1995. 26.
8. Texas Bicycle Coalition. Telephone interview. Austin, TX. 1995.
9. American Quarter Horse Association. Telephone interview. Amarillo, TX, 1995.
10. *Cyclosource.* Adventure Cycling Association. 1995.

Filling up before a long ride

IRON BUTT SADDLESORE

by Paul N. Yeager

Three-thirty A.M. comes early to a city boy working nine to five. That was the meet-time to join a group of motorcyclists trying for a Saddlesore 2000. The ride was to start at 4:00 A.M. on the Summer Solstice 2003 and cover over 2,000 miles in less than forty-eight hours. This entry-level jaunt for joining the Iron Butt Association had been organized by Beverly Ruffin of the Houston BMW club, and I figured if I was ever going to do anything official on a motorcycle, it would be because somebody else had set it up.

I left the house around 3:00 A.M., just as my kids were coming in for the night. I said I was glad they were home safely and they wished me luck on the ride. I knew they'd be sleeping the next eight or ten hours, and they knew I'd be out pounding wind somewhere in West Texas when they woke up. It was an odd moment for all of us.

The meeting place was a filling station on I-10 at mile marker 761. I rolled in shortly after 3:30, the last one to arrive. Six others were there, having already gassed up and gotten receipts. After a round of murmured hellos at my arrival, each went back to quietly poking around his or her bike. Three-thirty was too early for chatter. The other bikes included a thirty-year-old BMW slash-5, a twin cruiser with ape-hanger handlebars, a couple of older-model Honda Gold Wings, a cross-country BMW GS, a basic BMW R bike, and me on a K1200LT, so smooth and comfortable it's like cheating.

I filled the tank and paid with cash, and the hermetically-sealed attendant gave me a receipt which showed only the cash amount on it. As with any group of like-minded folk seriously dedicated to an idea or an ideal, the Iron Butt Association has its specific rules and rituals. For example, they require meticulous record generation and maintenance—receipts and sometimes photographs are needed to prove that riders were physically in a certain place at a certain time. To have my ride certified as a Saddlesore 2000, I needed a receipt showing the name and address of the gas station printed on it, and the time and date of the transaction. This is the ride's official start time. The amount of the purchase is irrelevant.

The attendant didn't accept that there was a practical difference in what he gave me and what I wanted, but he reluctantly humored me and after a couple of attempts, produced a suitable document. A side benefit was that the effort at tactful negotiation had helped wake me up. Beverly noted my mileage on her clipboard. For the beginnings and endings of rides, witnesses must certify your mileage in writing. The preferred start witnesses are firemen, judges, notary publics, or authorized Iron Butt members, and Beverly was our authorized Iron Butt member.

We waited until a few minutes after four to be sure no one else was going to join us, and then headed out. I realized that I had forgotten my camelback water carrier, so I peeled off from the group and headed back home. I had pre-packed the bike the night before, to keep from having to think too sharply at that time of morning, but I had put the camelback's water bladder in the freezer, out of sight and out of mind. I only thought for a second about blowing it off, knowing the forecast for the deserts west of Ft. Stockton was for temps over 100. I had a mental image of the arid land out there and knew I was going to need that water.

After momentarily stirring up the house again, I got back onto I-10 and headed east, mentally checking off the landmarks out of Houston—the big highway fork into Baytown, the olefin plant at Cedar Bayou and its astonishing smell, the San Jacinto River Bridge with the monument lit up off to the right, and then the high bridge over the Trinity. For me, the bridge across the Trinity makes the real demarcation line that separates Houston from not-Houston. Now I was really on my way. I felt pretty confident about making the first thousand-mile day. It was the second day I wasn't sure about.

Fatigue is the number-one enemy of long distance motorcyclists, followed by deer. Fortunately, rice fields cover much of the flat prairie east of the Trinity and there is no place for a deer to hide and suddenly, perversely, jump out in front of a bike in a kamikaze attack. I clipped along at a pretty good pace and kept expecting I'd come up on the other riders. I had added less than ten miles with my detour, but I didn't catch up with them until I pulled into the last gas station before Louisiana, over 120 miles away. They had already finished refueling and were heading over to the golden arches next door for breakfast. I thought to myself, Well it's clear I'm the rookie here, being late to everything. The elderly fellow on the thirty-year-old motorcycle wasn't having any trouble keeping up.

We pulled into the Tex-DOT Visitor Center at mile marker 880 a little after six. The Visitor's Center sits close by the Sabine River, the border between Texas and Louisiana, and for over ten years this has been the traditional starting point for the Texas Solstice Run, an event informally hosted by the BMW Club Motorcycle Club of Houston. Wheels roll at 6:14, the Official Crack of Dawn, and the goal is to ride across Texas and get to New Mexico before sunset. That's eight hundred and eighty miles if you stay on the 10.

The Run is always held on the Saturday closest to the Solstice, and with sixteen-some-odd hours of daylight, riders only need to average a little over sixty miles an hour to be having supper when the sun goes down. But that includes stopping time. Like most long distance events, the Run is more about having quick stops and as few of them as possible than it is about going extremely fast down the highway. It's about staying in the saddle and riding. As an endurance event, the competition is really with yourself.

All bikers are welcome in the Solstice Run and nearly a dozen riders were waiting there for us, including a couple of newish Gold Wing 1800s from Dallas and a fellow on a naked Harley who had ridden down from Ft. Worth. "Naked" means the bike had no wind protection of any kind. I wondered how he'd do over the course of the day. Beverly welcomed everyone and explained that some of the riders in the group were trying for a Saddlesore 1000. Those riders would take a detour in Van Horn that would add

Stopping at the Tex-DOT Visitor Center

some forty miles to the last leg. With the miles we had already ridden coming from Houston, we would log one thousand and thirty-four miles, give or take. She handed out a sheet of paper with the printed route, and as I stuffed it in my tank bag, Beverly looked down at her watch and said, "It's 6:14. Time to go."

The two new Wings were the first ones out, followed by the guy on the Harley. I was a little peeved at myself for not being ready to mount on the instant, but shortly got my earplugs in and my helmet and gloves on, and I was off too. Normally, riding at dawn makes me feel in synch with the coming day. To prepare for this ride I had been riding during the early morning hours for the last week or so, each day getting up half an hour earlier than the day before. On the last day I rode almost four hundred miles before I rolled in to work at 9:15.

Each morning I had been in a different place as the sun rose, out in the rural areas south and west of Houston. For many of us city folk, any apparent relationship between our jobs and the rising and falling of the sun is coincidental. It is exotic for me to be starting off the day with all the things that pay attention to the sun—the birds, the livestock, the country folks. That last morning, as I rounded a big sweeping turn, a flight of roseate spoonbills coasted over the treetops, blazing pink in the level sun. We locked into one of those perfect coincidences of time and place as my curving line of travel intersected their flight line like a dance.

However, the sense of dawn-as-a-new-beginning disappeared when I merged into the traffic on I-10. None of the magic of the earlier mornings infused the atmosphere on the Interstate. It was business-as-usual: get out of my way Charlie and devil take the hindmost. At least the pace was brisk, I thought. I couldn't stop the hope from popping into my brain that traffic might keep this pace all day and maybe I could make good time. And if I made good time today, would I have anything left for tomorrow?

Patches of fog hung low over the highway in the woods between Orange and Beaumont, and I passed the naked Harley in a clearing between patches. The fog evaporated on the approach into Beaumont and when the highway turned south in the middle of town, the sun was already pushing on my left shoulder. This was maybe 6:45 A.M., and the bike thermometer read 81. The air was tangibly humid and felt warm even in a mesh jacket. This was going to be a real summer day. I had a few sips from the camelback to test the system. The frozen block in the bladder was melting and the ice water was perfect.

The flat coastal prairie and rice fields between Beaumont and the Trinity River do not make very interesting countryside and there is little temptation to take your attention off the progression of the road. I tried to relax into the groove of the ride, thinking of the pacing of thousand-mile-a-day riding.

My brother Peter first told me about the Iron Butt Association and their eleven-day, 11,000-mile Rally that circles the continental U.S. "Do the math," he told me. You know those are eleven long days. Moreover, one doesn't ride from one corner of the U.S. straight to another. Oh, no. That would be too easy. Instead, one needs to ride into Nova Scotia or Alaska or something extremely out of the way in order to rack up sufficient bonus points to even place, much less win. People who hear the exploits of the Iron Butt riders for the first time often shake their heads in wonderment. "Why would anyone want to do that?" One of the highest compliments one Iron Butt rider pays to another is, "You're nuts." They are definitely a unique group.

Besides the Rally, the Iron Butt sanctions escapades such as the Ten Forty-eight Plus One, where you ride to all forty-eight lower states and then to Alaska in under ten days; and the 100 CCC, where you ride from one side of the U.S. to the other in under fifty hours, and then turn around and ride back in another fifty. Not long after I rode the Saddlesore Solstice, Tom and Rosie Sperry from California rode two-up from Mexico to Canada and back, over 3,000 miles in under forty-eight hours. They set the records for the first two-up BunBurner Gold 3000, and the first-ever border-to-border-to-border in under forty-eight hours. They also earned a laudatory, "You're nuts."

Not just anyone can enter these events, though. Riders have to already be members of the Iron Butt Association to officially attempt one of the big jaunts, and to become a member one has to make one of several entry-level rides like the Saddlesore or the BunBurner 1500 (1,500 miles in thirty-six hours).

These rides developed in the early 1980s, before the first Iron Butt Rally. Les Martin at the California Motorcycle Touring Association offered certifications for rides documented in California, Nevada, and Oregon. When he retired in 1993, he ceded the names to the Iron Butt Association, and certifications were then offered nationally. While the IronButt.com web site guidelines state that the Interstate Highway system offers the quickest and safest way to cover the miles, recent Saddlesore 1000 rides have been made entirely within the borders of most states and several cities, including Washington, D.C., Los Angeles, and New York. John Ryan made the New York attempt and at one point was pulled over by one of that city's finest. The officer was evidently perturbed at seeing Ryan pass by so many times in his circuit around the city, and wanted to know what the hell was going on. After a bit of back and forth, Ryan explained he was trying to see how many miles he could go inside the city in a 24-hour period. Happily, this satisfied the officer and he let Ryan ride on. "OK," he said, "I just wanted to know."

More than once I've heard, "Do you know how crazy all that sounds?" Most of the folks in our little group were hobbyists, like me. Our ride was the equivalent of Iron Butt baby steps, climbing a little hill, though even at that I had some questions about how I'd do on the second half—the thousand-mile ride back home. I wondered if I had the endurance to keep from getting drowsy on the bike. But that was tomorrow and I had a whole day of riding ahead of me today.

I came again to the Trinity River. Fingers of the river penetrate the woods all over, beautiful in that morning light to a swamp rat like me. A heron coasted lazily over the water and I slowed to savor the view across the Old and Lost Rivers and their many baylets and islands. The reverie ended abruptly at the end of the causeway as I plunged back into the greater Houston metro area and the universe of the world's petroleum capital. Suddenly tanker trucks were everywhere.

James McMurtry wrote a line in one of his songs, "Walk between the raindrops, dry as a bone," and that's how I tried to run the Houston traffic. Since it's my hometown I believe I have a sense of its pulse and rhythm, and I'll probably find out the hard way that that's blooey. I made it through fine, though, and was past the Brazos River a little after 8 A.M. So that's good, I thought, starting to do the math and smacking myself for again trying to jinx things.

I focused on the road, the bulk of my attention on getting through traffic safely, on achieving the horizon. With the stock tank, my bike will travel two hundred miles, more or less, before it needs gas. I visualized each stop as the end of a tunnel. I didn't watch the scenery go by so much as mark the steps of land between me and the next place my feet were going to touch the ground.

My first stop was in Columbus, on the Colorado River, regarded as the first western river as the traveler moves from eastern landscapes to the west. The Colorado crossing is about 190 miles from the Sabine, and the next tank took me out of the coastal plain across rolling hills to San Antonio and the Balcones Escarpment. I got in and out of these stops in under ten minutes, twice as long, I'm told, as the big dogs. Still, they were no-frills drills, all business. Without running, I wasn't sure how anyone filled a tank and drained a bladder in much less time.

West of San Antonio, I-10 climbs the Escarpment onto the Edwards Plateau and dives into the Texas Hill Country. This is one of the prettiest stretches of I-10 in the state, and I felt blessed that the sun was perfect and not too hot, and my mind could wander out across the landscape for a time instead of projecting itself down the road to the next scheduled stop.

Somewhere around Junction I slid out of my dream state and then rode head-down across the rest of the Edwards Plateau to Sonora. It was about a quarter to one, and I decided I was hungry enough to eat a gas-station cheeseburger. It's a good thing humans can belch. Eating a greasy burger in the middle of a long ride is not recommended, but I didn't know that then. It's better to eat something that's not going to hammer you as your body works to convert it to useful energy. A lot of riders eat power bars, nuts, dried and fresh fruit, jerky for the meat-addicted, and they drink lots of water.

After lunch, I unpacked a water-cooling vest and one of those crystal-filled neckerchief thingies and soaked them in the bathroom sink. The camelback was still at least half-full and half-frozen but the hottest and driest part of the trip was coming up, so I bought a bottle of spring water and the attendant let me load the bladder with ice from the soft drink fountain. "Technology" like the water vest, the camelback, and the earplugs extend a rider's limits. They put hours on the day, and in the case of the water vest, can be the difference between riding through an impossibly hot desert and arriving for drinks on the other side, and going stark raving loony from the sun pounding down on your head with the heat of a thousand demons.

Long distance riders in general and Iron Butt riders in particular know that properly applied technology lets them go farther without getting beaten to death, and in the case of Iron Butt Rally riders, that can be a competitive advantage. All the serious bikes have driving lamps that could start a fire if trained on something long enough. Little shelves and mini-holders abound, loaded with one or two GPS units (the laptop computer is in the top box that sits atop the auxiliary gas tank); a couple of radar detectors; a com center where the cell phone, CB, satellite radio, and other communications get plugged in; and extra mirrors turned to see the blind spots left by your stock mirrors. To read the map in the tank bag pocket at night a gooseneck map light with a rheostat switch is needed. Many bikes carry satellite transponders that tell people over the Internet where they are located. And then come the off-menu items, the little custom touches that each rider has put on his bike to give that little extra boost. I have a little shelf on my bike, too, but aside from the occasional radar detector the only thing on it is a statuette of a roadrunner, a paisano as they say in West Texas—a little buddy for good luck. That as much as anything shows me as a hobbyist rather than a really hard-core long distance

A paisano companion enjoys the Hill Country view

rider, a big dog. (I do have extra driving lamps, though, and they really do light up the road.)

The bike's clock said 1:30 and the thermometer showed 92 degrees when I pulled out of Sonora. I had taken nearly forty-five minutes on that stop, much longer than I'd intended. Still, I'd ridden nearly six hundred miles since four that morning, and back out on the highway I felt rested and strong. I decided to regard the time as well-spent spilt milk.

West of Sonora the hills drop away and flat-topped mesa-lands rise up, with tens of miles of flatland separating the bluffs. Where the Hill Country is semi-arid, the semi- part has evaporated out here. I had to go back and view the photos I took to be sure something grew out there—my memory is of a barren, brown land stretching from horizon to horizon, where nothing lives but the wind.

Wind farms have sprung up in considerable numbers on the bluffs around Ozona and Iraan (Ira-Ann), testimony to the force and constancy of the winds in those bleak lands. I remembered my first motorcycle trip out there years before. My wife, Janice, and I were on a fully loaded bike getting our first lesson in gyroscopic physics and inertia and how a two-wheeled vehicle counterbalances in strong winds. We were easily at a 45-degree angle running down the straight-line road, feeling it was our speed that kept us off the pavement and if we slowed down even a little, the wind would drop us like a hot brick.

The winds weren't blowing on this ride, though. The hot air was still riding across the desert. The thermometer on the bike read 98, but the water vest and neck cooler kept things just about comfortable under the mesh jacket. The camelback was essential now, and I thought of myself earlier that morning looking ahead to that moment when I would thank myself for going back to get it.

I hadn't seen any other riders, and wondered where they all were. I passed Bakersfield and its singular geologic icon, Squaw Tit Mountain, and pulled into Fort Stockton around 3:00 P.M. At mile marker 260, I had come almost three-quarters of the first thousand miles and once again started to count my chips before the game

Passing Bakersfield

was over. The next stop was around 4:30 in Van Horn, at mile marker 138. Because of the way the towns are spaced, both of the last stops had been only an hour-and-a-half apart.

As I coasted into the gas station I finally saw another rider from the Run. Curt Summers, one of the Gold Wing riders, was getting ready to pull out. We exchanged howdys and he asked if I was going to stay on the 10 for the Solstice route, or if I was going to take the Saddlesore route. I told him I was going for the Saddlesore, but thought I'd understood that it was actually shorter than staying on 10. In any case, I said, it went by the Guadalupe Mountains and was a much prettier route than the 10. Later, I found out that because I had really not been paying attention during Beverly's briefing that morning, I'd flipped the critical information— the detour didn't subtract the thirty-five miles, it added them. It *is* a prettier route, though. Curt climbed on his Wing and silently motored off towards the Guadalupes, and I hustled through the gas drill as quickly as possible and rode after him.

One of the most bizarre experiences I have ever had occurred several years earlier on this highway, just north of Van Horn. Janice and I were headed to the Guadalupe Mountains one sunny day, and in the distance I could see a huddle of turkey vultures picking at something on the left side of the road. They were unconcerned about us until we got pretty close. They began to waddle off in different directions and one of them slowly launched himself into the air. He reminded me of that cartoon vulture when I was a kid who sang, "I'm bringin' home a baby bumble bee . . ." He had the whole sky to fly in, but he turned to cross the road right in the path of the bike. Even as I watched him I didn't believe he was going to do it, but evidently this is a slow reacting species and he couldn't help himself. Perhaps he was target-fixated. I had slowed but still the bike's wind fairing thunked him.

Though it was a solid thunk, nothing on the bike sounded like it cracked and for a moment there I thought of just continuing on, no big deal. Then I realized something sufficiently odd had happened to warrant stopping and checking things out. Janice was wondering what took me so long. I pulled to the outside of the shoulder and we got off to check out the damage. The hair on the back of my neck stood up under my helmet. The front of the bike was covered with long, ropy strands of fresh meat, ghastly dreadlocks of red and pink and white strips piled in layers that conformed to the curves of the fairing, at once gross, disgusting, astonishing, and surreal.

I eyed the place of our encounter as I passed it this time, and rode on. Presently I came along side the Sierra Diablo, the Devil Mountains, and caught sight of Curt on his Gold Wing, a dot at the end of the road. I hustled to catch up, but at some point he saw me in his mirrors and took off. There is an unspoken rivalry between LTs and Gold Wings. They're both the biggest bikes on their teams, built for long distance touring with a passenger and all the bells and whistles, and powered by sophisticated and very potent engines. The road was not particularly well surfaced and there were many little hillocks and diplets, but it ran straight for ten miles at a stretch and we were the only two vehicles as far as the eye could see. We ran the ton for almost forty miles across those

Approaching El Capitan, the Guadalupe Mountains

low hills and shallow dips, and probably didn't see five other vehicles in either direction.

We approached the feet of El Capitan, the southern bastion of the Guadalupe Mountains, rising up red and majestic in the hazy westering light. Our highway T-ed into another and we turned left to head directly into the sun. The salt flats and cracked alkaline hills that flank the mountains feel like an ancient dune-land boundary between land and sea. From there we rode out onto an undulating surface that looks like the bottom of the ocean with all the water removed. I'm a swamp rat, and this looked like the bottom of the desert to me. The sun moved slowly down the sky, hot, hot, hot.

I thought since I was on the last leg of the trip I could spare the energy needed to ride as fast as I had while chasing Kurt, but as usual I discounted the reality. Moreover, after two successive hour-and-a-half legs, I wasn't mentally prepared for one that was going to take two-and-a-half hours. The mountains receded behind us and nothing rose up ahead to draw the eye and the mind forward. The flat land expanded and it seemed like we were riding on a giant treadmill, going nowhere. The sun fell lower and lower and I couldn't believe it was taking so long to get to the rim of El Paso. To make things worse, traffic lights started showing up every few miles. At one of the lights I pulled up next to Curt and nodded, and over the course of the next few stops we said howdy, complimented each other's bikes, agreed it had been a hot ride and that we were looking forward to mile marker zero and a cold beer. A shower would be good, too.

We finally got to the loop around El Paso and turned north toward the Franklin Mountains. Although the air was quite hazy, I expected something called the Franklin Mountains to be real obvious at that point and was discouraged that I couldn't see anything resembling mountains. I was definitely smelling the hay in the stables. We rode a few more miles and encountered increasing numbers of lights and a lot more traffic. I started getting impatient. At one light I asked a fellow in the car next to me which way it was to I-10. He said the quickest way was to go up two lights and turn left. Curt and I both thought we should be going straight rather than turning left. We puzzled over that for another light and then Curt asked the driver next to him which way it was to Anthony. "Oh, go straight," he said, "you'll come to the mountains. Drive right over the top and Anthony's on the other side."

That sounded exactly right. I was so glad Curt had asked *the right question*. Clearly, my brain was firing on even fewer cylinders than usual. In the Iron Butt Rally members rode days like this for eleven days, and after only one I was not asking the right questions. What would I be like on day eight or nine, for example? More to the point, what would I be like in the morning? The thought of nodding off on a bike scares me—you really don't want to lose your balance even for a second.

We stopped at a red light and suddenly the mountains were right there in front of us, backlit and shimmering in the thick haze. The stoplight changed and we crossed over onto the Woodrow Bean Transmountain Parkway and into the Franklin Mountain State Park. After all that flatland riding it was a kick to suddenly be rising up a curvy road to the top of a mountain, even if it was a little one. We crested the top and saw El Paso and Juarez spread out

Mile Marker Zero

below us, the river curving through and separating the U.S. from Mexico. We slowed to savor the view for a few moments, then headed down to I-10 at the bottom of the mountain. A few minutes later we were gassing up at mile marker zero and I collected my final receipt for the first leg, time stamped, location stamped, official. It was a little before 7:00 P.M., Houston time, for a total ride time of just under fifteen hours.

The vice president of our club that year was Floyd Crow. He checked my mileage at the end point of the first leg, and then Curt and I had that beer. We wandered around the motel parking lot, trying to adjust to not riding, then chugged the bottom half of the beer and broke for our rooms. I slept like a dead vegetable that night, and way too early the phone rang to wake me. For several minutes I grogged dizzily around the room trying to decide if I was going to do the second thousand miles, or get some more sleep and hope I could stay awake for the straight shot back home, only seven hundred and seventy miles.

As I moved around I gained momentum, and finally got to where I wasn't running into the furniture and things. What the hell, I thought, now that you can walk a straight line, go for it. The other Saddlesore riders had assembled outside. Unlike twenty-four hours earlier when everyone had been pretty quiet at the starting station, today we had a very chatty group. As the rest of the group gassed up, a fellow in a pickup pulling a trailered Harley drove in. It was a gleamy, creamy, custom showpiece bike, with a long front end and high handlebars. I wondered where he was going at 3:45 in the morning, and wondered what he thought about our group in our long-distance motley.

We pulled out at four and headed west into New Mexico. Between Anthony and Las Cruces, I-10 passes miles of dairy farms and feed lots. The stench is monumental and I wondered how many places on the face of the earth smelled that bad for that many miles at a stretch. I wondered if anyone made aux oxygen tanks for motorcycles. We arrived in Lordsburg a little before six, about twenty miles from the Arizona border. This was our turnaround point; from here we'd head back east to Houston. We rode around looking for a place to eat, but nothing was open. We gassed up and were swinging back toward the Interstate when golden arches blinked on nearby, like on Interstates all around the country.

The ride back was relatively uneventful and much of it was on auto-pilot. The high point of the day proved to be sunrise, coming up behind the Organ Mountains outside Las Cruces. The air was clear and cold and the light very crisp, and I felt extremely far away from Houston. The temperature would increase fifty degrees as we rode back across the state, to a high of 102, and again the camelback and the water vest were the difference between sanity and riding wildly out across the desert screaming.

Jim Green rode with me, on a cruiser with ape-hanger bars. The controls on handlebars like that are at head level, and holding your hands up that high gets very tiring after a while. I appreciated the extra effort it took to make a ride of two thousand miles with his arms held up like that.

My biggest fear for the return trip had been sleepiness, and I did get drowsy once, around four in the afternoon. We pulled into a gas station just outside Boerne, about thirty miles before my planned stop in San Antonio. This meant I would have to make one more stop than scheduled, but I felt lucky that that tingly, swimming-in-the-brain feeling that signals the cliff-drop of oncoming sleep had not crept over me until then. Even if I had to pull over every thirty minutes, I didn't want to drift into sleep even for a second.

We got back to the gas station at mile marker 761 a little after 9 P.M. We had ridden over two thousand and fifty miles in about forty-one hours, and we were pumped. And right then and there we were able to savor the fact that someone else knew what we'd just accomplished. I don't think there's a bigger answer than that to the question, "Why do you do that?" Just a private feeling of satisfaction, bolstered by knowing someone else knew what you'd done, and knew firsthand what the achievement really took to accomplish. In some ways it's a big deal, and in other ways it's not a big deal. My IBA number is in the 15,000s—over 15,000 folks joined up ahead of me, and there are uncounted other long distance riders who are not in that particular "club," riders who have circumnavigated nations and continents and the globe itself.

Riding the Saddlesore initiated me into some very good company and I feel like a kindred spirit in a way. I've learned some of the customs, rituals, and lingo of modern day long distance riders who mount their two-wheeled motorized thoroughbreds of amazing technological sophistication and ride across the continent. Two thousand miles in two days might be baby steps, but it's a great way to spend the weekend. And it made me want to take bigger steps, to go farther. Not necessarily in short periods of time, in Iron Butt fashion, but to go long distances nevertheless—to the edges of the continent and back, criss-crossing from side-to-side and then some day, top to bottom. Of all the continents. In the meantime I feed my daydreams of Janice and me wandering the globe as two-wheeled gypsies by taking a ride from some place here to some place there, and finding some loop that comes back around again.

Gretchen Lutz

THE UNSPOKEN CODE OF CHIVALRY AMONG DRAG RACERS

by Gretchen Lutz

At a typical race among "outlaw" pro mod drag racers, spectators see relentless competition among perennial rivals. During warm weather months, fans gather at local drag strips to see the show put on by Texas Outlaw Racing, an organization of pro mod racers. To the observer, it appears that a racer is single-minded in his or her need to beat the car in the other lane. And that is true. But that is not the whole truth. What the fan does not see is how the racers interact with one another before and after that four-second-pass down the track. Until the moment the tree goes to green, the typical pro mod racer will do anything he can to make a fellow racer's car go faster. An unspoken code of chivalry informs the way racers behave toward one another, creating an enigmatic, even genteel brotherhood that the unrestrained speed, power, and dazzle of the sport belie.

To the spectators, the pro mods are indeed outlaw racers, not being restricted by the rules imposed on bracket racers or even on the pro stocks. Pro mods can run with nitrous oxide, with blowers, with extreme scoops, or with outrageous wings, the functional features exaggerated by flamboyant paint jobs. With only the restrictions for safety and the requirement that the cars be "door slammers"—that is to say, have two doors—anything else goes. Some racers play up this outlaw business by racing under nicknames, such as Madman and Bounty Hunter, almost reminiscent of the WWF.

To the spectator, the outlaw nature of this brand of racing might imply that racers are sworn enemies, intent on doing anything to see the other car come in second. And for the four seconds that the opponents make their pass, that is true. What the spectator does not see, however, is how the racers treat each other in the times before and after the actual pass. Before the tree light goes to green, a typical outlaw pro mod racer will give his time, his advice, his expertise, his equipment, his tools, his sweat, and sometimes even his blood to make another racer's car go faster.

For all the super-trick technology and the awe-inspiring speeds, the typical pro mod drag race appeals in much the same way as the knightly tournament appealed, with the racers fulfilling the role of knights. Much as the well-configured steed was essential to a knight's success, for the racer the car is his all, trumping all personal, human desires in an effort to perfect the machine. To echo ZZ Top, the racers themselves, despite the showbiz swagger some appropriate, live their real lives in relative humility, adhering to the motto: "Let the machine speak."

Although each race car is a unique creation made especially for racing and not at all for the street, racers invariably make their cars appear to be modified stock cars, ones that might have been displayed on a showroom floor. Although pro mod racing would allow fully fanciful door slammers as creations of an individual's imagination, in actual practice the race cars look familiar, offering a nostalgic connection to the past for racers and fans alike, reminding them perhaps of a beloved family car, the car one first learned to drive, that first new car, or maybe even the longed-for dream car. At a national NHRA race, one will see scores of '69 Camaros. The '63 Corvette is also popular, as is the '53 Corvette. Though there is no real reason for it other than personal taste, approximately ninety percent of the Texas Outlaw Racing organization drivers race GM models. Despite having the option to have cars that look like nothing at all familiar, there is a sort of heraldry in place, a system whereby the racer says who he or she is by means of the apparent make and model of the car and the signature paint job.

Fans flock to their favorite kind of car, vicariously attaching to themselves the qualities and virtues of that particular car. Oddly, the driver himself is rather irrelevant. Once, at an NHRA national race I observed a car crash. The driver, a man known throughout the country for making beautiful car bodies, what the racers call simply "the car," walked away, and as he was leaving the track, the announcer asked the fans to give him a hand, declaring: "He is a credit to the kind of car he makes."

When I first attended a drag race as a guest of a racer, I was surprised to see that during the hour between the passes, during that short time the racer and crew have to "thrash" on the cars before making the next pass, racers visit one another in the pits, offering advice, parts, and tools, and working on the other person's car, even the very person who will be in the next lane. I have seen racers give fairly expensive consumable parts to an opponent. I have seen racers get sweaty, dirty, and bloody thrashing on the opposition's car. For the racers, making the car go faster trumps all other considerations, even if it is someone else's car.

During the time the racers are away from the track, it is not at all unusual for some of them to meet together to do what is called "bench racing," getting together to talk about racing, with the underlying theme always to make the car go faster. During the workweek, racers communicate by phone and on the Internet in private email or on the racing organizations' bulletin boards, offering advice, answering another racer's questions, and occasionally reliving past races. Sometimes on the various organizations' web sites there may be some "smack talk" about how a racer will beat another, but the emphasis is always on who has the better car, not on the character or even the driving skills of another racer. The unspoken code of chivalry dictates that one not speak ill of another racer personally.

And as a result of quite a few trips to the races as the guest of a veteran pro mod racer, Tommy Adams [name changed at the request of the actual driver], I decided that the general public should know how racers interact with one another during the time they are not roaring down the track. To do a little last minute research, I met my racer friend at Lonestar Raceway Park in Sealy, Texas, where he was competing in the sixth annual state championship.

It was a perfect day for racing, moderate with low humidity. We expected fast times, and we were right. My friend qualified, and while he was thrashing on the car for the first round of competition, I walked through the pits, observing racers helping each other out. A few racers, who had their cars adjusted to their satisfaction, walked from race car to race car, doing a little bench racing and offering help and advice to their fellows who were still thrashing to prepare for the next round.

My friend suggested that I go to the starting line to observe. The racers lining up in the starting lane would shake hands with their competitor and make calm small talk, sometimes about past races, occasionally about the condition of the car, frequently about the trip traveling to the track—all sorts of racing-related talk except the one subject they never discuss: the upcoming pass for which they are lining up.

When racer Adams got to the starting line, he began the rituals I had seen so often. First was the burn out, prepping the slicks so that they keep traction with the track. Then a crew member gestured him forward to the line. He expelled the nitrous and waited for the tree to go to green. When the tree went to green, Tommy got the hole shot as they say, meaning he was the first off the line. For about four seconds the cars howled down the track. Then right after the times (the e.t.a.'s) went up on the boards at the end of the track, the car in the right-hand lane crossed the center line and clipped the rear of my friend's '69 Camaro. The Camaro leapt into the air, rotating five times as it spun toward the field to the right of the track. When the car came down, it was crumpled beyond recognition but had not burst into flames.

The ambulance crew got to Tommy quickly. He had no serious lacerations or apparent broken bones; moreover, he was conscious. Following a crash like that, though, medical personnel were adamant that the driver be checked for head injuries. After opening up the wreckage with the jaws of life, the EMTs extricated my friend and put him on a stretcher and into an ambulance. During all this, the other racers and their crews had gathered.

Suddenly the focus was no longer on the car but upon the driver. The racers started talking about Tommy, commenting that he had been driving that '69 Camaro since he bought the prototype street car from a dealer back in 1969. One crew member of another racer asked me what Tommy did in his life outside of racing, what he did for a living, what family he had, what his life was like off the track. Everyone was telling a Tommy Adams story, sharing some memory of Tommy's long career.

After the EMTs determined that Tommy should be Life-Flighted to Hermann Hospital in Houston, some sixty miles away, the focus returned to the car. Tommy's crew chief was concerned about putting the mangled Camaro back into the trailer. Immediately, other racers and their crews started volunteering to help pick up the pieces and to get it all put back into Tommy's trailer for the trip home. One racer assured me that he would see to it that the car would get back to Tommy's home near Dallas, some 250 miles away. He urged me to drive to the hospital where Tommy was being transported by helicopter. The crew chief was going to stay with the demolished car and trailer and would drive it back. The racers had come to Tommy's aid, postponing the racing until both Tommy and his car were taken care of.

I drove east on I-10, getting into the sort of heavy traffic that Houston's Katy Freeway is known for. In a little over two hours I arrived at the hospital, where I was allowed in to see Tommy. When I approached and started asking how he was, Tommy stopped me, saying, "Did I win?" Despite all that had transpired and the possibility of death, to Tommy, the race was still the point. As it turned out, I told him, he had won. By that time the racer had become irritable because he had not yet been seen by a doctor and was still strapped into the head harness that the EMTs had put on him to keep him stable. It seemed that seventeen other patients had been brought by helicopter that night. I told Tommy that it was a good sign that he had not been seen by the doctor yet. That meant that the triage nurse had checked him over and decided his injuries were not life-threatening.

While we waited for the doctor, word came to us from the reception desk that Tommy's family was insisting to know what his condition was, having called the hospital's administrative offices. This news was puzzling and a bit disturbing in as much as Tommy had no immediate family. We later learned that the wife of one of the racers back at the track was using the family ploy to get information about Tommy's condition. She knew that the hospital would give out information to the immediate family only. Shortly after the mysterious call from the alleged family had come, several of the racers phoned me on my cell phone to check on Tommy. The racer whose car had clipped Tommy was absolutely beside himself. Everyone was saying that if there was anything they could do, they were ready.

Finally, the doctor came. X-rays showed our racer had some broken ribs but no other damage to his body. He was still experiencing dizziness, so the doctor decided to keep him in the hospital for observation. In the meantime, the crew chief had arrived with the trailer and the wreckage. He had had to park quite a distance away, at the Hermann Park Zoo parking lot, to find a place anywhere near the hospital large enough for the truck and trailer. When he found his racer was going to have to stay the night, he set out to find a hotel, again with the problem of finding a place that could accommodate trailer and truck.

Tommy stayed in the hospital for another day while an ear, nose, and throat specialist monitored the dizziness. The ENT doctor concluded that the otoliths, tiny "ear rocks" in the inner ear, had been dislodged, not unlike what happens when one turns over a snow globe. The dislodged otoliths were causing the dizziness. By the time Tommy got back from seeing the doctor, flowers had come from the family of one of the competing racers. Once in a regular room, Tommy was visited by a television celebrity, Dr. Red Duke, who was followed by an entourage of young doctors making rounds. Dr. Duke asked what had happened, and then the doctor and the racer engaged in talk about, what else? Racing. It seems that the famous doctor was a fan of motor sports, too.

By the time Tommy was ready to make the drive back to Dallas, he learned that his fellow racers had organized a fund-raiser to compensate him for the time he was going to have to lose from his business. Racers had donated goods and services for a raffle to be held the following week at the next race. Texas Outlaw Racing's website publicized the raffle, as more racers and fans contributed prizes and bought tickets. On Monday a week after the crash, racers gathered at Tommy's machine shop business to give him the funds they had raised on his behalf. For a change, the car was not the main thing. The human racer was. Racers came together without talking about it or thinking it over much in advance. They did what needed to be done for a fellow racer. And that is how it is among the outlaw racers on the pro mod circuit.

Now Tommy is gradually putting the pieces of his old race car together to make a new one. After thirty-four years of the '69 Camaro, Tommy is fitting his old chassis inside the body of a '53 Studebaker, thereby resurrecting his racing life, made possible in no small part by the chivalrous behavior of his fellow racers.

Advertisement for T-Bone's Truck Terminal and Restaurant, Amarillo, Texas (with handy mileage chart on back)

EATING UP ROUTE 66: FOODWAYS OF MOTORISTS CROSSING THE TEXAS PANHANDLE

by T. Lindsay Baker

———

From the mid-1920s to the mid-1960s, U.S. Highway 66 served as a major thoroughfare for motorists traveling between the Midwest and the Pacific coast. In the mid-1920s, the U.S. Bureau of Roads began designating highways in the forty-eight states with identifying numbers. In 1926, the agency gave number 66 to a combination of roads that started at Chicago and passed through St. Louis, Oklahoma City, Amarillo, and Albuquerque to reach Los Angeles, over 2,400 miles away. In Texas the roads that became Route 66 were dirt tracks parallel to the Rock Island Railroad across the Panhandle.

Few highways in America gave travelers such geographical and cultural diversity as Route 66. From the cornfields of Illinois, drivers went through the Ozarks in Missouri before entering the oil fields and red hills of Oklahoma. They then crossed the treeless plains in the Texas Panhandle before driving through the deserts and Indian country of New Mexico and Arizona. In their unairconditioned cars they proceeded through the Mojave Desert, passed by orange groves in southern California, and reached the Pacific shore at Santa Monica. By the hundreds of thousands, drivers made this trip on mostly two-lane highways that were not even fully paved until the 1940s.[1]

The collection of roads comprising Route 66 brought together travelers with specific needs and local people eager to satisfy those needs for the right price. Gasoline stations, auto garages, vulcanizing shops, hotels, tourist courts, and cafes sprang up where they had never operated before. Spending by motorists created entire commercial strips of businesses that catered to the needs of travelers. Many of these places offered food.[2]

Not all motorists could afford to buy prepared meals. Instead, they either carried food from home or stopped during travel to buy groceries. In the days before refrigeration they had fewer options in carrying fresh foods than we have today. In 1939, Linda Anderson traveled Route 66 with her family from the Midwest to California across the Panhandle, and she later recalled, "We would stop at the small independent grocery stores and pick up bread, lunch meat, and soft drinks for our lunches. . . . We . . . pulled off to the side of the road to eat our sandwiches. . . . It was cooler if we could find a place to picnic under the trees. . . ."[3] Not all travelers could afford the luxury of pleasant roadside picnics. During the Dust Bowl years thousands of dispossessed farmers and others from Oklahoma, Arkansas, and other states used Route 66 as their avenue of hoped-for escape from poverty through migration to California. In 1933, the City of Amarillo opened free soup kitchens for the indigent, while the Federal Emergency Relief Administration operated a Transient Bureau in the city twenty-four hours a day for two years to assist impoverished migrants on their way westward.[4]

Home-style eating-places sprang up the length of Route 66, with hundreds operating at one time or another across the Texas

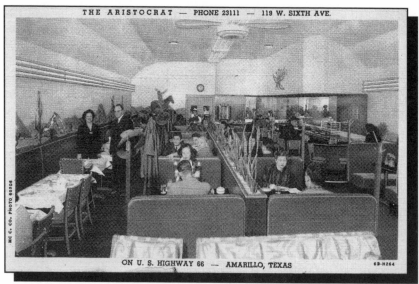

Postcard for the Aristocrat Restaurant, Amarillo, Texas

Panhandle. Many of these establishments, usually called cafés, functioned as free-standing businesses, but some of them fed travelers in conjunction with fuel and repair services at places that came to be known as truck stops. Others served meals to travelers near or alongside tourist courts, later known as motels. What sorts of meals did they serve?

Surviving historic menus give us windows through which to view typical Route 66 fare in the Panhandle. The Truck Stop Restaurant in Amarillo, actually more a café than a restaurant, about the time that old Route 66 was being bypassed by Interstate 40 in 1968, offered its customers breakfasts of eggs cooked any way, hash browned potatoes, and ham, bacon, or sausage with biscuits or toast for $1.25. Other breakfast options included steak and eggs, plain or cheese omelets, pancakes, and such sides as sweet rolls, cereal, cinnamon toast, and French toast. The cook could prepare every item on the menu except biscuits, just using a grill.[5]

Bob Dowell's Café, directly on Route 66 at Fifth and North Fillmore in Amarillo, offered its customers representative noonday and evening café fare during the 1950s. Its menu featured steaks and chops, deep-fried chicken, seafood, a limited range of what it

Postcard for Bob Dowell's Café, Amarillo, Texas

The menu is included on the postcard

called "Mexican Dishes," and a full selection of sandwiches and salads. Steaks and other entrées came with deep-fried "waffle potatoes" or "shoestring potatoes." The "kiddie's plate" consisted of hamburger, ice cream, and milk for 45¢, while the bacon-wrapped filet mignon for grown-ups sold for $2.50.[6]

Next on the "feeding chain" of Route 66 eating-places in the Texas Panhandle came restaurants. These establishments offered a wider range of meals beyond those that could be prepared on grills and in vats of hot grease. The Capitol Hotel Restaurant in Amarillo during the 1940s offered its overnight guests and others such refined choices as steaks, veal, pork chops, and seafood in season, together with vegetables like green peas, spinach, green beans, asparagus tips, and tomatoes. The sandwich selection included club, open-face chicken, and "home baked" ham, while patrons could choose stuffed tomato, lobster, and cream slaw salads. The most expensive item on the 1940s menu was the double sirloin steak with the trimmings for $1.75. Though we might chuckle about the prices today, this obviously was a high-end establishment, and it had operated continuously since the hotel opened in

January 1928, just a year-and-a-half after Route 66 received its numerical designation.[7]

A handful of restaurants on Route 66 in the Panhandle specialized in particular fare. This was the case of the Long Champ Dining Salon at 705 Northeast 8th in Amarillo, which starting in the 1940s and for two decades featured seafood flown in for freshness. With a neon sign that beckoned, "Tourists Welcome," the Long Champ offered its diners such meals as broiled Florida pompano, broiled Texas flounder, fried individual catfish, and whole Maine lobsters. Acknowledging its location in the Panhandle, in the heart of cattle country, the menu also offered a full range of steaks, allowing customers to select their own piece of meat before it was cooked. Vegetable options at the Long Champ included candied yams, sautéed green peppers, buttered beets, and green peas, with soups ranging from French onion to New Orleans gumbo. Dining for travelers at the Long Champ clearly was a treat.[8]

Some restaurants on Route 66 became visual as well as culinary landmarks for travelers. This clearly was the distinction of the U-Drop-Inn of Shamrock in the eastern Panhandle. It came into existence as a consequence of an early-1930s change in the alignment of U.S. Highway 66 from downtown streets to a new location several blocks north. L. R. Randall discovered that he owned all four corners of the prime real estate that would become the intersection of U.S. 66 east and west with U.S. 83 north and south.

After Randall's death, Amarillo businessman James M. Tindall approached his widow with an offer in 1934. He agreed to build for her daughter and son-in-law, Bebe and John Nunn, a new building on one of the corners if she would sell him some of the valuable land. John Nunn then described the combined service station and restaurant that he wanted. Architect Joseph Champ Berry then created a fanciful concrete and glazed tile masterpiece of Art Deco design. Bebe Nunn remembered, "Back in the '30s, neon was all the go. Our sign and tower was all bordered in green and red neon. . . . It shined so bright that you could see it from way back past McLean." Soon, the new eating-place became known as

The menu for the Long Champ Dining Salon, Amarillo, Texas

"the swankiest of the swank" restaurants. All up and down Route 66 motorists came to know its reputation.

The sophisticated kitchen included walk-in coolers where John Nunn kept sides of aged beef from which he personally cut meat. "We had a great number of steak eaters," Bebe Nunn explained, "so they knew they could ask for a certain thickness and get it." Years later Lou Kofton stopped in Shamrock in 1952 on a cross-country drive from California. "I remember this gas station because it had a tower and was elegant. . . . I also had something to eat at Nunn's Café, at the other end of the same building. . . ."

About 1960, the bus company serving Shamrock shifted its station to the restaurant. Grace Brunner, who had become the owner, recalled, "Back then . . . We had about ten [bus] schedules a day. We kept sandwiches made up and put them on the counter before a bus was due, as there wasn't time to order from the kitchen. . . . We had to have several waitresses. We also kept plenty of pies and apples. Of course, candy, cookies, chips and gum."

The venerable station and café operated commercially until 1995. It then stood vacant for several years, before being restored in 2001 to serve as a visitors' information center for Shamrock.[9]

Travelers today find that many if not most of the places where they choose to dine are "chain restaurants" or franchises of national firms. One of the earliest such eating-places on Route 66 in Texas was the Jones Brothers Drive-In that sold franchised "Chicken in the Rough" in two Amarillo locations. The specialty had its origin in Oklahoma City. There Beverly and Rubye Osborne had opened a six-stool diner in 1921, serving hamburgers, fried chicken, and other grilled and fried fare; in time their business prospered and grew. In 1936, the couple took a trip to California when a bump in the road sent their lunch, a meal of fried chicken, spilling onto the seat. Rubye joked to Beverly, "This is really chicken in the rough." The incident led them to an innovation in American dining.

Once they returned to Oklahoma City, the Osbornes started serving what they called "chicken in the rough"—pieces of cut-up

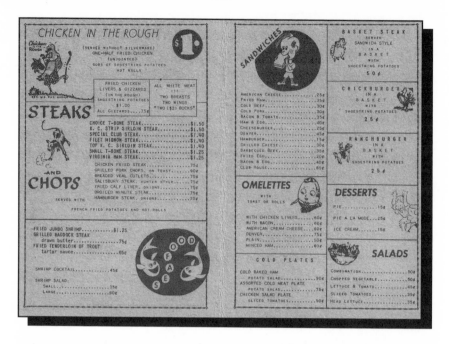

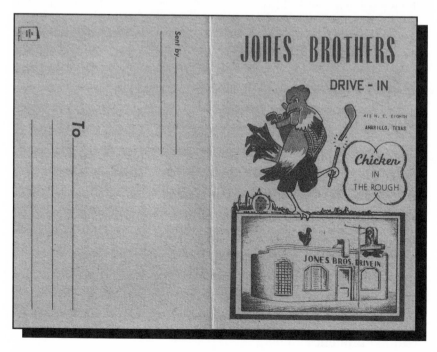

Postcard for the Jones Brothers Drive-In, Amarillo, Texas (with menu on back)

deep-fried chicken on a bed of French fries with a buttered roll and honey—**with no silverware.** They did this at a time when proper etiquette required the use of a knife and fork for eating chicken. With a price of 50¢ for half a chicken and the trimmings, and using a copyrighted cartoon of a rooster holding golf clubs, their idea of casual dining caught on. It *really* caught on. By World War II, the Osbornes were running seven restaurants in Oklahoma City, the largest of which, on Route 66, seated 1,100 diners.

By this time they had begun franchising the "Chicken in the Rough" restaurants, eventually seeing them in 234 locations across most of the country. Claude A. and J. Marvin Jones of Amarillo purchased an Osborne franchise and opened two drive-in restaurants at 413 Northeast 8th and at 208 West 6th, both on Route 66. Later known as the Jones Brothers Village Inn, the eating-place survived into the 1960s.[10]

Some restaurants became Route 66 attractions in themselves. The major example in Texas is the Big Texan Steak Ranch, established by Bob Lee in 1960 on Northeast 8th in Amarillo. For hundreds of miles each direction from the city, its billboards today advertise, "Free 72-Oz. Steak Ahead!" The eating-place began as no more than an ordinary barbecue cafeteria with western décor that happened to be on Route 66 near the Amarillo Livestock Auction. One day a horse managed to get out of one of the auction cowboy's trailers in the parking lot. As the owner struggled to jump onto the horse, passing motorists almost ran into each other as they watched. Bob Lee recognized the sensation that the man on horseback had caused. He approached one of the cowboys and said, "Look, you come back tomorrow. I'll pay you twenty-five bucks just to sit on your horse and wave to people." The wrangler thought he was crazy but took the money. The gimmick worked. Route 66 travelers started pouring into the restaurant. Lee dressed his employees like cowboys and had them carry little six-shooters at their sides. Then he put up a huge metal sign in the shape of a cowboy. Still more tourists came.

Working cowboys from the livestock auction intrigued the out-of-state guests, so Bob Lee started cashing their paychecks on Fridays and offering them twenty-five-cent beers just so that they would hang around the restaurant and provide local color. Son Danny Lee remembered, "They were such pigs when they ate." Seeing how much the men could put away at the tables, the elder Lee made the auction cowboys a memorable offer: "I'll tell you what. Next Friday night, when you guys get paid, everybody come up here and put up $5. I'm going to serve you one-pound steaks for one hour, and whoever eats the most gets all the money in the pot." The cowboys came, and so did the news media. Danny Lee continued the story, "Sure enough, the cowboys showed up and my dad started serving them one-pound steaks for an hour. One guy was ahead of everybody, and he said, 'Well, bring me a salad, too. What else you got there? Bring me a shrimp cocktail and bring me a roll.'" By the time the hour was up, he had consumed four-and-a-half pounds of steak plus the trimmings. Bob Lee, realizing that the cowboys had given him yet another gimmick to attract customers, declared to the media, "From this day forward, anybody that comes in here and eats a seventy-two-ounce steak, complete with side orders, will get it for free." The Big Texan boomed.

The day in 1968 that traffic in Amarillo diverted from historic Route 66 to Interstate 40, Bob Lee and his family saw their business drop an estimated eighty percent. They knew that they had to move or go bust. The family purchased five abandoned barracks from the old Amarillo Air Force Base, relocated them to a new site at the east side of Amarillo on the Interstate, and used them to create a new Big Texan Steak Ranch. With a 450-seat dining room, a full menu, live Western music, a shooting gallery, and waiters still dressed as cowboys, the eating-place remains a major attraction for interstate travelers.[11]

For the most part the traditional eating-places on Route 66 have gone the same way as Bob Lee at the Big Texan. As Interstate 40 bypassed their towns, they either made do with a trickle of trade from motorists and locals on the old business routes, they went out of business, or they relocated to the side of the new roadway. Motorists pour off the highway in search of sandwiches, salads, steaks, and seafood, just the same as their Route 66 predecessors did during the decades before. Their trade today perpetuates many of the same foodways that their parents and grandparents enjoyed as they took the Mother Road across the Texas Panhandle.

[Prepared for Texas State Historical Association, 4 March 2005.]

ENDNOTES

1. Michael Wallis. *Route 66: The Mother Road*. New York: St. Martin's Press, 1990. 5–11.
2. Catherine Gudis. *Buyways: Billboards, Automobiles, and the American Landscape*. New York: Routledge, 2004. Gudis examines the phenomenon of "corridors of consumption" along American highways.
3. Linda Anderson. "Memories of Route 66." *Route 66 Magazine* 6, no. 1 Winter 1998–99: 10.
4. David L. Nail. *One Short Sleep Past: A Profile of Amarillo in the Thirties*. Canyon, Texas: Staked Plains Press, 1973. 95; Wallis, 131, 133.
5. Truck Stop Café, Amarillo, Tex., *Good Morning: Breakfast Now Being Served* (Eastland, Texas: VC Menus, 1970): menu in personal research files of the author. Ernestine Linck and Joyce Roach make clear the distinction between cafés and restaurants in Texas in their book, *Eats: A Folk History of Texas Foods*. Fort Worth: Texas Christian University Press, 1989. 231–36.
6. Bob Dowell's Café, Amarillo Texas, *Bob Dowell's Café: Fifth at No. Fillmore[,] Amarillo, Texas* (Amarillo: privately printed, ca. 1955): menu in personal research files of the author.
7. Capitol Hotel, Amarillo, Texas, *Snuffy Says,* (Amarillo, Texas: privately printed, ca. 1945): menu, unpaged, in personal research files of the author; Richard Hamm, "Days of Capitol Hotel, $2 Rooms Gone Forever." *Amarillo Sunday News-Globe* (Amarillo, Texas), 11 September, 1977, clipping available in "Amarillo Texas, Hotels" Vertical File, Texas Collection, Baylor University, Waco, Texas; Daryl McKee, "Capitol Hotel Stands as Testimony to Past Elegance." *Amarillo Globe-Times* (Amarillo, Texas), 1 February 1973. 22.
8. Long Champ Dining Salon, Amarillo, Texas, *If It Swims We Have It! Long Champ Dining Salon[,] AAA[,] on Hwy. 60 & 65[,] Amarillo, Texas[,] Recommended by Duncan Hines,* (Amarillo, Tex., Privately printed, ca. 1950): menu in personal research files of the author;

H. H. Hutson, *If It Swims—We Have It[,] Long Champ[,] 705 N.E. Eighth in Amarillo[,] U.S.A.,* (Amarillo, Tex., Privately printed, 1948): paper table placemat in personal research files of the author; Long Champ Dining Salon, Amarillo, Tex., *Recommended by Duncan Hines[,] Longchamp[,] Recommended by AAA,* Publication 9B-H686 (Chicago: Curt Teich Company, 1949): postcard in personal research files of the author; Long Champ Dining Salon, Amarillo, Tex., *Recommended by Duncan Hines[,] Long Champ Dining Salon—East of City on Highway 60 & 66—Amarillo, Texas,* Publication 8B-H70 (Chicago: Curt Teich Company, 1948): postcard in personal research files of the author.

9. Kerry Campbell. "Café Still a Landmark." *Amarillo Daily News* (Amarillo, Texas), 11 March 1991, A1, 2. (first four quotations); Kerry Campbell. "Route 66 Landmark: Owners Look Back Fondly at Café's History." *Amarillo Globe-News* (Amarillo, Texas, ca. 1992), available as clipping in Scrapbook 3, Old Route 66 Association of Texas, McLean, Texas; Jay Firshing. "The Incomparable U-Drop Inn/Tower Station to Be Restored." *Route 66 Federation News* 7, no. 1, Winter 2001: 9–13 (sixth quotation); Jay Firshing. "News on the U-Drop-Inn Café." *The 66 News* (Springfield, Ill.), Winter 2000. 18; John Kofton. "My Girl Lou: A Story of Love, the Mother Road & East in 1952." *Roadsigns* (La Verne, Calif.), 11, no. 1, Winter/Spring 2001: 14 (fifth quotation); Bob Moore. "The U-Drop-Inn: An Art Deco Masterpiece." *The Mother Road Journal* (Lakewood, Colo.), #10, October 1993: 16; Jimmy J. Pack, Jr. "Images of the U-Drop Inn." *Route 66 Federation News* 9, no. 4, Autumn 2002: 11–12; Barry Penfound. "Shamrock, Texas" *Route 66 Magazine* 4, no. 3, Summer 1997: 16–18; U-Drop-In Café, Shamrock, Texas, *U-Drop-Inn Café[,] Shamrock, Texas[,] Hy-Way 66 and 83[,] Delicious Food Courteously Served,* (n.p.: privately printed, ca. 1940): paper serviette in personal research files of the author.

10. Marian Clark. "Oklahoma City Is Home to a Route 66 Classic Eatery." *Route 66 Federation News* 1, no. 2, Autumn 1995: 15–16; Jones Brothers Drive-In, Amarillo, Tex., *The World's Most Famous Chicken[,] Jones Bros. Drive-In,* (n.p.: privately printed, ca 1945): match cover in possession of the author; Bob Moore. "Chicken in the Rough: Road Food Supreme." *Route 66 Magazine* 3, no. 4 (Fall 1996): 28–29; Beverly Osborne, Oklahoma City, Okla., *Where You See This Sign, It's Genuine Chicken in the Rough,* Publication 6B-H2576 ([Chicago: Curt Teich Company, 1946]): postcard in possession of the author.

11. Jane Bernard and Polly Brown. *American Route 66: Home on the Road.* Santa Fe, N.M.: Museum of New Mexico Press, 2003. 90–91; Mary C. Bounds. "It's a Feat to Eat This Much Meat." *Dallas Morn-*

ing News (Dallas, Texas), 3 March 1985, A49, 55; Jesse Katz. "Price, and a 72-Ounce Steak, Will Make a Real Texan Out of You." *Fort Worth Star-Telegram* (Fort Worth, Texas), 19 October 1997, 13 (seventh quotation); Larry O'Brien. "Eatin' the (Big Texan) Steak." *Route 66 Magazine* 10, no. 1 Winter 2002/03. 11; Cynthia Puckett. "Big Texan Continues in Lee Family Tradition with Big Plans for Future." *Amarillo Sunday News-Globe* (Amarillo, Texas), 10 February 1991, B5; Laura Raitman. "The Best Little Steak House in Texas." *Route 66 Magazine* 9, no. 2 Spring 2002. 24–27; Jean Simmons. "No Wimpy Burgers Served at Amarillo's Big Texan." *Dallas Morning News* (Dallas, Texas), 4 February 1990, G2; Bob Stevens. "Touring Route 66: Part 5." *Cars & Parts Corvette* 4, no. 2 February 2001. 54; Rick Storm. "Get Your Kicks: Famous Road Changed Way Nation Traveled." *Amarillo Globe-News* 24 June 2001. A9.

A typical Sonic Drive-In

THERE'S LIFE BEYOND THE SONIC: GROWING UP CRUISING

by Charlie McCormick

On Friday and Saturday nights in Snyder, Texas, my high school friends and I cruised the strip—what we called making the drag. We bought gas with dollar bills and change so that we could drive our chromed trucks and dirt-caked cars around the strip's mile-long, imperfect loop. We turned around at the Sonic Drive-In on one end of the strip and in the Bar-H-Bar Western Wear parking lot on the other. In between, we passed our classmates, potential dates, and occasional fights. We played our music too loud. We drank Pearl Light and Lone Star beer from cans as our cars entered the shadows between the street lamps, hoping that the cops wouldn't see us and that our friends would. The drag, at least for those few hours after dark, belonged to us. The next morning, it would belong to our parents, our bosses, and our teachers, and we would drive down it again as we ran errands or went to school or work. But not on Friday and Saturday nights. At night we had our own reasons for cruising the strip. And driving around our imperfect loop—twenty, maybe thirty times in a row—we knew that, despite the fact that we were going nowhere, we were on our way.

Our enthusiasm notwithstanding, teenage drivers in Snyder were hardly cruising's initial pioneers or greatest proponents. In its glory days in the 1960s, cruising could be found on commercial strips throughout the country: on Woodward Avenue in Detroit, on Colorado Boulevard in Pasadena, and on the Sunset Strip in Los Angeles. In recent years, cruising has remained the recreational activity of choice for many adolescents around the nation: from Salt Lake City's State Street to Kansas City's Prospect Avenue, and from Denver's Federal Boulevard to Atlanta's Stone Mountain Park. Though the street names are different in each locale, the performance of cruising has remained basically the same. It continues to involve groups of adolescents driving in automobiles around a predetermined route on Friday and Saturday nights, occasionally parking in a lot or stopping for food, and attempting to see and be seen by their peers as they figure out who they are and who they might be.

In the 1990s, I studied cruising in Abilene, Texas. What I saw there was what I had seen in Snyder a decade before. For example, as in Snyder, Abilene's adolescents knew there was a "cool" side (read as: "teenager's side") to park on and an "uncool" side (read as: "adult side"), even when it really gets crowded on Friday and Saturday nights. I knew which side to park my car on as I conducted my fieldwork. But I did not mind the "uncool" side of the Sonic because it afforded me a better view of what was happening with the adolescents across the way.

I saw that some of the teens laughed openly and often, fully enjoying their time "out." Some adolescents were more cautious with their displays, wanting to be noticed but not so badly that they would run the risk of actually being noticed and therefore subject to the possibility of jokes, humiliation, or disinterest. Others—usually males—maintained a steely gaze, glaring at anyone who dared to meet their stare. Almost everyone on the "cool" side had busy eyes—eyes always on the lookout for someone to "hook up" with, eyes always aware of who else was there and what was happening. Occasionally, all eyes focused on the same spot— the hollered threat ("What the hell are young looking at!?!"), an engine revving, or the car peeling out of the Sonic, kicking gravel up and out behind it, reaching the posted speed limit on North 1st (40 mph) in seconds.

During my fieldwork, a uniformed officer patrolled the Sonic. Rarely did teen eyes focus on him. When a parking place on the "cool" side opened up, it was immediately filled with a car or truck loaded with multiple teens. Adolescents ordered cokes and occasionally hamburgers, French fries, slushes, tater tots, or foot long coneys smothered in chili and cheese. They drove wrecks and vehicles that easily cost over $40,000. Some were modified (lowered Caminos or jacked-up F-150s), and some belonged to their parents. All of their automobiles, for a few hours at least, were sites of possibility.

What I learned about adolescent cruising from my research in Abilene is—at least in part—what I knew. Kids cruised North 1st because it was part of their traditional repertoire. They cruised because they had grown up seeing their teen-elders do it. They cruised because they had heard their parents talk about cruising "back when." They cruised because they could get a little crazy when they did it, because it was fun.

Back in Snyder, when I was in high school, our parents tolerated our weekend ritual of cruising, finding it a better alternative than lots of other things we could be doing, and seeing in it distant memories of their own youth. Tolerate it though they did, they were not above the occasional jibe at our expense. A smirk at the outfits we had so carefully donned before we left the house to go "out." Rolling eyes every time they saw where a scratch-mark had been left on the road by the too-fast acceleration of a teenager's car. And occasionally—I'm not old enough yet to concede too much to the adults of my youth—a flash of real wit. Take, for instance, Patsey Massey's admonition to her teenage daughter—a phrase so pithy it became the mantra for a whole generation of parents in this small corner of the world: "There's life beyond the Sonic." We teenagers were not so dense as to miss the joke. She meant that we were wasting our time on something more or less irrelevant, that we should quit attributing so much significance to cruising and get on with the business of living. I doubt, though, that she meant to suggest the phrase's other meaning which my friends and I seemed to assume was a better interpretation: cruising—for which the Sonic was emblematic in Snyder—was the necessary first step, a drive-through threshold, beyond which we entered the mysterious and promising realm of *Life*, where there were no more curfews, homework, or adolescent restrictions. Of course, we were all correct. She was right for the obvious reasons, and we were right, too.

Folklorists argue whether traditions develop in order to shape individuals to social and cultural norms or to liberate individuals from those social and cultural norms. In the case of adolescents, cruising seems to serve both functions. In traditional coming-of-age and rite-of-passage experiences, adolescents are prepared both for their passage into conventional adult roles and statuses, and for the uncertainties and negotiations that accompany typical adult life. These coming-of-age and rite-of-passage experiences are difficult and dangerous rituals because they help "good" kids become "good" adults. Of course, the values and behaviors of good kids are not the values and behaviors of good adults. Good kids go to bed on time, exhibit deference and cooperation, and are far removed from sexual activity. Good adults stay up as late as necessary, competitively pursue their interests, and have healthy sex lives. Coming-of-age and rite-of-passage experiences frequently open up safe space for "good" kids to play "bad" and therefore to prepare for their future lives as "good" adults. Cruising on main streets and commercial strips is one important way that many of us could act up and act out in relatively safe spaces in order to mature.

Cruising frequently has evoked concern in local communities, but it is precisely as a result of this concern—not despite it—that cruising is established as an appropriate site for acting up and acting out. If no concern was expressed, adolescents could hardly maintain the illusion that they were acting up and acting out. Still, the mundane conclusion of almost all researchers of cruising—at least in the 1950s, '60s, and '70s—is that adolescents who cruised were not fundamentally deviants. When "good" kids played "bad" during cruising, they were only enacting the legend of cruising.

The legend of cruising is a story that is constructed locally, but it shares narrative elements with the wider cruising tradition. The narrative on which the cruising legend is based is unarticulated in its whole, but its basic themes can be reconstructed based on the patterned behaviors and artifacts of its performers and audiences across time and space. Included in these themes are various forms of rebellion (drinking, violence, smoking, and drug use), courtship (sexual behavior), and resistance to authority. However inarticulate the trans-local cruising narrative may be, though, its impact on local performances is significant. Fred Setterberg, in an essay in *The Automobile and American Culture,* describes the significance of this narrative for the adolescents who cruised in San Leandro, California, like this: "There's not a single kid cruising up and down East 14th Street . . . who is not decidedly aware of the role he is playing and the responsibilities he has inherited. As a young American primitive whose image must be kept as finely tuned as his automobile, the Strip cruiser bears the weight of a thousand complicated notions about kids, cars, and the romance of 'just hanging out.'" He continues: "The legend [the unarticulated cruising narrative], it seems, has created its own demand—and the kids keep coming back for more."[1] Adolescents perform the menace of cruising—they act the way they do—not because that is fundamentally who they are or even what they want to do, but because that is how they have been taught to tell the legend or story of cruising. And local communities teach adolescents to tell this legend through the sanctioning of the coming-of-age and rite-of-passage experience by traditionalizing it.

Without experiences like cruising and cruising itself, "good" kids would have a difficult time becoming "good" adults. Ritual failure—misbehaving—is a typical failure of the rite-of-passage experience and serves the dual purpose of separating the developing adolescent from his or her former self and opening the adolescent to the possibility of life alternatives and of introducing the developing adolescents to their new capacities by showing that old competencies—children's competencies—cannot adequately address the situations one will find in life. Through an experience like cruising, acting up and acting out—a failure for "good" children—serves a developmental function, preparing adolescents for their lives as adults.

When I first told my mom about what I was studying, she said that it sounded to her like I was just trying to justify all the time I wasted during high school riding around with my friends. She echoes the refrain I heard in my youth and cannot forget even as I approach middle-age: "There's life beyond the Sonic." Her comments warn me not to over-exaggerate the importance of cruising. But the more time I spend learning from cruising, the more I have come to believe that it deserves our attention as much as any other artistic genre, social situation, or cultural expression. To paraphrase a colleague, cruising is one more example of the human capacity for gregariousness, a capacity without which we would be merely life's spectators instead of its participants. Cruising remains today, just as it was yesterday, an example of the everyday artistry which we humans produce as we make ourselves, our futures, and our places our own. I still believe I can see Life, just beyond the Sonic.

ENDNOTE

1. Fred Setterberg. "Cruising with Donny on the San Leandro Strip." *The Automobile and American Culture*. David L. Lewis and Laurence Goldstein, Eds. Ann Arbor: University of Michigan Press, 1983. 318–19.

F. E. Abernethy is Secretary-Editor Emeritus of the Texas Folklore Society, having edited or co-edited over twenty volumes of TFS publications in his thirty-three years leading the organization. He's a world traveler, and still continues to venture to foreign countries studying cultures all over the world.

T. Lindsay Baker holds the W. K. Gordon Endowed Chair in Texas Industrial History at Tarleton State University in Stephenville, and also directs the W. K. Gordon Center for Industrial History of Texas, a museum and research center located at the Thurber ghost town. He has written over twenty books on the history of Texas and the American West, and has previously contributed to TFS annuals.

Kenneth W. Davis, a past president of the Texas Folklore Society, is Professor Emeritus of English at Texas Tech University, from which he earned a Bachelor of Arts degree in English before attending Vanderbilt University for a master's degree and then a Ph.D. in English. For many years at Texas Tech University he taught undergraduate and graduate courses in American and Comparative Folklore. In retirement he remains much interested in Texas folklore and in the literature and history of the West and Southwest. He is now serving on the Lubbock County Historical Commission and is on the Board of the West Texas Historical Association.

Lucille Enix works with book and magazine publishers as a management consultant and editor, as well as with writers to help them shape creative works into publishable form. She holds a master's degree in journalism from Northwestern University, and a bachelor's degree in Science from Oklahoma State University. She worked as a features writer for the *Chicago Tribune,* as a reporter for a Washington news service, and as Features Section Editor for the *Dallas Morning News*, where she developed a new format for the Features Section and created the concept, format, and editorial direction for the weekly Entertainment Guide. In addition, she served as editor of *Vision* and *Dallas* magazines, and taught at Southern Methodist University. She co-authored *The Ultrafit Diet* (New American Library, 1990), with Dr. Joe Davis, and also *Joseph Imhof Artist of the Pueblos: A Biography* (Sunstone Press, 1998), with Nancy Reily. She has traveled extensively throughout the continents of Africa, South America, Asia, and Europe. Ms. Enix formed her own editorial consulting business and worked with clients in Europe, Mexico and the United States for over twenty years. Journalistic honors include: The Southwest Journalism Forum Award for Professional Excellence, two Dallas Press Club Katy Awards for Best General Interest Magazine, a Texas Medical Association Award for excellence in communication, the Women in Communication Award for outstanding journalistic contribution, and the *Art Direction Magazine*'s Creativity Distinction Award. Before and after she retired, she became a long-distance cyclist, biking 50–100 miles per day on bicycle tours.

Newton Gaines, a physics professor at TCU, was President of the Texas Folklore Society from 1928–1929.

Carol Hanson was born and raised in Dallas, Texas—the child of August and Mary Helen Stanglin. She has four brothers and one sister—two of her brothers, Phil and David, accompanied her on the Sesquicentennial Wagon Train in May, 1986. Carol received her Masters of Library & Information Sciences from North Texas State University in Denton in December, 1979. She has been a librarian at Dallas Public Library, Zula B. Wylie Library in Cedar Hill, and the Betty Warmack Branch Library of Grand Prairie. In 2004, she returned to Dallas Public Library to be Assistant Manager at the Kleberg-Rylie Branch Library. On June 17, 1989, she married Pete Hanson in Cedar Hill, Texas, where they still live with their son Erik. Carol joined the Texas Folklore Society in 1985, after being a member of the Dallas corral of the Westerners' organization—several members had encouraged her to attend a TFS meeting. Carol attended the 1985 meeting with Ruth Lambert, and has been hooked ever since. Most anything associated with history interests her, which explains her long-time dabbling with her family's genealogy for 20+ years; she is considered to be the family historian for the Stanglins. She also has interest in photography, scrap-booking, and gardening—and, of course, reading.

Jim Harris was raised in Dallas and taught college English in Texas, Louisiana, and New Mexico, where he has lived with his wife Mary and son Hawk since 1974. He is a runner, photographer, and fisherman. Retired from teaching, he has been the Director of the Lea County Museum in Lovington, New Mexico since 2002. He has given many presentations at TFS meetings and is a past president of the society.

Mary Harris has been a member of the TFS since 1973 and has served as President, Program Chair, Director, Councilor, local arranger, session chair, presenter, and designer of a half-dozen programs for TFS annual meetings. She is a retired classroom and special education teacher, and since earning a doctorate in Higher Education Leadership, Mary serves as Dean of the School of Education at College of the Southwest in Hobbs, New Mexico. She is married to Jim Harris, and she is the mother of Hawk Harris, who is also a long-time member of the TFS.

L. Patrick Hughes is a Professor of History at Austin Community College, where he has served on the faculty since 1977. A graduate of the University of Texas, he is an active member of numerous state and regional organizations, including the Texas Folklore Society. He is also a guest lecturer for UT's Elderhostel program.

W. C. Jameson is the award-winning author of fifty books, 1,500 published articles and essays, and over 300 poems and songs. In addition to writing, he performs his songs and music at folk festivals and concerts throughout the country. He has written the musical scores for two PBS documentaries and one feature film, and he wrote and performed in the musical *Whatever Happened to the Outlaw, Jesse James?* An actor, Jameson has appeared in five films, including a co-starring role in *Spoils of War.*

James B. Kelly was born in Ft. Worth, Texas, and raised and educated in the public schools in Sinton, Texas. He earned a BBA Degree from Texas A&M University in 1952. He was commissioned a 2nd Lt. in the U.S. Army, and served during the Korean Conflict with the 30th Regimental Combat Team, 3rd Infantry Division, from 1953–1954. He worked in the ranching and insurance industries, was Chairman and CEO of Kelly Land & Cattle Company, and served as a bank director for over ten years. He retired in 2002, and he joined the TFS and attended his first annual meeting in 2000.

Jerry B. Lincecum, a sixth-generation Texan, is Emeritus Professor of English at Austin College. He holds the B.A. in English from Texas A&M University and M.A. and Ph.D. degrees from Duke University. A past president of the Texas Folklore Society, he has presented many papers at annual meetings of the society and co-edited *The Family Saga: A Collection a/Texas Family Legends* for the TFS in 2003. Since 1990, he has directed "Telling Our Stories," a humanities project at Austin College that aids older adults in writing their autobiographies and family histories.

Gretchen Lutz lives in Houston, where she teaches reading at Cesar E. Chavez High School. A native of Bowie, Texas, she has a B.A. in English from Texas Christian, an M.A. in English from the University of Houston, and a Ph.D. in English from Rice University, where her dissertation was on women in the F. J. Child collection of traditional ballads.

Charlie McCormick is the Dean for Academic Affairs and an Associate Professor of English and Communication at Cabrini College in Southeastern Pennsylvania. Although it's a long way from his home of Snyder, Texas, Cabrini College encourages his ongoing analysis of adolescent cruising on Main Street in Texas and beyond.

Archie P. McDonald has taught history at Stephen F. Austin State University for forty-three years, and he serves as director of the East Texas Historical Association and editor of the Association's *Journal*. He is a past president of the Texas State Historical Association, past vice-chair of the Texas Historical Commission, and is the author/editor of more than twenty books on historical topics—and one book of humor titled *Helpful Cooking Hints for House Husbands of Uppity Women*.

Charlie Oden began work for the T&NO (SP) Railroad in 1940 as an extra telegrapher clerk towerman. Three years later his company promoted him to train dispatcher. He worked as train dispatcher and chief train dispatcher for the next thirty-seven years. When he began work, steam engines were pulling the trains; when he retired, diesel electric units were pulling them. When he retired, Charlie was familiar with all of the names and locations of the rail yards and side tracks and knew what the different classes of engines would pull all along the Gulf Coast, on the prairies, or over the mountains, knowledge he used in planning and moving trains. Beginning in 1955, Charlie attended Navarro College at Corsicana, S.M.U., and the University of Houston until he had accumulated 90 of the 120 semester hours required for a degree in accounting. Because the 30 hours left to graduate were all electives, Charlie elected to quit school. He has contributed to TFS publications *Hoein' the Short Rows* and *Between the Cracks of History*.

Ellen Pearson was born in 1941, in Houston, a year before Fannie Marchman began her account of her life. Raised in Waxahachie, she spent her formative years, alternately, prissing around town in a

red and white Pontiac Bonneville Convertible (with the obligatory
ooga horn and glasspac mufflers), and whooping it up with
cowhands on the family ranch in Central Texas, working cattle on a
fine string of King Ranch-bred quarter horses. She dated bad boys
with double first names, all beginning with "Billy." Ellen encountered the Marchman clan through her stepdad, Riley Laurens
Marchman, the grandson of Fannie Marchman. Her only Marchman memories are of the diminutive Riley G. Marchman, Fannie's
firstborn, swinging his mid-sized dog around his modest backyard
in Waxahachie, the dog tenaciously gripping a towel in his mouth.
Ellen discovered the Matriarch of the Clan long after her death,
during a visit to her brother Rusty's house in Waxahachie, when
they unearthed an ancient scrapbook containing Fannie Marchman's account. She now lives on a sidehill farm in Western Massa-
chusetts, where she enjoys the last Belgian draft horse of a long line
of steady workers, plus his new companion, a bay quarter horse
mare, named Brandy, who helps her to remember the days on the
KbarRanch in Texas.

Barbara Pybas lives in Cooke County, Texas on a ranch twenty
miles from Gainesville, bordering the Red River. She immigrated
to Texas from western Oklahoma in 1949 by marrying a Marine
veteran and coming fresh from Oklahoma A&M University. From
that time she has been active in community organizations, county
politics, and as a committee member from Cooke County for the
Texas Historical Commission. She has focused on Texas History
and has several stories in the Handbook of Texas/My Texas
Online: *www.tsha.utexas.edu/mytexas.* She has been a presenter at
Texas Folklore Society meetings and at the Morton Museum in
Gainesville serving, as well, on their board of directors. She attends
the Sivells Bend United Methodist Church, established in 1869.
This small country church has been the site for three daughters'
weddings and several grandbabies' baptisms. There are six Pybas
children and eleven grandchildren who think the ranch is a Bed

and Breakfast. Barbara has for several years attended the Telling Our Stories classes conducted by Dr. Jerry Lincecum in Sherman, and is included in his publications.

Consuelo Samarripa shares her performing art of storytelling and pubic speaking in various venues. As a second generation Texas native born in the West side *barrios* of San Antonio, she shares history, folklore, personal stories, poetry, multicultural tales, and myths. Her repertoire also includes ghost stories. She has appeared in lead roles of various theatrical productions. Consuelo's programs entertain audiences in English, Spanish, and her own bilingual blends. She conducts workshops for children and adults, is on the Texas Commission on the Arts Touring Roster for 2006–2008, and is registered with the Mid-America Arts Alliance.

Jean Granberry Schnitz was born in Spur, Texas. She graduated from Raymondville High School in 1948 and from Texas College of Arts and Industries College (now Texas A&M University in Kingsville) in 1952. She and Lew Schnitz were married in 1953. They have three sons and four grandchildren. A retired legal secretary, she lives near Boerne. As of 2007, Jean has presented eight papers to the Texas Folklore Society. She has been a Director on the Board of the Texas Folklore Society since 2002, and was elected Vice-President for 2005–2006. She became President at the 90th annual meeting in Galveston, Texas, in April of 2006.

Jan Epton Seale is a poet, essayist, and fiction writer. Born in Pilot Point, where Bonnie and Clyde robbed their first bank, she grew up in Gainesville and Waxahachie. She lives in the Rio Grande Valley of Texas, where she writes, teaches creative writing, and enjoys helping call attention to the unique flora and fauna of South Texas. She has authored a number of books, the latest being *The Wonder Is: New and Selected Poems 1974–2004*, published by Panther Creek Press.

Janet McCannon Simonds, born and reared in the Rio Grande Valley of Texas, is the Office Secretary and Treasurer of the Texas Folklore Society, and a long-time resident of Nacogdoches. Although she studied art and design for her bachelor's degree and has a master's degree in Education, she spent most of her career evaluating and managing social service contracts (and writing lengthy reports) for the State of Texas. After retirement from the State, the fun began—first, she had a five-year adventure in the College of Education at Stephen F. Austin State University, and then she discovered the Texas Folklore Society. A life-long love of Texas history and folklore and the written word has found a very congenial home.

John O. West taught English and folklore at the University of Texas at El Paso for thirty-nine years and is a retired Professor Emeritus. His publications include *Mexican American Folklore, Cowboy Folk Humor,* the introduction to Jose Cisneros' book *Riders Across the Centuries,* and *Jose Cisneros: An Artist's Journey.* In 2002, he was made a Fellow of the Texas Folklore Society.

Paul Yeager is a filmmaker, television producer/director, and interactive multimedia developer. In 1999, *A V Video Producer Magazine* named him one of the Top 100 Producers in America. Yeager's adventures by motorcycle began in 1974, when he and his wife Janice headed for Mexico on a grossly overloaded Honda 175. The following year they bought one of Honda's new four-cylinder bikes and pounded out some 75,000 miles over the next few years. They retired that bike, had three children who grew up and left home, and then began riding again in 1999. Writing has always been central to Yeager's work, and in 2000 he began a series of stories about his motorcycle travels. These have been published in *Cycle World's Adventures Magazine, BMW ON Magazine,* and the premiere issue of the *Iron Butt Association Magazine,* among other places. Most of his stories can also be found online at *www. bmwclub.org* in the Ride Tales section.

INDEX

A